THE
SPY'S
SON

THE
SPY'S
SON

The True Story of the Highest-Ranking CIA
Officer Ever Convicted of Espionage and
the Son He Trained to Spy for Russia

Bryan Denson

Atlantic Monthly Press
New York

Published simultaneously in Canada
Printed in the United States of America

FIRST EDITION

ISBN 978-0-8021-2358-9
eISBN 978-0-8021-9131-1

Atlantic Monthly Press
an imprint of Grove Atlantic
154 West 14th Street
New York, NY 10011

Distributed by Publishers Group West

groveatlantic.com

15 16 17 18   10 9 8 7 6 5 4 3 2 1

In memory of my father,
Kenneth Earl Denson,

and dedicated to Holden Miles Denson,
my son, my wingman, my pride and joy

"I used to advertise my loyalty and I don't believe there is a single person I loved that I didn't eventually betray."

—Albert Camus, *The Fall*

Contents

THE
SPY'S
SON

Prologue

Suspected Spies in Chains

Portland, Oregon, January 29, 2009

I'm sitting in Satan's Pew, the name I've conferred upon the torturously narrow courtroom benches in the Mark O. Hatfield United States Courthouse. As I squirm in my seat, reporter's notebook dandling on my lap, I notice a curiously high number of deputy U.S. marshals in the gallery, mostly buff guys with steely gazes and Glocks under their sports coats. Behind me, wearing blazers and striped clip-on ties, stands a knot of court security officers. Next to them, FBI agents squeeze together on a bench against the back wall. I haven't witnessed court security this tight since the feds rolled up Theodore Kaczynski, the Unabomber, and hauled him before a judge in Helena, Montana. A courthouse contact has already tipped me that today I'll witness something groundbreaking here in the cheap seats of American justice.

Keys jangle behind a paneled wall to my right, where I can hear the clank of a metal door. Deputy marshals are queuing today's prisoners, who will appear one by one to face their charges before a magistrate judge. The weekday parade of pathos, known to courthouse denizens as Mag Court, normally features a tedious cast of freshly arrested miscreants, some scratching from withdrawal. Now and again the show comes alive with stone killers, cops gone bad, diamond thieves, outlaw bikers, cockfighting impresarios, ecoterrorists, grave robbers, or the corner-cutting captains of industry.

On this foggy Thursday afternoon, I've come to write about two suspects—an international spy, and the son who joined him in the family business of espionage.

My editors at *The Oregonian*, the daily newspaper several blocks away, are holding space on the front page for my father-son spy story. But the duo—whose names I'd never heard until this morning—will be arraigned separately, consigning me to a hellish deadline. I look at my watch and silently curse the docket gods. A hapless bunch of schnooks are scheduled ahead of my spy suspects, and the judge will take her good old time reading them their rights.

First up today is an accused scam artist from California who sold central home vacuum cleaning units across North America; apparently he was brilliant at sales and collecting money, but not at delivering the goods. Now comes another genius, a career bank robber arrested yesterday just twenty-one minutes after knocking off a Bank of America for a lousy $700; he's already calculating how much time he'll serve in prison. Up next is a guy who drank himself stupid out on the Umatilla Indian Reservation and threw some playful karate kicks at a buddy, who hurled him to the ground, whereupon Junior Jackie Chan blew a gasket, picked up *two* knives, and stabbed his pal nearly to death. Then come two men accused of illegally harboring a luckless El Salvadoran woman; she turned up, like so many, on the wrong side of the U.S. border.

Today's guest of honor is Harold James "Jim" Nicholson, who in 1997 became the highest-ranking Central Intelligence Agency officer ever convicted of espionage. Nicholson, serving time at the federal prison fifty miles from where I sit, sold the identities of hundreds of CIA trainees to Russian spies. Now he's accused of betraying his country again—this time from behind bars. The Rolex-wearing spy nicknamed Batman, having recruited countless foreign assets to betray their own countries for the CIA, is suspected of sending the Russians his youngest son, twenty-four-year-old Nathaniel James Nicholson, as his emissary. Nathan, a partially disabled Army veteran, took basic lessons in spycraft from the old man, then smuggled his dad's secret messages out of the prison visiting room to

Russian spies on three continents. For the trophy-conscious FBI, securing another conviction against Jim Nicholson would be a major prize.

A heavy door swings open, and here he is.

Jim wears a khaki prison uniform and a faded T-shirt the color of broiled salmon. His pale blue eyes sweep the room with an expression that shifts abruptly, as if he'd expected something grander than this feckless rabble of court staffers, lawyers, and a few scribbling journalists. Jim moves for the defense table with the short-step shuffle of a man who knows the sting of a jaunty stride in ankle chains. He eases into a high-back chair. Jim sports a soul patch and mustache, gray hair sweeping over the tops of his ears. I take a mental note. *This guy would look right at home playing tenor sax in a jazz quartet.*

I've gazed at hundreds and hundreds of suspected felons in courtrooms across the country, but Jim Nicholson carries himself differently. He's not eye-fucking the prosecutors or sneaking glances into the gallery for a friendly face. There's no swagger, no tapping foot, no nervous smile that might offer some kind of tell. The man doesn't even appear to be breathing. He wears an expression of captive resignation, like a golfer on a tee box watching the foursome in front of him swat cattails in search of a lost ball.

Then I see something. The chin. It tilts upward ever so slightly and guides his gaze, regally, a few inches above the eyes of everyone else on the floor of the courtroom. It's a look that tells me everything I need to understand: This guy just knows he's the smartest man in the building.

At this moment, I have no clue that I will spend the next five years contemplating the life and crimes of Jim Nicholson, piecing together his tangled human narrative, the wreckage he left of his family and the CIA, and his unique role in the ongoing hostilities between Washington and Moscow. And I cannot possibly know that I will learn this story with the help of Nathan, his family and friends, prison inmates, former spies and counterintelligence agents, national security lawyers, public policy makers, hundreds of pages of investigative files, wiretaps, court records, prison and military papers, Jim's correspondence, excerpts from his personal journal, and a colorful band of investigators with the FBI and CIA who twice brought him to justice.

Already my questions are many: How on earth could a man devote decades of distinguished service to his country only to betray her? Why would he reach out to Russia again? Why would Moscow still care about its former mole nearly two decades after the Cold War? What could Russian spies hope to gain by making contact with Jim a dozen years after his treachery was unmasked? And why would he send his youngest son into the breach, risking his freedom? What kind of a dad does that?

When I hustle out of the courtroom to make my early evening deadline, I run into David Ian Miller, the special agent in charge of the FBI's Portland Field Office. Dave, who has always been a straight shooter, tells me that Jim Nicholson was a skilled and worthy adversary.

"At the end of the day," he says, "this will prove to be a story of family, trust, and betrayal."

And, as it happens, so much more.

1

Hola Nancy

"The integrity of the upright shall guide them; But the perverseness of the treacherous shall destroy them."
                              —Proverbs 11:3, The Holy Bible (ASV)

Eugene, Oregon, fall 2008

The morning of October 10 dawned cold and gunmetal gray in Eugene, a college town so accustomed to autumnal gloom that the young man with sleepy blue eyes gave it scarce notice. Nathan Nicholson hiked across an elevated walkway from his drafting class toward the Lane Community College library, which sat in the middle of campus in the aptly named Center Building. Behind him, a thicket of towering evergreens carpeted the coastal mountains, which stretched fifty miles west to the Pacific Ocean, clouds draping their rounded shoulders like tattered shawls.

Nathan wore his hair razor-close on the sides, with a little longer patch on top, a style his barbers back in the Army called high and tight, and which, not by accident, disguised his receding hairline. He moved with an infantryman's gait, chest out, head and shoulders barely rising, stocky legs chewing up ground. But there was a slight hitch in his stride, as if his left leg were stepping over imaginary glass, a parting gift from the parachuting injury that ended his military career. He had turned twenty-four that summer.

The air felt cool on Nathan's face, his strong brow and broad chin, and he could see his breath. The first rains of winter had begun early in the Willamette Valley, where even longtime residents herald the onset of the soggy season with low-grade despair. Soon would come a monotonous series of drizzles, rolling off the Pacific as if by conveyor belt, delivering the valley so many short, gray days that by February, some folks would begin to joke about eating the barrel of the nearest gun.

Nathan was not a native Oregonian, and he sometimes missed the more exciting climates of his boyhood. His dad's foreign assignments sent the Nicholson family to punishing places. Manila, with its blistering humidity and electrical storms you could feel under your feet. Bangkok, often called the hottest city on the planet. Kuala Lumpur, where monsoons deliver a hundred inches of hard rain a year. And Bucharest, with its pipe-bursting winter freezes. He also missed the rotations, traveling from embassy to embassy, uprooting every few years to start fresh someplace new.

Outside the library, Nathan slipped a black-and-gray Alpine backpack off his shoulder and knelt on the cool brick walkway as if to tie his shoe. He hunched over the pack for an instant, letting his eyes casually sweep the commons, panning faces and forms. One intense glance from anyone and he would bail, circling back later for another try. But he saw nothing suspicious.

Nathan unzipped the pack's front compartment and lifted out a small notebook with a blue, marbled cover. He flipped through its pages until he reached a twenty-eight-word notation that began, "Hola Nancy." He studied it for a few moments and climbed to his feet, satisfied he could e-mail the message just as the Russian had dictated the previous winter in Peru.

His gut was tormenting him again. For many months, stabbing pains deep beneath his breastplate had intermittently doubled him over. He was convinced that the stress of the last year had given him stomach ulcers. His meals bunched in his belly like piles of tacks. He'd seen a doctor at the college's health clinic, who told him to drink green tea, carry Pepto-Bismol, and avoid tomato juice. Nathan thought she'd seemed unconcerned, even dismissive of his pains, as if she considered college students exempt from the titanic stresses that produce big-boy ulcers. She had not appeared to comprehend the depth of his anxieties, nor could she. There was no way for her to know that for two years he had traveled the Americas as his father's agent to Russia's foreign spy service, and now feared he might be under surveillance by the Federal Bureau of Investigation.

Inside the library Nathan followed tan-gray industrial carpet past bookshelves topped with busts of famous literary and historic figures. From across the room, the figures of Will Rogers, Benjamin Franklin, and Frederick Douglass were locked in a perpetual stare-off with Ernest Hemingway, Albert Einstein, and Kate Greenaway. Nathan pushed through a doorway into an adjoining classroom that doubled as a computer lab, eyes scanning the room for anyone out of place. He settled in front of one of two dozen Dell monitors spread across rows of white desktops. It had taken him weeks to find this spot, the only computer lab on campus where students weren't required to log in.

Nathan pulled up the Yahoo home page, with its familiar red logo, and tapped in the user name "Jopemurr2" and the password "Florida12." He typed the e-mail from memory, wincing at each word. The sentences looked more ridiculous on the screen than when he jotted them down inside a soundproof room at the Russian Embassy in Lima. His fingers froze for an instant over the keyboard as he listened to the words in his head. They sounded as if someone with clumsy English were speaking a pass-phrase in an old spy movie. Such obvious code. He resisted the urge to revise the words into something approximating authentic human correspondence. The Russian had been specific that he stick to the prescribed text, and Nathan stuck to the script. Yet he couldn't stop himself from waking up the prose with a forest of exclamation marks:

Hola Nancy! It is great to receive your message! I love you too. I hope
to see you soon!
The best regards from my brother Eugene!
—Love,
Dick

The Russian had assigned them code names. He called himself
"Nancy" and gave Nathan the name "Dick." He conferred the sobriquet
"Eugene" on Nathan's father, whose years spying for the Russians had
brought them all together.

At precisely 9:58 a.m., Nathan saved his e-mail into the draft folder
of the Yahoo account. He cleared the web page off his screen and sneaked
a casual glance to his side. Earlier he had spied a woman standing behind
him. She was still there, eyeing his workstation like someone stalking
a stool in a crowded bar. When he stood and reached for his bag, she
practically dove for his seat.

Nathan's e-mail, safely parked in the draft file, would remain sus-
pended in cyberspace until the Russian—God only knew where—logged
into their shared account and opened the folder to read his message. The
note would never travel from one computer to another, leaving a messy
trail across the Internet that could link them. The draft folder served as
a modern-day dead drop, a spy tool as old as espionage.

Spying, sometimes called the world's second-oldest profession, is
complicated business. But the essence of covert communications hasn't
changed since a Mesopotamian potter stuck a secret formula for glaze into
the hidden compartment of a clay tablet thousands of years ago. Spies
use signals—a chalk mark on a bridge, a beer can on a country road, an
X on the post of a streetlamp—to let their handlers know they will meet
at a prearranged spot. Now they use high-tech gadgets such as Internet
remailers and codes embedded in digital photos. But new isn't always
better. Old and new tricks work, right up until they don't.

Nathan didn't fully comprehend the risk posed by his face-to-face
meetings with the Russian. He was unaware the old man who called

himself "George" had been tossed out of the United States, persona non grata, at the apex of the Cold War, or that the meetings George arranged exposed only Nathan to arrest.

There was genius in their Yahoo cyber exchange. It was such a simple hideaway that nearly anyone could pull it off, even a grandfatherly Russian spy born nearly forty years before the advent of e-mail.

Nathan's note confirmed that in precisely two months, he would stand, as instructed, outside a restaurant on the island of Cyprus clenching his backpack in his right hand. There he would meet the Russian, share the latest messages from his dad, and walk away with another bundle of Moscow's money.

Hola Nancy, indeed.

On the first Saturday in December 2008, a metal door clanked behind Jim Nicholson as he peered across a vast rectangle of scuffed linoleum looking for his youngest son. Visiting hours at the Federal Correctional Institution in Sheridan, Oregon, were just under way. Prisoners and their guests took seats on rows of blue plastic chairs, which were bolted together airport-style so that they sat thigh to thigh and faced the same direction. Uniformed guards stationed behind a crescent of painted cinder blocks kept watch over the room. Surveillance cameras spied from above, as families shared snacks and stories, the din of their conversations punctuated by the occasional squeal of a toddler leaving the adjoining playroom.

Jim Nicholson, who had recently turned fifty-eight, was serving the back end of a twenty-three-year stretch for espionage. He stood six feet and weighed 194 pounds, with sloping shoulders and strong arms. A mane of salt-and-pepper hair, more salt than pepper, fell over the collar of his khaki prison shirt, his inmate number—49535-083—ironed above the left breast pocket. He wore a tattoo on his right forearm, an Army Ranger emblem inked decades ago and now faded to a greenish glob. On the underside of the same arm was a fresh tat that read "O POS," his blood type.

Jim was a bona fide celebrity among the more than one thousand prisoners at Sheridan, a medium-security prison known as soft time for its standard cohort of bank robbers, cocaine dealers, and identity thieves. The federal lockup ten minutes east of Spirit Mountain Casino has long drawn its share of celebrity prisoners. A parade of them have passed through the complex, including Stacey Koon, the ex–Los Angeles police sergeant convicted for his role in the Rodney King beating, and Marion "Suge" Knight, the founder of hip-hop's iconic Death Row Records. Michael Swango, the serial-killer physician who poisoned at least four patients, turned up at the prison in 1999, the same year *Blind Eye: The Terrifying Story of a Doctor Who Got Away With Murder* hit bookstores. Later came Robert "Spam King" Soloway, whose botnets corrupted computers worldwide, and Duane R. Moore, the adult film star better known as "Tony Eveready, the Gangsta of Porn."

As it happens, Jim wasn't even the first spy locked up at Sheridan. He had served time with James D. "Jim" Harper Jr., doing life for selling missile secrets to Poland from 1975 to 1983, and Christopher Boyce, who sold satellite secrets to the Soviet Union in the 1970s. Boyce's exploits—espionage, breaking out of a federal prison, and an audacious series of armed bank robberies—were documented in two books and a hit movie, *The Falcon and the Snowman*.

Jim stood out at Sheridan. He was bright, well traveled, and served as a father figure for younger inmates. He had worked as a quality control inspector in the prison furniture factory, and emceed Sunday worship services in the prison chapel. He cut a charismatic figure as a long-haired, moccasin-wearing, born-again Christian. But he suffered from the deadly sin of vanity. He spent a long time primping in his cell, especially before weekend visits with his family. One of his former cellmates, a Las Vegas bank robber named Phil Quackenbush, snickered when Jim combed dark shoe polish into his beard to look more youthful for his kids.

Nathan was a week shy of thirteen when he first came to see his dad in prison. Hundreds of times since then he had passed through the gates, topped with gleaming coils of razor wire, navigating sign-ins, a metal detector, and a hand-stamp station, to be ushered by corrections officers, room by room, into the bowels of the institution, heavy doors buzzing and slamming behind him, just to reach this scuffed-linoleum visiting room with bars on the windows to spend time with the old man. Nathan considered this his second home.

When Nathan saw Jim across the floor, he stood and hugged him fiercely, kissing his dad's cheek. Seventy-four miles separated Nathan and Jim, save for their every-other-Saturday visits. Their phone conversations were routed through a special line at the CIA and Jim's letters were copied and analyzed before being mailed forward. In spite of the encumbrances, perhaps because of them, father and son had grown extremely close.

Jim had missed much of Nathan's first seven years of life. He was serving on the front lines of the Cold War, a covert operator working to derail and defeat the Soviet Union's influence in the Philippines, Thailand, and Cambodia. Jim's adversaries in the KGB dubbed the U.S. their main enemy. The competing spy services played a high-stakes game of cat-and-mouse as an atomic sword of Damocles—thousands of nuclear missiles—dangled over the planet.

Jim's blind devotion to the CIA kept him working late at night, meeting assets and writing reports. His early exploits in Manila earned him the nickname "Batman," and he was thrilled by his rising star in the agency. But the demands of his work meant that he saw little of his wife and three kids.

Nathan barely knew his father until his parents' marriage shattered in the early 1990s. He and his older brother and sister moved in with their dad in Kuala Lumpur, Malaysia, where they witnessed a monumental shift in his personality. Jim seemed to relish his new role as single dad, joyfully making up for lost time with them.

Years later, Nathan often reminisced about his childhood days with his dad. He remembered lying in bed as Jim settled onto the floor next to him, adjusting a pillow behind his back to read the woodsy sketches of humorist Patrick F. McManus. Jim would clear his throat with comic flair, animating McManus' comic characters with a wide range of voices. The nighttime readings often left them laughing so hard that Nathan had to grab his gut as the old man fought to get the next sentence out.

The bedtime stories would end a few years later, when the rubric of their father-son narrative would divide into the time before Jim's arrest in 1996 and everything that followed. But Nathan would never let go of the dad he remembered in his youth, as Jim turned from U.S. intelligence officer to convicted spy, and eventually a federal prisoner.

Nathan gestured toward a bank of vending machines, which sat on the other side of a red stripe on the floor. Inmates were forbidden from crossing the line.

"Hey, Pa, you want anything?"

Jim ordered his usual, and Nathan trooped off with a handful of bills. He returned from a microwave moments later with two jalapeño cheeseburgers in steaming plastic bags and a pair of ice-cold Coca-Colas. He set their meal on the tray between them. Jim tore open a packet of taco sauce and got right down to business. He wanted to review Nathan's travel plans, and make sure he was completely prepared for his trip to Cyprus. He needed every detail. Departure times. Layovers. Arrivals.

Nathan walked his dad through every leg, sounding like a determined Army clerk briefing the base commander. On Monday he would fly out of Portland to New York's JFK International Airport, connecting in Istanbul for a Turkish Airlines hop across the Mediterranean Sea to Ercan International Airport, on the island of Cyprus. As Jim had instructed, Nathan had reserved his airline tickets with a credit card, but paid for them with $1,584.41 in cash to avoid a paper trail. Jim had told him to find a high-class hotel, which would be safer, and Nathan had used his Visa Citi Platinum card to book a room at the Cyprus Hilton, the best hotel in the capital city of Nicosia. He would pay that tab in cash, too, and ask the desk clerk to delete records of his credit card. Nathan had tucked an extra $294 into his Delta ticket papers for spending money on the six-day trip.

Jim nodded approvingly. He explained to Nathan that the Ercan airport sits in northeastern Cyprus, the Turkish side, which meant he would pass through an armed checkpoint at the Green Line on the taxi ride to his hotel on the Greek side of the capital city. He gave his son a primer on the long conflict between the Greeks and Turks, how Nicosia remained the world's last divided city. Jim leaned closer, asking Nathan in a near whisper to walk him through his cover story.

Nathan quietly explained that if he was stopped by the feds, by anyone, he would say he had flown to Cyprus to meet Army buddies and tour a few castles.

Jim told him that when he checked into the Hilton, he should ask a desk clerk if any of his buddies—phantoms though they were—had left a message for him. He told his son to stop by the desk daily to ask about his friends, solidifying his cover. Jim reminded Nathan that throughout his stay in Nicosia, he needed to remain keenly alert for tails. It was crucial that he not be followed into his meeting with the Russian. The Mediterranean city has long been a hot spot for spies and counterspies, and Jim knew the FBI kept watch on the Russian Embassy. Nicosia had served as a key locale for Cold War spying between the U.S. and the Soviet Union, partly because of its nexus to Europe, Asia, and the turbulent Middle East. Spies on both sides liked tours there. The sandy beaches at nearby Larnaca were heavenly.

The key thing to pack, he said, was the letter Jim had mailed him that summer; it was intended for the Russian. Jim also reminded him to carry the address for his fiancée, Kanokwan Lehliem, who had served as his interpreter—and a great deal more—during a bloody 1980s border war in which Cambodian refugees spilled in waves into her native Thailand. Kanokwan had pledged to wait for Jim until he got out of prison, and he wanted Nathan to wire her some money from Cyprus.

Nathan listened obediently as the old man laid out his to-do list, but he was way ahead of him. Stuck to the fridge in his apartment was a yellow Post-it with a long checklist of things to pack, including all the items Jim reminded him to bring. The first item on Nathan's list, however, was the Holy Bible his dad bought him for his eighteenth birthday. He carried it for inspiration.

With Christmas approaching, Jim urged Nathan to use some of the money the Russian would pay him to buy gifts. He wanted Nathan to wrap two presents with his name on them for his oldest children—a Wii game system for Jeremi, who was serving in the Air Force in Florida, and a bottle of Armani Code perfume for Star, who lived forty miles east of the prison, in Beaverton, Oregon.

Just then, Star walked into the visiting room.

Nathan and his dad shot to their feet, breaking off all talk of Nathan's trip. They had agreed not to tell anyone about their contact with the Russians, deciding early on that Nathan—and Nathan alone—would serve as Jim's courier. Jim told his youngest son that the Russians were paying him out of fealty for his past service, and that Nathan's primary role was to deliver financial succor to his brother and sister, both buried under mountains of debt, and to make payments on his own car and credit card. Nathan had plunged into Jim's scheme with no misgivings. He trusted his father, who rewarded his loyalty with praise. In a letter that summer, Jim applauded Nathan's brave step into what he called the "unseen world," one that he described as sometimes dangerous, always fascinating.

"God leads us on our greatest adventures," Jim wrote. "Keep looking through your new eyes."

On the morning of December 8, 2008, a Monday, Nathan stood in baggage screening at Portland International Airport, arms straight out, wearing the timeless look of the defeated traveler. A beefy Transportation Security Administration officer with a shaved head patted him down, having seen an "SSSS" notation on the young man's boarding pass. The acronym stood for Secondary Security Screening Selection. When the TSA officer was finished, he began pawing through Nathan's backpack and passed him over to the manager.

This wasn't Nathan's first trip through secondary, and he was beginning to think he'd been flagged because he was Jim's son, and that maybe his luck was running out.

Officer Donald Headrick, who managed the TSA's behavioral detection team, was middle-aged with a broad face, thinning hair, and glasses. Headrick sat Nathan down to quiz him about his travels. *Where are you heading today? What's the purpose of your visit? Are you meeting anyone?*

Jim had coached Nathan on how to handle situations like these. He labored to keep his breathing even and reminded himself that the guy in the royal blue TSA uniform with the gold badge was human, too. He looked Headrick in the eyes and regaled him with a spectacular run of lies about heading to Cyprus to meet battle buddies and tour castles he'd read about. Nathan was lying for a living now, just like the old man. He used all the charm he possessed to sell his story to the TSA manager, trying to sound excited about his trip. But much as he tried, Nathan couldn't get a good read from his inquisitor's face.

His head swam with doubt. Was someone onto him? On the way back from his last meeting with the Russian in Peru, Customs officials in Houston put him through a half-hour search and disappeared into an office with his blue notebook and other gear. Recently, his Chevy Cavalier had begun to make unusual beep tones when he keyed the remote, an indication someone had bumped into or entered the car. A few times recently, he had returned to his one-bedroom apartment to find it marinating in the smell of human body odor, and not just any B.O., but the B.O. of someone having a really bad day. Then, just the previous Saturday, a clean-cut guy, midforties with a little paunch, had glommed onto him at the prison as they made the long trek through the metal detectors and heavy doors to the visiting room. The guy had planted himself in a row of seats in front of them, his back to Nathan and Jim, and seemed to be listening in on their their conversation.

Headrick thumbed through Nathan's wallet, asking how much money he was carrying. Then he rummaged through his bag.

Nathan figured maybe it all ended here. But suddenly, Headrick was handing him his wallet.

"Enjoy your trip," he said. "Have a nice flight."

For sheer whimsy, you had to give it to the Russian. He summoned Nathan ten time zones from home, to Nicosia, a city known for its old-world cuisine, just to rendezvous in front of a T.G.I. Friday's. Nathan stood on a wide sidewalk at 12 Diagorou Street as darkness fell over a palm-flecked shopping district choked with Greek nightclubs and restaurants. Towering streetlamps bathed him in light as he fidgeted in front of the Texas-based chain restaurant's familiar red-and-white awnings. He looked for all the world like any other hayseed American tourist, another cultureless Yank who had stumbled into the exotic crossroads of Europe and the Middle East only to forgo the local fare and feast on Jack Daniel's pork chops, New York Cheesecake, and six-dollar Budweisers.

He wore jeans, sneakers, and a camel-colored baseball cap. The Russian had presented him with the hat at their last meeting, instructing Nathan to wear it outside the restaurant while grasping his backpack in his right hand. He completed the tourist getup with a map of Nicosia, which he snatched from the Hilton's front desk on his way out. When Nathan left the hotel for his appointment, he had launched himself down Archbishop Makarios III Avenue, named after the first president of the Republic of Cyprus, toward the T.G.I. Friday's. He hiked down side streets to avoid being tailed, and he doubled back a few times, pausing at shop windows to check their reflections, making sure he wasn't being followed.

Nathan's walk took such a circuitous route that he blundered off course and got lost. But being the earnest sort, he had left the Hilton so early on the evening of December 10, 2008, that he still arrived an hour early for his meeting with the Russian. He stood on that wide sidewalk trying to look casual as the sun went down on a cool evening two weeks before Christmas. The moon, almost full, shone brightly in the clear island sky.

Jim had told his son that his meetings with the Russian were potentially dangerous. "Risky," he had said, "but not illegal." But Nathan now suspected that couldn't possibly be true. The evidence, he knew, would show he had smuggled his dad's notes out of the prison, then carried them to first-name-only Russians in diplomatic stations in San Francisco, Mexico City, and Lima. They had paid for the information with bagfuls of hundred-dollar bills. Both his dad and the Russian had repeatedly cautioned him to keep an eye out for surveillance, and the old man had taught him basic spy skills to avoid detection. It was abundantly clear to Nathan that he and his dad were no longer just father and son, but co-conspirators tempting fate each time he met the Russian.

At precisely 7 p.m., Nathan caught a glimpse of a short, gray-haired man walking toward the restaurant. He forced himself to look away until he heard the Russian's unmistakably precise English, words that came almost in a whisper.

"Do you know the way to the federal post office?"

Nathan turned and looked at him as if they had never met. His handler stood at five-foot-six, a couple of inches shorter than he, with white hair, dark gray eyes, and a thick neck. Nathan was supposed to speak his end of the recognition dialogue, an exchange Russian spies call a *parol*. But it felt pointless to him. They had now met on three continents, spent hours talking in soundproof rooms. They were, by anyone's measure, *acquainted*. But Nathan wouldn't disappoint him.

"It should be around here somewhere," he said, lifting the prop in his hand: the map of Nicosia. "Let me show you the way."

Before Nathan could finish the line, the Russian was tugging at his sleeve to move them along. They strode in silence past the Epi Topou Café, toward the sprawling Megaland computer game store, and turned left down a poorly lit side street, where a dark European sedan hugged the curb.

The Russian leaned close.

"Don't say anything in the car," he said.

The Russian opened one of the sedan's rear doors and instructed Nathan to curl himself into the well behind the front seat. Nathan felt the car lurch into gear and pull away. The Russian and his driver chatted in their mother tongue over the drone of the engine. It sounded like a serious conversation.

Nathan's dad and his Army instructors had drilled him on situational awareness, the art of evaluating landscapes and keeping track of time to protect himself and complete his objective. Nathan's immediate objective was to know where in the hell they were taking him. But he was clueless, scrooching in the back with no way of identifying streets or landmarks. They drove along lighted thoroughfares and dark ones, making turn after turn, sometimes rumbling across stone streets. They seemed to be traveling in a wide arc, but the car eventually paused at a tall gate before passing through and into a garage.

Nathan climbed out of the sedan and stood. He knew not to talk until they were alone. They climbed a narrow staircase to a circular landing lit by a sparkling chandelier. The Russian guided Nathan into a tiny office with sofas flanking a coffee table. Nathan took a seat, his back to the heavy door, as the Russian rustled up refreshments. After a moment, the older man presented him with a plastic bottle of Coca-Cola. In all their meetings, the Russian had offered him coffee first and had always seemed humored when Nathan asked for Coke. Ordinarily, he began their meetings by asking how Nathan's father and the rest of his family were doing. But tonight he had something else on his mind.

He wanted to know if Nathan saw anything suspicious in his travels, including his walk from the Hilton to the T.G.I. Friday's. Nathan explained that he had walked a basic surveillance detection route on the way over, running into a pair of guys with Russian accents who asked where they might find someplace to eat. The Russian nodded, as if in deep thought. Nathan said he had turned around at one point to see if he was being tailed and caught a glimpse of a short man abruptly ducking out of sight.

The old man smirked.

"I was tailing you," he said.

Nathan hadn't recognized him.

"Do you have any new messages for me?" the Russian asked.

The question put Nathan on his heels. The Russian had cautioned him in their last meeting not to carry more of his dad's handwritten notes out of the prison—"Too dangerous," he had said—and now seemed to have changed his mind. Nathan tried not to look flustered. He pulled out the letter Jim had mailed him that summer—it was intended for the Russian—and handed it across the coffee table.

Jim was permitted to send letters from the prison, but all his correspondence—peppered with hand-drawn emoticons—was routed through the CIA's headquarters at Langley. Analysts there reviewed Jim's mail to ensure that he wasn't sharing classified information still etched in the coils of his brain from sixteen years in the agency.

The Russian now read the letter.

"Hi Tiger! I want to thank you for your very moving letter of 10 August. I want to also tell you that the qualities you said you had received from me—respect for others, discipline, endurance, faith, patience, love, and sheer will power—are very much qualities that apply to you, whether you received them via me or not. I am so very proud of you, son. You are a man of great courage and a blessing to our entire family."

Jim's missive then veered weirdly into his latest health exams. He listed his height, weight, age, and notes about his excellent physical conditioning, right down to the results of his latest EKG, blood pressure test, and prostate cancer screening. The letter also mentioned the status of two bills before Congress that Jim hoped would get him out of prison sooner. Then came a line with no ambiguity. The words were clearly intended for the Russian, whose countrymen had long stood behind those caught spying for Moscow.

"We've waited a long time for a miracle, but patience is what we've learned instead," Jim wrote. "I have much to do for those who have stood by me."

The six-page letter noted the financial struggles facing Jeremi and his Russian wife, Nastia, who lived in Panama City, Florida. Jeremi, weighted down with student loans, worked at Tyndall Air Force Base. "He's a [staff sergeant] now," Jim wrote, "and still would like to be an officer—which he would have been if they hadn't sat on his security clearance for so long, no doubt because of me." Jim pointed out that Star, who had a decent job at a Portland software company, had accumulated even bigger student loan debts. He wrote how proud he was of Nathan for working as a draftsman while attending college.

"I've probably not told you anything you didn't already know," Jim wrote, "but it's good for me to review all these blessings from time to time lest I forget and become melancholy from wandering around this old prison for a twelfth year. You know. But, I still have dreams and goals and I don't see me sitting back in retirement mode once I am free again. . . . Too much wasted time has already passed for me to waste the future too."

The old man closed by advising his son to put half his savings in euros, owing to the precarious U.S. dollar. Then, with a final wink to the Russian he knew would read his words, Jim wrote: "Take good care of yourself, son, and please extend my very best to those with you. We will have our day. With pride and love, Pa."

The Russian looked up from the letter and asked Nathan if he had any other messages from his father.

"That was all I was instructed to carry," he said.

Nathan knew his dad wanted to set himself up in Russia after serving his time. The old man clearly wanted to live the adventurous life again, this time in luxury, on Moscow's dime.

The Russian wound down the meeting by asking Nathan a few questions about The Farm, the CIA's covert training center. Jim had taught tradecraft, the art and craft of espionage, at the base along the Virginia tidewater. He wanted to know the circumstances that got Jim assigned to the center in Camp Peary in the mid-1990s, where the Nicholson children lived in a government house. The CIA does not publicly acknowledge its nine-thousand-acre training center, one of the government's worst-kept secrets.

"This is the next assignment," the Russian said, pulling out an envelope. They would meet again a year later, on December 18, 2009, in Bratislava, Slovakia. The Russian slid a black-and-white photo in front of Nathan, and smiled.

"Tell me if you see a woman in this."

The photo pictured an abstract sculpture. The piece looked like a human with a halo of hair and massive knees, but there was a gash sliced from hip to sternum. Nathan saw little in the piece to suggest a woman. The Russian noted that she was supposed to be pregnant. This, too, offered no help.

"I don't see it either," the Russian said.

The two men laughed.

The Russian told Nathan that the sculpture sat in a park at Bratislava's Račianske mýto, a major transportation hub, and it was to be the site of their next rendezvous. They would meet at 7 p.m.

The Russian made Nathan repeat the instructions for their meeting, including the coded phrase he was to drop in their Yahoo account in the event he couldn't make it.

"My brother Eugene is ill," Nathan said.

The Russian nodded. He opened a folder and withdrew a paper pouch, out of which he pulled a rectangular envelope. He spilled its contents—a bundle of U.S. hundreds—on the table, careful not to touch the currency.

"Please count it," he said.

Nathan protested, saying it wasn't necessary; they were all friends.

"I insist," the Russian said.

Nathan carefully counted out $13,000, much more than he expected.

"Too much," he said.

The Russian looked puzzled.

Nathan tutored him on U.S. law, explaining that it's illegal not to declare more than $10,000 in cash when reentering the country. That meant he would have to burn through a few grand in the following days so that he came in under the limit. This seemed wasteful to Nathan. The Russian, who had lived through generations of austerity in the former Soviet Union, insisted that the broke American college student take the money. This commenced a comical round of reverse haggling. In the end, Nathan agreed to accept $12,000—not a penny more.

With Christmas coming, Nathan wanted to know what the Russian had planned for the holidays. The two men had made little in the way of small talk in their past meets, and Nathan could see the question made his handler uncomfortable. But the old spy let his guard down, saying he hoped to get home in time to spend the New Year holiday with his wife and son.

It occurred to Nathan that he had no earthly idea where the Russian lived. He knew better than to ask, and it wasn't in his nature to pry.

The two men made their way to the garage and climbed into the sedan, where Nathan folded himself onto the floorboards again. The car rumbled through the south side of the city, all done up for the holidays, Christmas lights sparkling from tree trunks and white globes strung above Makarios Avenue. They drove in silence for a long time before the car slowly came to a stop. The Russian gave a nod, and Nathan climbed out wordlessly. He stood on a parking lot a few blocks from the Hilton trying to orient himself. Suddenly, the sedan kicked up gravel behind him and vanished.

Nathan spent the next couple of days knocking around Nicosia, ordering room-service sushi, gorging on the Hilton's all-you-can-eat buffet, and hitting Pizza Hut, where he sampled the Mediterranean pie with stuffed cheese. As a former deliveryman for the pizza chain, he liked to see how they made their pies in other countries. Nathan stayed on the swanky side of Nicosia, but toured the bastions of the ancient city, deciding he liked the cobblestone streets and solar panels, a splendid collision of old and new. Empires had fought over the city for thousands of years. They had thrown up stone walls and battlements until the latest of them—thanks to a simmering truce between the Turks in the north and the Greek-backed Cypriots in the south—apparently agreed to propagate the town with shopping malls and beige high-rises and to cover every horizontal surface with satellite dishes and antennas.

Before he left Nicosia, Nathan wired Kanokwan $500 and paid his hotel bill, which ran just over a grand. Later that day he landed in Istanbul, where he wended through a serpentine line. He presented his passport to an unsmiling window clerk and walked toward a brightly lit red sign reading, "Duty Free." There he dropped about $100 on the bottle of Armani Code that Jim wanted him to buy Star for Christmas.

Then he flew backward in time, toward Oregon and his one-bedroom walk-up in the Heron Meadows Apartments.

Nathan reached Portland International the first hour of Monday, December 15, and slogged to his Chevy. He drove south toward Eugene in a rare snow shower, which threw a brilliant white blanket over the valley. He reached his apartment at 3:30 a.m. and stashed $9,500 cash in his nightstand. Nathan climbed into his rack knowing his dad would be pleased with the latest payment and with another meeting set for Slovakia the following year. Then he collapsed in the loopy delirium known only to those who've flown halfway around the world in coach.

At precisely 1:20 p.m., a loud pounding woke him. He lay in bed for a few seconds, his eyes adjusting to the light. Someone was knocking so hard on his metal door it reminded him of his sergeants back in the Army.

Nathan lurched out of bed and lumbered barefoot across the carpet toward the door.

The pounding persisted.

He pushed an eye against the peephole and saw the fish-eye forms of two middle-aged white guys standing on his stoop. They were serious-looking men in jeans and heavy winter coats. One of them chewed gum.

Feds, he thought. Had to be.

Nathan stood frozen behind the door. For an instant, he thought maybe they would just walk away, hoped they would.

The gum-chewing man pulled out a phone and began to dial. Nathan turned from the peephole and sprinted on tiptoes toward his bedroom. He was closing in on his flip phone when suddenly it rang. He pounced on the silence button before it could ring twice. Then he waited, praying for the men to go away.

Moments later, the pounding resumed.

The hell with it, Nathan thought, moving for the door. It's now or never.

He exhaled and reached for the doorknob.

2

First CIA Tour, Manila Station

"Manila is the cradle, the graveyard, the memory. The Mecca, the Cathedral, the bordello. The shopping mall, the urinal, the discotheque."

— Miguel Syjuco, *Ilustrado*

Manila, Republic of the Philippines, 1982

The U.S. Embassy compound sits on Manila Bay, a complex of sun-scrubbed buildings overlooking a wide promenade lined with coconut palms along Roxas Boulevard. Just up the harbor sits the Manila Yacht Club, and next door is a busy shipping terminal that sends massive vessels churning toward the tadpole-shaped island of Corregidor and the wide-open waters of the South China Sea. To the north of the embassy, a colorful patchwork of buildings rises from both sides of the Pasig River, a sluggish tidal estuary that bisects the city and runs in opposite directions on the whims and seasonal water levels of nearby Laguna de Bay. Everywhere, knots of mosquitoes hunt for blood.

The embassy compound's chancery, which sat a block from Manila's largest red-light district, Ermita, had served as a jail after World War II, its basement a makeshift court to try Japanese war criminals. Jim's desk, little more than a prop, now occupied an office upstairs. There the first-tour spy posed as a diplomatic officer in the mornings and slipped out in the afternoons. He filed reports behind a heavy wooden door marked "Office of Regional Affairs," a well-known euphemism for CIA stations around the globe.

Manila was a playground for a young CIA man in those days. The operations officers in Jim's station enjoyed a decent relationship with the host government of Ferdinand Marcos Sr., and seldom worried about being revealed, caught, or arrested for their espionage. They also didn't fear Filipino counterintelligence officers, who were too clumsy and overmatched by their CIA counterparts. The spies in Jim's wing focused their intelligence gathering on the KGB and its cohorts from Cuba, China, and Vietnam.

Marcos ran one of the world's most corrupt governments, famously telling ABC News, "I have committed many sins in my life. But stealing money from the government, from the people, is not one of them." Of course, Marcos and his famously shoe-hoarding wife Imelda were busily siphoning billions of dollars from public programs at the time, parking much of it in North American banks. Marcos so detested communist groups working to overthrow him that he fell into lockstep with the U.S. government and its efforts to thwart the spread of communism. Marcos had imposed martial law in 1972, closing the nation's congress and news outlets, and ordering the arrest of political foes. By the time Jim reached Manila, Marcos had presided over a decade of brutal human rights violations.

Jim was assigned to the CIA's internal branch, which spied on the emerging Communist Party of the Philippines and its armed splinter group, the New People's Army. The NPA, with assassination units scattered up and down the nation, was growing. Its gun-toting killers served as shakedown artists, extorting money from local businesses and foreign-owned mining and logging companies in hopes of fomenting a communist revolution.

Marcos' principle antagonist, former Filipino politician Benigno "Ninoy" Aquino Jr., had aligned himself with the left in hopes of overthrowing the regime's ruthless government. Aquino, once expected to ascend to the presidency in 1973, was instead imprisoned. When he suffered a heart attack, the Marcos regime allowed him to fly to Dallas for bypass surgery. He remained there in exile as his people fell into years of withering poverty. In the summer of 1983, Aquino flew home to the Philippines to confront the sagging political climate and talk to Marcos about a peaceful restoration of democracy. Aquino told journalists he was returning of his own free will, and was prepared for the worst. "A death sentence awaits me," he prophesied in an undelivered speech. And he was right.

The assassination of Aquino triggered angry protests across Manila, and many Filipinos believed Marcos had ordered the slaying. The Communist Party's labor and women's movements organized massive demonstrations outside the U.S. Embassy and other spots across the city, calling for the end of the U.S.-backed Marcos government and carrying posters emblazoned with the hammer and sickle. Jim and other officers dressed down in casual clothes and launched themselves into the daylight demonstrations. Jim posed as an American sympathetic to their cause.

Jim and a fellow case officer, one of his closest friends, often paired up to wade into the raucous crowds. Their job was to observe and report on conditions. Armed gunmen halted them from time to time for questioning. "We always did talk our way past them," Jim's former partner told me. "A former supervisor began calling us 'Batman and Robin' after one of these episodes."

Jim ate up his superiors' bon mots, delighted to be thought of as the station's caped crusader. He worked doggedly to develop assets who could provide him entree to key figures in the communist insurgency and the NPA, according to Norb Garrett, who served as the CIA's station chief in Manila from 1984 to 1988.

"He had the reputation of being kind of an up-and-comer," Garrett said. "A bright kid. Hard worker."

Jim worked like a journalist trying to learn what the protesters might do next, gathering intelligence and filing real-time reports. Embassy officials had a stake in the doings on the street. They feared demonstrators might breach the gates of their compound like the student protesters who overtook the U.S. Embassy in Tehran in 1979, holding fifty-two hostages for more than four hundred days.

Jim's workdays didn't end on the streets. He and other ambitious CIA officers rounded out their days in bars and other nightspots, cultivating new contacts and working old sources as they mixed business with beer and other pleasures. One of Jim's brother officers in the internal branch remembered beaching up with Jim and other colleagues at the Hobbit House. The popular bar, opened by a fan of J. R. R. Tolkien, was staffed almost entirely with dwarfs and other little people. It was a popular spot for Americans, especially young, good-looking, ambitious CIA officers trolling for intel to get ahead in the agency while drinking San Miguel.

But the extracurricular nights out played hell on marriages, including Jim's.

Laura Sue Cooper hadn't seen him coming that day in early 1973.

She was eighteen years old, a freshman at Oregon State University, weighing in before fencing class. She stood on the gymnasium scale after a short workout on the universal weight set. Jim sidled up, noting that the scale read ninety-three pounds.

"Getting a little heavy," he remarked.

Miss Cooper responded by slugging Jim in the arm. Love at first swing.

She stood five feet tall, a fair-skinned hazel-eyed blonde with a sprinkle of light freckles. She was born in the seaside dairy country of Tillamook, Oregon, but raised mostly in Eugene, home of the University of Oregon Ducks.

It was a little before Valentine's Day when Jim called. Laurie had no idea how he got her number. She learned he was a twenty-two-year-old senior on a four-year ROTC scholarship. She was curious enough to say yes to a date. What she didn't learn until later was that

Jim had made a bet with a roommate that he could get her to go out with him.

Laurie, who had never been outside the U.S., was smitten from the start. Jim stood a foot taller than she, dark-haired and handsome. He had traveled the world, growing up on Air Force bases as far away as Japan. Jim was as charming and gregarious as Laurie was shy and circumspect.

He proposed less than a week later.

That spring, Jim graduated third in his ROTC class at Oregon State, fulfilling a lifelong dream to earn his commission as a second lieutenant in the Army. He had shaped himself into a low-keyed leader, commanding a unit called the Raiders. His four-year ride in the Reserve Officers' Training Corps coincided with some of the bloodiest fighting of the Vietnam War.

Combat troops had pulled out of South Vietnam three months earlier, returning to a largely ungrateful nation. Meanwhile, Washington and Moscow had closed out the first quarter-century of a nuclear and geopolitical standoff that posed grave consequences for the planet. Amid this chaos, Jim charted his future.

He married Laurie on June 10, 1973, in Eugene. Laurie wore a white floor-length wedding dress with a cathedral veil made of tulle. Jim wore his Army dress uniform with a bow tie. The newlyweds walked under an arch of dress swords. But the wedding marked only the beginning of Jim's dead run into adulthood. He had already taken Army Ranger training in the ROTC and, with no war left to fight, he would plunge himself into military intelligence to help defeat communism.

Jim was a child of the Cold War. He was born in Woodburn, Oregon, on November 17, 1950, the day after President Harry S. Truman declared an emergency crisis caused by the threat of communism. Jim's mother, Beatrice Marie "Betty" Adamson, had married Jim's father, Harold James Mesick Jr., in 1949, while she worked as an Army cryptographer. But

Betty's marriage to Mesick, an Air Force sergeant, never took. Mesick showed little love for her and never bonded with Jim. He was sent to Okinawa, Japan, to serve as a gunner on combat missions in the Korean War. When later he walked away from his family, Betty didn't object. She remained married to Mesick in name only until 1956, when they formally divorced. Betty got full custody of Jim, who hadn't laid eyes on his namesake since he was an infant.

Betty became a single working mom at a time when such circumstances surely fed the small town's scandal-hungry gossips. She opened Elite Beauty Salon and remodeled her life. Her parents looked after Jim while she worked. They were Presbyterians who had fled North Dakota in the early 1930s, victims of drought, swarms of crop-killing grasshoppers, and black blizzards of dust that finished off what the Wall Street Crash of 1929 had commenced.

After Betty had been juggling work and motherhood for a year, her sister introduced her to an airman living at an air base in Klamath Falls, Oregon. Marvin "Nick" Nicholson was nearly five years younger and a few inches shorter than Betty. They fell in love during a historic autumn in American history. John Wayne and Sophia Loren lit up movie screens in *Legend of the Lost*, Elvis Presley's song "Jailhouse Rock" hit number one on radio charts, and Cold War tensions between the U.S. and U.S.S.R. literally soared when the Soviets launched the world's first artificial satellite. The technology that powered a twenty-three-inch sphere called Sputnik 1 into outer space was also capable of delivering a nuclear warhead to the continental U.S.

Jim served as ring bearer at his mother's wedding on March 22, 1958, in the Presbyterian Church in Woodburn. Betty sold her beauty shop and they moved to Klamath Falls, where she enrolled Jim in second grade. Jim balked when he learned the school roster listed him as Harold James Mesick. He thought he'd already become a Nicholson. "Mom," she recalls him complaining, "*we* got married." Nick put the matter to rest by formally adopting Jim. The couple would eventually give Jim siblings, sister Tammie and brother Robert.

Air Force bases and other military installations would serve as Jim's backyard playgrounds for the next dozen years. He made the awkward turn into his teens at Edwards Air Force Base on the western edge of California's Mojave Desert. In January 1965, Jim met Len Beystrum in an eighth-grade history class, and the two would become lifelong friends. They were inseparable for about three years at Edwards, hiking into the desert to dig forts, riding bikes, swimming in the base pool, and playing board games. Jim later played football with the Desert High Scorpions. Like most of the Edwards kids, he was steeped in patriotism. He stood at attention when the base intercom played "Taps" each evening.

It was a scary time for Americans. Cities handed out nuclear evacuation pamphlets, homeowners built bomb shelters, and schoolkids were forced into duck-and-cover drills as alarms blared. But parents at Edwards had little truck in fear. Nick Nicholson and other airmen were already doing their part to ensure the U.S. stayed on top of the Soviet Union. Nick spent his days as an aircraft technician maintaining the Air Force's SR-71 Blackbird spy planes, which hurtled at supersonic speeds to collect intelligence on communist adversaries.

It was likely that Nick's work and Betty's talk of code breaking ignited Jim's passion for spying. While other boys stuck their noses in *Mad* magazine, Jim pored through library books on intelligence operations. He idolized James Bond, played on the big screen by Sean Connery. The early 007 dressed sharp, piloted an Aston Martin with twin machine guns, and burned women down with charm and dry martinis. Spies were the new heroes of Cold War culture in America. Napoleon Solo in *The Man From U.N.C.L.E.*, Kelly Robinson in *I Spy*, and Maxwell Smart in the spy-spoofing *Get Smart* thwarted countless communist villains.

The notion of spying for one's country as an act of patriotism took such deep root in Jim that by the time he and his young bride set off to chase his military intelligence career, he was already dreaming of missions in foreign ports of call. Laurie, who had just completed her first year at Oregon State, quit school to help Jim follow his ambitions. They spent the first few years of their marriage at Army bases in Georgia and

Kentucky, humid hellholes where Jim took airborne training and Laurie got up every morning to make sure the seams of his shirt, belt buckle, and trousers were aligned. Jim's big move came in 1975, when he was shipped off to Fort Devens, in Ayer, Massachusetts, where he studied cryptology, the art of code breaking. Jim's superiors, clearly impressed with the young officer, later assigned him to the Army Security Agency field station in Okinawa, Japan.

Jim knew Okinawa well. He and his mother had moved there temporarily in September 1959 to join Nick, who was stationed in Sobe, at the edge of the East China Sea. The Nicholsons took residence in an un-air-conditioned concrete-block house with grass rugs, bamboo furniture, and mosquito netting. Jim slept on an Army cot, his life a perpetual camping trip. He and his chums spent their days exploring the island, a wild, tropical place crawling with venom-packed snakes and spiders as big as your fist. Ghosts of World War II haunted the place, where U.S. Marines fought for eighty-two days to establish military bases. Jim and his buddies ran across live ordnance, and once, while exploring a cave, stumbled over a skeleton with a rifle and helmet.

Jim's adult years on Okinawa were a steady climb in his intelligence career. The Army Security Agency was responsible for securing military communications and running electronic countermeasures. Jim advanced to first lieutenant, then captain, and won commendations. He also attended school at night, earning a master's degree in counseling from the University of Maryland's University College program in Asia. He later volunteered as a counselor for military personnel and their families.

Laurie resented Jim's focus on his career, which turned her into an officer's wife. She was tired of attending military parties, where she felt ignored. Tired of turning down job offers to chase *Jim's* career. Tired of serving as Jim's chef, housekeeper, and doormat. It galled her that he had earned his master's before she'd gotten a bachelor's. She took classes in Japanese, sociology, and oceanography. But when she asked Jim if she could return to college full time, he told her that was just an excuse to divorce him.

Jim and Laurie also began to suspect each other of cheating. Jim thought she was sleeping around on him, and she was convinced he had bedded an enlisted woman. Before things could spin out of control, Jim's tour of duty on Okinawa came to a close. The Army relocated him to Fort Huachuca, Arizona, home to the U.S. Army Intelligence Center and Strategic Communications Command, a good post for an up-and-coming intelligence officer. It was there, in the middle of 1978, that Laurie gave birth to their first child, Jeremiah, whom they named after the biblical prophet. Laurie picked their son's middle name, Dei, the Latin word for God. They called him Jeremi.

The Army presented Jim an array of intelligence-gathering disciplines, from satellite surveillance to human-to-human spying, known as HUMINT. Laurie recalled years later that Jim had no interest in the field of human intelligence, which is where his talents lay.

The peacetime Army and its lousy pay left Jim at a crossroads. During his next posting, at Fort Ord, near Monterey Bay, California, he made a bold move to leave the only career he knew. He plunked down $500 for some proper business plumage, choosing a three-piece pinstripe suit tailored with medium-weight wool. Laurie sent him off to a job fair looking deadly handsome. Jim mailed résumés to potential employers, including Alcoa, Frito-Lay, and the CIA, and left the Army on August 13, 1979.

Jim thrilled at the notion the CIA might call him for an interview. But he leaped at his first job offer, uprooting Laurie and Jeremi and moving them to a rental home outside Kansas City, Missouri. Jim went to work making decorative candles and votives for Hallmark Cards. Laurie recalled that Hallmark, impressed with Jim's work, wanted to send him to Hong Kong as a production manager for its injection-mold operation. But the Nicholsons stayed put as Jim prayed the CIA would call. They bought a house in Lee's Summit, Missouri, where Jim joined the Church of Jesus Christ of Latter-day Saints and grew a beard. When Jim told his parents he'd become a Mormon, his mom, who raised him Presbyterian, wasn't pleased.

"It's up to you," said Betty. "But you'll never convince me I'm a second-class citizen."

"We don't believe that," Jim told her.

Betty didn't buy it, but she let it rest.

Jim's CIA application stalled, although he was precisely what the agency wanted. He was smart, charming, and possessed a good mix of creative problem-solving skills and executive functioning; his military intelligence background was a bonus. He read up on world affairs, Laurie recalled, and practiced naming the world's top political leaders. But Jim was the victim of poor timing.

The CIA had spent the last few years curbing clandestine operations and drawing down its roster of on-the-ground spies. Stansfield Turner, the CIA's director, believed that the future of global intelligence gathering was in electronic surveillance. "We only need spies," Turner famously observed, "where satellites can't go." Turner slashed more than eight hundred jobs from the payroll, a two-year bloodletting commenced in the autumn of 1979 that came to be known as the Halloween Massacre. His Cold War strategy was to expand the machinery of intelligence gathering, especially signals intelligence, to identify nuclear missile silos and intercept radio transmissions behind the Iron Curtain. But the Soviets' war in Afghanistan and their backing of communists in Nicaragua soon changed Turner's thinking.

In the waning months of Jimmy Carter's presidency in 1980, the CIA commenced a hiring blitz to cover its Cold War action in the Middle East and Central America. The agency funded Afghanistan's Islamic mujahideen in their war against the Soviet Union, and they provided support to Nicaraguan rebels in their efforts to overthrow the Soviet-backed Sandinista government in Managua. In early 1980, the CIA flew Jim and many other prospective operations officers eastward for interviews.

Laurie picked Jim up at the Kansas City Airport when he returned from his interview. They made small talk on the way home in their Jeep CJ-7 Renegade. Inside the little orange car, Jim would not talk about how things went. Only at the house, behind closed doors, did Jim confide that he'd accepted a job with the CIA. Laurie recalled that he was practically bouncing off the walls, a life's dream come true. Jim explained that she could be a stay-at-home mom or join him, under contract, to support his spy work as part of a husband-wife team. But with a baby in the house, Laurie didn't feel comfortable taking a part-time job with the agency. She would consider it later.

The Nicholsons packed Jeremi and the family's Australian shepherd, Morning Dew, into the Jeep and drove to northern Virginia, eventually settling into a drafty frame rental house in Alexandria. Jim entered duty with the CIA on October 20, 1980. Fifteen days later, voters sent Ronald Reagan to the White House—good news for Jim's new employer. The Reagan administration reinvigorated the CIA with enough funding to combat the Soviets at every front in the global spy war. The agency dispatched Jim and hundreds of other men and women to The Farm, 150 miles south of their home, for basic training as spies.

Laurie discovered the loneliness of the long-distance CIA relationship during Jim's ten months at The Farm. As Jim learned how to make disguises, detect surveillance, and recruit foreign assets, Laurie learned how to keep house with a potty-training toddler. As Jim took the agency's paramilitary course, parachuting out of planes, firing machine guns, and rigging handmade explosives, Laurie scrubbed toilets and paid the bills. When her husband came home for short weekends, he couldn't talk about his training. Jim was obsessively secretive about his work, maintaining his cover as a Department of State diplomat even with his parents. Laurie wearied of the separations, and she sometimes felt like a single mom. The Nicholsons spent enough time together to conceive Star, born in October 1981. But in time, Jim's constant travel and the secrecy of his work would grind them toward a showdown.

When Jim's training at The Farm concluded, the agency sent him home to Alexandria, where he commuted to a language class nearby. He spent his days with several other men in a high-rise in Rosslyn, Virginia, studying Tagalog, the primary language of the Philippines. Jim's classmates were newly minted diplomats with the U.S. Foreign Service, and it was obvious the government planned to post them in Manila for their first tours abroad. The students drew close, eating together and sharing life stories. But they noticed that Jim grew uncharacteristically quiet when they'd discuss the State Department's grueling A-100 class, which taught the building blocks of diplomacy. When someone finally asked Jim which class he'd taken, he told them he was in a special program that allowed him to bypass the course and go straight into the political end of the Foreign Service.

Classmate Tom Reich had never heard of such a thing. Curious, he and another student later checked with someone in the State Department personnel office, who thumbed through a roster of junior officers, found no one by Jim's name, and declared, "You've got a spook in your class." Jim's concealment didn't sit well with Reich. Foreign Service employees were supposed to help CIA officers maintain their cover, and Reich found Jim's lie off-putting. He knew there was no reason for Jim to keep up the unnecessary charade. It was as if he enjoyed the lie.

On the last Tuesday in January 1982, Jim took the oath of office, promising to defend the Constitution against all enemies, foreign and domestic. He also signed papers acknowledging that he held top-secret security clearance and that disclosing U.S. secrets was a crime that could gravely damage his nation.

Early that March, as the six-month Tagalog course wound down, Jim invited his classmates and teachers to the two-story rental in Alexandria. Reich watched the dynamic between Laurie and Jim. Laurie was cute and meek as a mouse, and she appeared to live under Jim's thumb. Jim held court with his guests throughout the evening. Whenever he asked if anyone needed fresh beverages, it was Laurie who jumped up to fetch them. Jim never lifted a finger. Laurie might as well have been the maid.

Jim did not explain to Laurie how he spent his days and many evenings in Manila. He typically got home after she had read the kids to sleep. Laurie, pregnant with their third, was mostly homebound. Sometimes

Jim took Laurie to embassy parties, some of them mandatory. They often found themselves at swanky residential homes in one of Manila's sixteen cities, Makati, where the men dressed in *Barong Tagalogs* and sipped tropical cocktails. From time to time, Laurie recalled, they ended up at suit-and-tie affairs where Jim—keeping to his cover as a political officer—made friends with Soviets he considered "developmentals."

From time to time, Jim brought potential assets home, phoning Laurie on short notice to say he had extended a dinner invitation. He had told her that recruitment of a KGB officer was rewarded with a full bump in pay grade. She worked hard to make their guests feel at home, rustling up food and cocktails, which were reimbursed by the CIA. One of the couples had children roughly the same age as Jeremi and Star, and Laurie figured the husband was KGB. Jim and the Soviet got along famously and became good friends.

This cat-and-mouse action played out daily in cities across the globe, one spy working to recruit another spy—or a government official, a business maven, or someone inside the corridors of power and influence. They tried to learn their targets' vulnerabilities—alcoholism, for instance, or marital infidelities, money problems, gambling addictions, hidden homosexuality, or drifting ideologies. They worked months, sometimes years, to craft a recruitment pitch. Sometimes they resorted to blackmail.

Once at an outdoor party, Laurie recalled, a Soviet man drew her aside for a pitch of his own. Russian men were famous for their flirtations. But this man's wife was nearby, visibly pregnant, and he'd clearly been drinking. Soon he made a graceless offer to take her for a ride in his car, just the two of them. Laurie berated him for his boorish move. While he might have been a KGB officer sidling up to Laurie to learn more about Jim, she took it as an unwanted romantic advance and told him, as nicely as she could, to go fuck himself. "I probably blew it for Jim," she said.

Though Jim spent night after night away from her and the kids in hopes of finding a source capable of penetrating the KGB, Garrett didn't recall his developing any sensational assets during his years in Manila, and he was certain that Jim brought no spies—those from the Soviet Union or other communist countries—into the CIA's fold. Although it wasn't for lack of trying: Jim's reputation in Manila was that he was out on the town, but not stepping out on his wife. The city was full of sultry, flirtatious women hunting for husbands. Many of the men they pursued turned philandering into an art form, and Garrett remembered nearly sending one of Jim's brother officers home—meaning back to the U.S.—for bringing unauthorized women into the CIA station. The agency's spies were supposed to report their relationships with foreign nationals, even those in which all that passed between them were bodily fluids.

Laurie took an entirely different view of Jim's nights on the town. Late in his Manila tour, she recalled, their maid confessed to her that she and Jim were having an affair, and that she was pregnant. Laurie recalled that the Filipino housekeeper wanted her husband, her kids, and the family dog. Their maid wasn't the first to throw herself at Jim, but she was the first hell-bent on breaking up the marriage. Laurie confronted Jim, and he quickly summoned the housekeeper for an intense conversation in Tagalog. Jim neither confirmed nor denied the affair to his wife. Many years later, he would deny ever cheating on her. But rumors about Jim's affair with the housekeeper passed through the CIA station, according to one fellow officer.

On the last day of July 1984, Laurie gave birth to Nathan in a hospital in Makati. The Nicholsons named him Nathaniel after the Old Testament prophet. It would have been easy at that point for Jim, with three kids in the house, to put his ambitions on the shelf and coast. But it might have been career suicide.

The following year, the CIA posted Jim to Bangkok, Thailand, to take part in a covert program in support of the Cambodian resistance movement against communist Vietnam. The Vietnamese, backed by the Soviet Union, had seized Phnom Penh in the late 1970s and were at war with Cambodia. The bulk of Cambodia's opposition movement—supported by the U.S.—had fled to the jungles of its western border with Thailand. The CIA needed bodies on the ground.

Jim was thirty-four years old. He had sat out the Vietnam War in classrooms back in Oregon. Now came his chance to run paramilitary operations against the occupiers. Garrett, who supervised Jim in Manila, said the new assignment played to Jim's strengths as a soldier. He recalled that his young subordinate was excited about running cross-border ops in a hot zone with a Kalashnikov rifle slung over his shoulder.

Part of the CIA's mission was to ensure that Cambodians fleeing the bloodshed safely reached international refugee camps in Thailand. In a tricky arrangement, the U.S. supported the coalition forces of exiled leader Norodom Sihanouk and the anticommunist Khmer People's National Liberation Front. The third leg of the coalition at odds with the communists was the Khmer Rouge, a guerrilla force led by Pol Pot, who had superintended genocide in Cambodia in the 1970s. Many of the Cambodian refugees spilling into Thailand wanted food, asylum, and one-way tickets to the West. The CIA sent Jim and his colleagues to the border to train Sihanouk's soldiers and make sure they reached safety.

Jim shared no details of his new assignment with Laurie. He moved his wife and three kids into a house near the U.S. Embassy compound in Bangkok, hired a maid and a cook for them, and vanished. He took up residence in a CIA house in Aranyaprathet, Thailand, a border town more than 130 miles east of his family, where he spent much of the next three years. Jim was supposed to come home to Bangkok four days out of each fortnight, but his stretches on the border grew longer. At one point, he didn't come home for months, leaving the kids heartbroken.

The separation effectively turned Laurie into a single mom. She spent exhausting days making sure Jeremi caught his bus to and from the American School, packing Star off to preschool, and taking care of Nathan, still in diapers, as she took a weekday gemology class in downtown Bangkok. Nathan grew into toddlerhood scarcely knowing his dad. He was a terror: rebellious, tempestuous, the family daredevil. He seemed to find the highest spots in the house, often beds, then jump up and down until he fell. He was an unrepentant show-off who wore skinned knees like service medals. Nathan was, in almost every way, Jim's mirror image.

Meanwhile, Jim lost himself at work on the border, gathering intelligence alongside a young Thai interpreter, Kanokwan Lehliem, whom Jim would later credit with saving his life on a few occasions as they moved between troops and gunfire. Eventually they fell in love.

Laurie and the kids paid a visit to Jim in Aranyaprathet one weekend, their driver carrying them past Buddhist shrines and green fields bleached by sunlight. When they reached Jim's government house, Jeremi, who was just nine or ten, took one look at the place and thought it didn't look like a man's dwelling. The house was spotless, and it was abundantly clear to Jeremi and his mom that someone else was living with Jim.

"There was a female in there, you could tell," Laurie recalled in an interview years later. Yet there was no sign of a maid—not so much as a toothbrush. It was clear that whoever lived there had cleared out. Laurie couldn't confront Jim with her suspicions in front of the kids. So she let it go. But the visit told her everything she needed to know. "He had his mistress there," she said. "He had a house there. Why would he want me and three kids?" Laurie was torn apart by the latest of what she was starting to see as Jim's serial infidelities. Still she wouldn't leave him, clinging to the hope that Jim would overcome the demands of his job to make the most of their marriage.

When Jim's tour ended in 1987, the CIA shuttled Jim and his family off to Tokyo for a two-year hitch marred by the ambassador's disdain for the agency. The CIA rotated Jim stateside in 1989. The Nicholsons bought a town house in Burke, Virginia, eighteen miles from agency headquarters.

The CIA promoted Jim to chief of its station in Bucharest, where he would run intelligence operations against the communist bloc. This was a declared position, meaning Romanian officials would learn that he was the agency's top spy in their country.

Laurie didn't want Jeremi to learn from outsiders that his dad was a CIA officer. So she sat down with her oldest, now twelve, asking him what he thought his dad did for a living. When Jeremi said his dad worked in government, Laurie helped guide him through a series of questions that steered him to Jim's specific job. She swore Jeremi to secrecy and explained that Star and Nathan were too young to know.

The Nicholson children had reached an age where Laurie felt comfortable taking a part-time job with the CIA to help serve her country and support Jim's operations in Romania. She took some classes in the D.C. area—a couple of weeks of radio training and a course on how to identify surveillance—before they flew overseas.

Bucharest, Romania, 1990

The big house in Bucharest seemed like a palace to Nathan, who turned six that summer. The first-floor living space was cavernous, with stone floors, tall pillars, a fireplace, a servants' staircase, and a large dining area with a built-in liquor cabinet. The table sat twelve. The basement had a wine cellar and cloakroom, with an overflow passage that held two refrigerators, where Jim—a fiend for chocolate—squirreled away Reese's Peanut Butter Cups. Star took a small room with a domed ceiling. Nathan took a large room with Jeremi on the second floor, which had its own balcony. But he lived in the downstairs TV room playing Super Mario Brothers 3 on the game console.

The house served as a party palace for the Nicholson kids and their classmates at the American School. Friends popped in for raucous games of hide-and-seek, making use of a massive attic where maids had once slept during the curfews imposed by malevolent communist leader Nicolae Ceauşescu. The Nicholsons threw an annual Halloween bash for kids in what Nathan recalled as their especially creepy basement.

Jim's posting in Romania put him nine hundred miles from Moscow, a choice spot to run operations against his nation's primary communist targets. But once again, Jim's timing was poor. Anticommunism had already swept Europe, taking down regimes in Czechoslovakia and Poland. In East Germany, the Berlin Wall fell in November 1989. A month later, Ceaușescu's rule over one of the most repressive nations in the Soviet bloc came to a dramatic close. He had made the mistake of ordering his KGB-like intelligence service, the Securitate, to open fire on antigovernment demonstrators. Ceaușescu's own military hunted him down with his wife, Elena, capturing them on Christmas Day 1989, hastily trying them for genocide and public corruption, and summoning a firing squad. Hundreds of soldiers reportedly offered to deliver the fatal bullets.

Jim was just thirty-nine years old, and his star shone brightly at Langley. He was practically a shoo-in to one day join the agency's Senior Intelligence Service, the CIA's top echelon. But he had a devil of a time in Bucharest, where his position was known to Romania's intelligence service.

Communism had fallen with Ceaușescu. But much of the Securitate's rank and file—a secret police force once estimated at eleven thousand agents and a half-million citizen informants—still kept tabs on foreigners. Jim was tailed in his maroon Volvo and sometimes needed Laurie to sneak him around, dropping him off and picking him up at prearranged spots. She and Jim took hikes on streets near the embassy looking for dead drops, the secret hiding spots that spies and their assets used to communicate and exchange money.

Laurie's primary job was to man a radio monitoring system inside the embassy. She worked in a drafty garret, headset muffs clamped over her ears, as she tried to detect surveillance devices planted in the building. She sweated through Romania's summers in her attic cubbyhole and wrapped herself in a blanket during its frozen winters, her antennas pointed down into the guts of the embassy to ensure that the offices of the CIA and the U.S. ambassador weren't bugged.

Laurie had hoped Jim's new position in Bucharest would put him on something approximating a nine-to-five schedule. But once again, she found that his career came first. He worked long hours at the office, slipped out in the evenings, and occasionally left town on business. Laurie was certain he was playing around on her. She recalled that just two months after their arrival, Jim told her, "No matter what anyone says, I did not have an affair." Laurie felt herself pulling away.

She struck up a friendship with a polite young veterinarian named Radu, who was smart and good-looking and who, like so many eastern European vets, made house calls. He stood a little over six feet tall, about a foot taller than Laurie. Radu looked after the Nicholsons' dog, Max, which was half wolf, and George, the stray orange-and-white cat that turned up on their doorstep. Radu treated George's mange, and Laurie helped Radu with his English, correcting his pronunciation and teaching him American slang.

Their friendship rattled Jim.

It was late one evening when seven-year-old Nathan found his dad at the top of the staircase listening to Laurie and the young vet. They were seated on a sofa in the living room below, having an animated conversation. Nathan could see his dad eavesdropping with a furrowed brow, and he was curious. Jim motioned him over with a forefinger.

"What's up, Dad?"

"That guy," Jim said with a nod to the doings below, "really makes me uncomfortable."

That was all Nathan needed to hear. Before his father could say another word, he trotted downstairs and announced to Radu that he had overstayed his welcome and that it was time to hit the road. Nathan stood defiantly, his mom looking bewildered as Radu pulled himself to his feet. The young vet smiled uncomfortably and excused himself for the night.

Not long after that, Jim confronted Laurie about the budding relationship. Their stories differ on what was said. Jim's version, as he told it to his parents, was that he chewed her out for growing close to the young Romanian, saying it was precisely the kind of relationship the CIA had warned them about—one where she might be blackmailed into disclosing classified information. Laurie's version is that Jim flat-out accused her of disclosing secrets to Radu, scolded her for being so stupid, and told her he'd been handed an inch-thick file on her misdeeds. It remains unclear what bothered Jim more—Laurie's crush on the vet or her uncomfortable ties with a man he feared was a foreign spy.

The Nicholsons' marital bed wasn't exactly on fire. Over the years, Laurie found Jim impatient in the sack, always wanting things his way. This was perhaps forgivable. But after all of his betrayals—his virtual abandonment of his family in Bangkok, his schtupping his way across much of southeastern Asia, at least in Laurie's mind—his accusation that she'd been unfaithful to her country was the straw that broke the marriage's back.

In a kind of cosmic reorganization, Jim and Laurie's union began to disintegrate just as one of the most feared superpowers in history imploded over the next border. On Christmas Day 1991, Mikhail Gorbachev resigned as president of the Union of Soviet Socialist Republics. Boris Yeltsin accepted the launch codes of the former empire's nuclear missiles and became president of what would be called the Russian Federation. After decades of cruel leadership, systemic corruption, and austerity, the U.S.S.R. was dead. An obscenely expensive war in Afghanistan, tipped in the mujahideen's favor by none other than the CIA, had helped to ruin the Soviet economy and end the Cold War.

Back at CIA headquarters, the Soviet/East European Division threw a party that spilled into the fourth-floor hallways of the Original Headquarters Building. Many of the revelers, intoxicated by the global paradigm shift and the free flow of booze, pinned buttons to their suits. The buttons were circular and white, and featured a red hammer and sickle with three words stamped prominently:

THE
PARTY'S
OVER!

Jim's attention in Bucharest stayed fixed on Moscow. He kept a laser focus on the foreign intelligence wing of the former KGB, now the Sluzhba Vneshney Razvedki. The Communist Party and the KGB were done. But its successors in foreign intelligence, the spies of the SVR, had merely tempered their hatred for the "Main Enemy," the KGB's nickname for the U.S. Now they called Americans their "Main Adversary." The boys and girls in the SVR, many of them former KGB officers, weren't holstering their Makarovs just yet. Their spying would now be a grudge rematch against the West, which had quietly knocked their dicks in the dirt. Jim saw Romania as a battleground in a new era in which the SVR and Romanian intelligence would surely pose a threat.

But Jim's take on things seemed paranoid and even delusional to John R. Davis Jr., who on March 11, 1992, became the new U.S. ambassador to Romania. Davis soon discovered that the CIA's chief of station was, in his words, a bit odd.

"For one thing," Davis recalled, "he was seeing Russians under every bed. It was very strange. He tried to persuade me that the Romanians were still working for the Russians and that they shouldn't be trusted under any circumstances. That they were up to no good in Romania."

Davis didn't see it that way. He had spent thirteen years—scattered over three decades—in Poland, where he witnessed firsthand the revolution that ended its piece of the Cold War. He believed that once the Soviets let go of the reins, the locals would scramble to ingratiate themselves with the West. It was something he'd seen all across eastern Europe. Davis was nearly certain that members of Romania's Securitate, to assure their own survival, would do the same. He and Jim argued this point a few times before they agreed to disagree.

Laurie continued to spend time with Radu, causing Jim personal and professional headaches. He probably felt that Radu posed a security threat—that he was a Romanian spy using Laurie to steal his office's secrets. But he turned his anger directly at Laurie. He flew into a rage in early 1992, telling her never to see the veterinarian again. Jim promised her that if she did, he would take her, sexually, any way he pleased.

The venomous attack came out of nowhere, Laurie recalled, leaving her confused and hurt. All that she and Radu had ever done was talk and maybe flirt a little. European men flirted perpetually. Jim's response to her befriending the handsome vet wasn't to lose his temper, to walk out on her, or to threaten to kill the bastard. He bullied the mother of his children into believing he would savage her if she disobeyed him, making Laurie feel like a whore.

Perhaps it was spite, but she waited until Jim left town on a trip to Moldova to invite Radu over to the house. It was nighttime, and the kids were asleep, when she took him to bed in the attic. She made love to Radu another day, when the kids were at school. Laurie later confessed the affair to Jim, who demanded to know all the details. She recalls telling him, "A hundred times in a hundred places," knowing it would piss him off.

Just before Easter 1992, she got tipsy drinking wine with one of the embassy wives, and shared a few details of the discord in her marriage. Eventually she lost her temper, slipped off her wedding and engagement rings, and pitched them across the kitchen floor.

In June, Laurie told Jim she wanted a divorce, and he said she could have it.

"Fine," she told him. "Get me on the first plane out of here."

Laurie recalls that Jim tried to dictate the terms, saying he would take the boys and she would take Star. But she wasn't budging. She and the kids flew to Virginia, where Jeremi celebrated his fourteenth birthday, then traveled to upstate Washington to live with her brother. Jim stayed behind in Bucharest.

They spoke about once a week, typically with Jim phoning to rant at her. She remembers speaking little, weeping much, and going numb during those chats. Later, she recalled, Jim confessed he was having a nervous breakdown. When the CIA reassigned Jim to Kuala Lumpur, he phoned her to demand that she and the kids move to Malaysia and join him, or that she finally divorce him.

On July 27, 1992, Laurie filed dissolution papers in Shelton, Washington. Jim flew to the Pacific Northwest later that summer, where Judge Toni A. Sheldon granted him temporary custody of the kids, partly because Jim had a good job and Laurie was unemployed. The judge ordered him to pay for Laurie's college education and send her $700 a month to get her back on her feet. In the interim, she would have the kids every summer and Christmas vacation, regular contact by letter and phone, and a say in their religious upbringing. It would take years for Jim and Laurie to reach a divorce settlement, an excruciating journey for the Nicholson clan.

When the summer of 1992 came to an end, Laurie, living in the Pacific Northwest, packed the kids up to go live with their dad in Malaysia, where Jim was now stationed. She returned to Oregon State University to pursue the dreams she had abandoned two decades before to help Jim chase his. She studied geology, walling herself off like a prisoner to rebuild her life brick by brick. After a full-time course load and laboratory sessions that stretched long into the night, she dragged herself home to her little apartment and crumpled into bed thirteen time zones from her kids. She woke many mornings with eyes cemented shut from tears. To survive, she recalled, "I had to seal off my heart."

Jim rarely put the kids on the phone. When she did reach them, she could hear the changes in their voices. She sensed them growing up without her, and it made her feel powerless. She longed to hug them, to smell their hair, see them smile. As often as possible, she placed overseas calls hoping that Jim wouldn't pick up. His voice only reminded her of that long, brutal chapter in her mortal education. She hated him, and in her weakest moments wished him dead. Jim had created malleable women—the meek Laura Sue Cooper he married, the compliant Laurie Nicholson who stayed. All she wanted was to become someone else, someone she could respect. In fact, when the divorce became final two years later, Laurie would legally change her name to Al'Aura Jusme. The new surname formally redefined her place in the world. Just me.

She blamed Jim for their miseries and sensed he was grooming the kids for a life apart from her. Laurie tried to convince herself that the children would see through his attempts to slowly turn them against her, and that they would be strong enough not to play along. But Jim was powerfully deceptive. He'd been professionally trained at duplicity and deceit. He was, in so many ways, precisely what the agency created.

3

"Batman" Switches Teams

"History has many cunning passages, contrived corridors
And issues, deceives with whispering ambitions,
Guides us by vanities"

—T. S. Eliot, *Gerontian*

Kuala Lumpur, Malaysia, 1994

Sometime in early 1994, Jim's superiors cabled him with his new assignment. The CIA was sending him stateside later that year, where he would report to The Farm to teach tradecraft.

"I think the living environment there will be better for the kids than up in Washington," Jim wrote in his personal journal. He had kept a diary since the 1970s, and it now filled several volumes. "The housing and living there is very good, more affordable than in D.C. and more attractive. The schools are smaller, also an advantage. I may have been able to do better career-wise in taking a job at headquarters this time, but the operations training will probably be better for the family as a whole, plus it will make best advantage of my experience for the future of our organization. Teaching is something I have thought would be interesting. I am a little nervous about it, nevertheless. Still, change is often interesting and usually good for me."

The agency liked to rotate veteran spies through The Farm, where their skills and real-world espionage experience would inspire and embolden students. Jim was a likely pick for one of the plum jobs. He had put in a dozen years overseas, and his supervisors at Langley probably thought a little time on The Farm would reinvigorate him.

As a deputy chief in the CIA's Kuala Lumpur station, Jim oversaw the office's spy operations. He was assigned to the U.S. Embassy, which sat on the northwest corner of the Royal Selangor Golf Club, in a swanky part of downtown called the Golden Triangle. Near the embassy, workers were completing the superstructure of the Petronas Twin Towers, an architectural wonder that would eventually stand taller than the Empire State Building.

Nathan would turn ten that summer. He liked the International School of Kuala Lumpur, where he wore a uniform of navy blue shorts and a white polo shirt with the school's Panther logo over the pocket. His life in Malaysia marked a crossroads. He had grown up with an absentee dad who returned from time to time bearing gifts. "He was more of a Santa Claus figure," Nathan recalled. But the father who was always vanishing into taxis and airport terminals was now at his disposal. Jim coached Nathan's soccer, basketball, and softball teams, and he shuttled his youngest to and from an introductory tae kwon do class.

Jim supervised his kids' homework and chauffeured them from one activity to another, thrilling in their accomplishments. Jeremi earned his Eagle Scout medal. Star had become an excellent equestrian. Nathan was a dynamo on the soccer team. They ate late dinners together, slopping up curry with the popular local flatbread, *roti canai*. Jim often drove them out to the swimming pool at the exclusive Raintree Club of Kuala Lumpur. Nathan's siblings spent many summer days reading indoors, but he couldn't hack it inside. He hurled himself outdoors with school friends, searing golden brown in the tropics.

Jim spent the spring of 1994 finalizing his divorce, drawing closer to his kids, and trying to jump-start his love life. He had gotten serious about a Chinese Malaysian named Lily, who worked at the U.S. Embassy.

But his oldest kids detested her. Star and Jeremi saw their dad's sweet young trophy girlfriend as a barnacle they hoped to pry loose before things got too serious. Lily worsened matters by presenting them with trinkets that made them feel as if they were being bought off. Nathan was still young enough to appreciate Lily's attention. He liked the little pewter spaceship figurine she bought him. But Nathan missed his mom and hoped his parents would reconcile. Unlike his siblings, he was grateful to Lily for doting on him and making his dad happy again.

As Jim's tour in Malaysia drew to a close in the middle of 1994, he sat the kids down to tell them he planned to propose to Lily. "I'm gonna put you guys first," Nathan recalled his dad saying. "If any of you don't like Lily, that's it." Star and Jeremi immediately voted no. Nathan would never forget the look of heartbreak on his dad's face. While Nathan voted yes, the deal was already sealed. Jim would slowly break things off with Lily. She stayed around for a time, but Nathan remembered that she and her dad now said their goodbyes outside the house.

When school ended that spring, Jim flew the kids back to Oregon to spend the summer with Laurie and his extended family. Laurie and her lawyer were now making noise about money, forcing Jim to consider the financial implications of years of alimony and child support, college tuition, and twice-a-year airfare for the kids to see Laurie. They fought over community property—cars and furniture and keepsakes, along with a few small patches of undeveloped land they owned in Texas and coastal Washington, and the equity in their northern Virginia town house. But their biggest tilts involved custody: Both sought primary care of the kids.

One of Jim's greatest faults, Laurie recalled, was that he had somehow accustomed himself to champagne tastes on a Budweiser budget. She used to tell him, "You have holes in your pockets as big as your pockets." Jim was almost a fetishist about acquiring electronic gadgets. He bought top-shelf TVs, stereos, computers, and video-game systems, swapping them out as they lost their luster. While most of his colleagues bought their clothes off the rack, Jim preferred hand-tailored suits from

Hong Kong. Early in his marriage, he had flown off on an overseas assignment and returned wearing a silver Rolex watch. Perhaps knowing Laurie would flip, he'd picked her up a pair of cheap vases.

With his looming divorce decree sure to break the bank, Jim devised a plan.

The CIA authorized Jim in the spring of 1994 to meet face-to-face with the SVR's top official in Kuala Lumpur, Yuri P. Vlasov. (This was perhaps a pseudonym, since this also was the name of a Soviet Olympic gold medalist in weightlifting who famously denounced the KGB.) Vlasov served as *resident* in the Malaysian city, the equivalent of a CIA station chief. Jim's official meetings with Vlasov at the SVR's *rezidentura* were intended to throw open the door to dialogue between the two spy agencies. But Jim's underlying goal, tacitly approved by the agency, was to offer the Russian intelligence chief a chance to work secretly for the CIA.

Russians had jumped ship in droves after the collapse of the Soviet Union to secretly work for the CIA and FBI. The going rate for U.S. intelligence agencies to bring one of the valuable traitors aboard was about one million dollars. It was a buyer's market. So much so that U.S. intelligence officials had put limits on how many of these volunteers they would put on the payroll.

The CIA kept some of these voluntary turncoats, known as "walk-ins," as agents in place. This meant they kept their jobs in Russian intelligence services, but leaked secrets to the agency. The United States and the Russian Federation, now democratic partners in the global marketplace, found themselves clumsy at making nice after decades of head-to-head battles. While they continued to spy on each other, it behooved them to team up on issues such as counterterrorism, which threatened both nations. It was the right time for the U.S. and the Russian Federation to quit acting like the playground bullies who'd been forced to shake hands after the fight.

Higher-ups in the CIA and SVR had agreed to share intelligence on Islamic terrorist organizations, such as Hezbollah, which threatened

Russian and U.S. interests. Muslim extremists had bombed New York's World Trade Center in 1993, and Russia—having lost its war against Afghanistan's mujahideen—was now hip deep in an undeclared war against Islamic guerrilla forces in the breakaway region of Chechnya.

Jim made his way to the Russian Embassy. It was a mile away from the U.S. diplomatic station, walking distance if you didn't mind soaking through your shirt on the way over. It may never be clear whether Jim and Vlasov discussed terrorism in their first meeting, but it would have been timely. Not quite six years later, a group of Arab terrorists—some battle-hardened by the Soviet war in Afghanistan—met in that very city to plan a series of attacks attributed to a group that came to be called al-Qaeda.

What is known about Jim's meeting with Vlasov is that the CIA had given their man permission to offer the Russian—just between gentlemen—an opportunity to switch teams.

In spy parlance, this is called hanging out the shingle. This wasn't a formal pitch, simply the CIA's way of opening the door, a smidge, to see if Vlasov would take a peek at the pile of money on the other side. Jim knew that developing the *resident* into a mole for the CIA would be next to impossible. But he also knew that were he successful, his star would shoot through the roof at Langley, and he'd likely earn a bump in pay. The same went for Vlasov: Recruiting Jim would be a major coup. Both spies were high-level officers who held the positions, and security clearances, necessary to breach some of their nations' best-kept secrets.

What Vlasov couldn't have known is that Jim had been daydreaming about switching teams even before their meeting. He imagined himself selling his country's secrets in exchange for piles of cash—money that could solve his problems. He would pay off Laurie in the divorce and possibly gain primary custody of the kids. Jim tried to rationalize such a betrayal. He figured the CIA had long ago turned him into a criminal. He had broken into houses, planted bugs for the agency. He had paid people to steal their own countries' secrets. Besides, as he noted years later in an interview with author David Wise, he didn't see Russia as the "bogeyman" of yesteryear. But Jim was tortured by nightmares of going to prison.

Jim should have had nightmares. A few weeks back, in a courthouse near his old rental house in Alexandria, a federal judge had sentenced former CIA officer Aldrich Ames to prison for the rest of his life. Ames' Russian handlers had given him the code name Kolokol ("The Bell"), paying him a staggering $2.5 million as their agent inside the CIA. Ames apologized during his sentencing hearing in Alexandria's federal courthouse. But he told the judge he'd grown disenchanted by the U.S. government's extreme political shift to the right and accused the CIA's careerist bureaucrats of deceiving generations of Americans and their policy makers about the necessity and value of their spying.

Years later, from inside the U.S. Penitentiary in Allenwood, Pennsylvania, Ames would acknowledge in a letter to me that the odds of someone inside the CIA selling the agency's secrets and getting away with it was, and remains, quite poor. Ames wrote that the CIA's spies are paid as well as comparably qualified civil servants. Like other Americans, they save money, buy houses, send their kids to college, and take vacations. Still, like other professionals, they come up short, suffer financial crises, and divorce. "Only a very, very few try to solve these problems illegally, robbing banks or getting money for secrets," he wrote. "Loyalty of one sort or another, fear and conventionality, keep most on the straight and narrow."

Jim knew that Ames had been captured, convicted, and sentenced to life. His colleagues in the CIA considered Ames a disgrace for embarrassing the agency and betraying his government's secrets. Ames' betrayals had helped Russia identify and execute spies inside its own intelligence operations. But Jim took a different view of Ames' treachery and arrest. He figured that with Ames out of the way, the SVR might be in the market for another highly paid mole inside the CIA.

By sunset on June 17, 1994, one of the longest days of the year in Kuala Lumpur, Jim would have taken his first irreversible steps toward becoming the CIA's new Judas. While meeting in Russia's embassy, Jim told Vlasov he was in trouble. His tour in Malaysia was ending, he said, and he was up to his jugular in an expensive divorce and custody fight. Soon he would have to resettle his kids in the United States.

"I need twenty-five thousand dollars," he said.

Vlasov sat for a moment, taking it all in. He had gray hair and a nice suit. His English was good.

"That should not be a problem," he said.

The Russian's face betrayed no emotion. But he must have been ready to burst into song over his good fortune. Jim had required neither flattery nor coaxing. There would be no seduction necessary to get the CIA man to betray his country for cash. Jim had simply volunteered to spy against the very nation he had served with distinction for twenty years. Vlasov, however, was trained to be suspicious. Guys like Jim rarely volunteered. Vlasov knew that CIA and FBI counterintelligence personnel sometimes posed as potential spies against the U.S. The long-term strategy of these "dangles" was to play the Russians, learn what kind of operations they were running, and give them useless tidbits to string them along. Moscow's spies had done the same thing for generations.

Vlasov wanted to know what Jim could do for Russia, and Jim explained that he was being sent to The Farm as an instructor. Vlasov had to grin.

"What did you do wrong?"

Vlasov knew Jim could help the SVR. In his new position at The Farm, Jim would learn the true identities of hundreds of Career Trainees, known as CTs, many of whom would be sent overseas on their first tours—some to spy on Russia. If Jim gave up the identities of those CTs, the SVR would know them on sight. This meant Moscow wouldn't have to waste time and countless rubles identifying CIA officers in foreign nations. This would turn Russia into a toothy cat in its global cat-and-mouse games with the CIA. The SVR could set traps for the young CIA officers all over the world, bugging their homes and tailing them.

Russian spies were notoriously patient. They often gathered information on foreign intelligence officers for years before pitching them to commit espionage against their own countries. A walk-in windfall such as Jim Nicholson could keep SVR spy operations hopping. With his new job in the CIA, Jim would be strategically placed to become the next Aldrich Ames.

But Vlasov was left to wonder whether Jim could deliver the SVR the names of deep-cover American spies. Officers with nonofficial cover, known as NOCs, operated alone, often posing as businessmen. This work was dangerous. Intelligence officers with embassy cover caught in the act of espionage in a foreign country were typically expelled. But the unmasking of NOCs was a different matter. They could be arrested and sentenced to long prison terms, even killed.

A week after Jim's pivotal meeting with Vlasov, they met again at the Russian Embassy. Vlasov handed Jim a stack of hundred-dollar bills, $25,000 in all, and told him that Moscow was holding $75,000 more to pay him later. They met again on June 29. This time, Vlasov told Jim that Moscow had approved their arrangement, and that he would meet his new SVR handler in New Delhi, India, at Christmastime. Vlasov gave Jim a mail-drop address in Harare, the capital of Zimbabwe, and instructed him to send a postcard, signed Nevil R. Strachey, to signal the meeting in Delhi. Someone in the African nation would pick up the mail and alert his handler that the meet was on. The use of the mail drop, which spies call an accommodation address, would put layers of distance between Jim and the man he would meet in India.

Before Jim left the Russian Embassy, the SVR snapped his photo. This would be forwarded to his new handler, who would be told to watch for the CIA man in the lobby of Le Meridien Hotel in downtown Delhi. Vlasov instructed Jim to wear his Rolex on his right wrist and carry a magazine and shopping bag. He would wait for his handler to greet him first before responding with a pass-phrase.

During four visits with Vlasov in June 1994, Jim did his part to show the SVR he meant business. He turned over the names of more than a dozen assets cultivated by his CIA colleagues in Kuala Lumpur, some of them agents working inside Malaysia. All of Jim's meetings were authorized by the CIA. The agency had no reason to suspect Jim of secretly using the meets to chart his course as the CIA's new betrayer.

As far as the CIA knew, Jim was performing bona fide intelligence work in Kuala Lumpur. The very month that he switched teams, the director of Malaysia's spy service, known as the Special Branch of the Royal Malaysian Police, awarded Jim a gold ceremonial dagger, a kris with a serpentine blade.

On the last day of June, Jim wired $12,000 into his savings account at the SELCO Credit Union in Eugene, Oregon. This put him in position to square things with Laurie. That summer, they would finalize the terms of their divorce. Jim was ordered to pay Laurie $4,000 for her share of their land, and $2,000 for her legal fees. The judge thought Jim and Laurie were both good parents. But Jim was a steady government worker with an excellent salary, and Laurie was a broke college student. The judge ruled that Jim would serve as the primary caregiver, and that he must fly the kids home to spend Christmas breaks and summer vacations with their mother.

Camp Peary, Virginia, summer 1994

The CIA's covert training center stretches more than nine thousand acres across the Piedmont flats along the York River in southeastern Virginia. A tall fence corrals much of Camp Peary, named for the North Pole explorer Robert E. Peary. The base has a 1,500-meter airstrip, a helicopter pad, shooting ranges, classrooms, running trails, a swimming pool, a clubhouse, a Holiday Inn–like dormitory to house trainees, and nice homes for its instructors.

CIA officials do not formally acknowledge the place. But to residents next door in Colonial Williamsburg, where actors in tricorner hats carry muskets and women wear bonnets and colonial skirts, Camp Peary is an open secret. The property had variously served as the indigenous home of the Shawnees, the hunting lodge of the last British governor of

Virginia, a Civil War field hospital and, during World War II, a training center for Seabees and a stockade for German POWs. Now it was home to one of the world's best spy schools.

Jim had the right mix of skill and charisma to lead the next generation of the agency's CTs. He was assigned to teach tradecraft. The course ran about five months, with a slightly shorter paramilitary course. Between those disciplines, CTs learned how to parachute out of a plane, write and decipher secret messages, shoot pistols and machine guns, drive a car through a roadblock, break into a house to plant bugs, and recruit and handle foreign agents. The CTs would also be dispatched to nearby towns, such as Richmond, for mock operations that taught them how to cultivate assets, set up secret communications, and put the slip on surveillance teams.

The Farm was the ultimate gated community, a kind of secret national park, for the instructors and their families who lived there. Parents never worried about pedophiles or kidnappers, who would rue the day they trespassed on such a heavily secured and devilishly armed facility. The first thing instructors with children were told when they moved onto the base was to buy them bicycles to get around. While portions of The Farm were kept off limits, there were trails and creek beds through vast tracts of hardwood forests open for exploration.

Nathan turned ten the month that his dad moved to Camp Peary. Star would turn thirteen in a few months, and Jeremi was sixteen. The base was so sprawling and clean that Nathan had no clue he lived in a private community inaccessible to the general public. He had spent almost his entire life in government housing in Asia and Europe and had no idea what living in the U.S. was supposed to look and feel like.

The Nicholsons took up residence in a two-story government house with a splendid deck and big backyard at the end of a cul-de-sac. The house was marked M-16, an address that doesn't exist outside The Farm. Nathan chuckled when he first heard the house number, because M-16 also was the name of the military rifle his dad carried in the Army. Jim sometimes regaled Nathan with tales of his days in the Army's elite corps of airborne Rangers, of jump training and small-arms fire. Nathan ate it up, convinced that he, too, would one day wear the spit-and-polish boots of an Army Ranger.

Nathan spent summer days lazing in the base's outdoor swimming pool, nights playing hide-and-seek amid the fireflies. On Saturday evenings, he and other Camp Peary kids gathered in the base clubhouse for movies. They hiked and biked countless miles, exploring the ruins of abandoned houses that—like the boys themselves—were beaten by sun and salt air. They were tough boys, and mischievous.

Early one Saturday evening, Nathan and his friends pedaled out to the airstrip, a restricted space next to the York River, about ten miles from the brackish waters of Chesapeake Bay. Some of the older boys posted Nathan and his friend Mike as lookouts. Nathan couldn't fathom why an airfield held any allure. But they stood point as the others ditched their bikes on the runway and hiked toward a cargo plane. Nathan watched them, astonished by their cheek. The lights of a security station shone on the other end of the strip. What if someone saw them? What if a plane came in for a landing? Nathan could see the boys climb into the cargo plane. Soon, a security officer drove straight toward him and stopped.

"What are you kids doing?" the security man asked.

Nathan explained that he had no idea.

"So how many of your friends are in the plane?"

"Three."

The guard took Nathan's name and drove over to roust the other boys and jot down their names. The boys pedaled back to the base clubhouse to await their fates. Some of them broke into tears as their parents, who'd been notified, rang the clubhouse phone. One by one, the boys took their brief calls, waved weak goodbyes to the others, and headed home to face the music.

Finally, it was Nathan's turn. He sat sick with dread. He could only imagine how disappointed his dad would be. Jim's occasional upbraiding, unlike Laurie's, was neither shrill nor violent. Laurie often shouted and gave them a choice of being either grounded or paddled, the former being so abhorrent to an adventurous kid like Nathan that he frequently took the paddling. Jim's method was to sit Nathan down for discussions. With crisp diction and a wrinkled brow, he walked his youngest through the elements of his transgression. These discussions did not end until Jim was certain Nathan fully understood the gravity of his trespasses. Jim's look of betrayal and words of admonishment were all the punishment he needed.

"Nathan, it's your dad."

He took the phone.

"Son," Jim said, "I understand you were questioned here earlier."

"Yeah."

"Are you all right?"

"Yeah, Dad."

Nathan admitted his role as lookout for the other boys.

"You're not gonna do this again, are you?"

"No."

"All right," he heard his dad say. "I think you've had enough of a scare."

And just like that, it was over. The fright of being caught and questioned by base security, as Jim had said, *was* punishment enough.

That conversation stitched Nathan and Jim ever closer. But his father had never shared with him the family secret, nor had anyone else. Nathan knew his father held a government job, laboring in and around U.S. embassies. But he'd never been curious enough—or perhaps old enough—to ask the nature of his work. And he was slow to pick up on the abundant clues that his father wasn't an ordinary bureaucrat.

Nathan entered fifth grade that fall, and his yellow school bus seemed to be the only one at Queens Lake Elementary that passed in and out of Camp Peary. He heard someone say the driver had a special security clearance to enter the gates of the camp. The children who lived at the training center, and who knew what their parents really did for a living, were instructed to tell their classmates they lived on a Department of Defense base. It was a small lie perpetuated by signage. But there were more obvious clues, too, that Camp Peary was no ordinary suburban community.

The neighborhood was the only one Nathan ever saw with its own shooting range. Jim gave Nathan trigger time at the range, where he fired a .22-caliber rifle, a crossbow, and one of Jim's big-bore pistols. His dad sometimes took him and his siblings to what he called "demonstrations." Nathan recalls watching a group of men blow up a hillside. Another time, he witnessed a car, closely pursued by another, hurtling down what appeared to be a racetrack. Suddenly, both cars skidded to a halt, with the driver of one pulling a pistol and firing at the other. This was part of the CIA's "Crash Bang" course.

Car crashes, muzzle fire, explosions—to a ten-year-old boy, these were the Siren calls of manhood. But no one offered Nathan any context for these demonstrations.

Nathan mined fragments of his memory for details that might explain why they lived on this strange military post. He recalled a conversation, on the sidelines of a soccer match in Malaysia, in which his father was telling a friend about tailing someone, or maybe of being tailed. His dad had uttered a name, and Nathan could see it bothered the old man to have spoken it in front of him. Jim had said, "I need you to not remember this, all right?" And later, when Jim had quizzed him about the name, he seemed pleased to see Nathan hadn't remembered it.

It's unclear why Jim left Nathan in the dark about his job. Perhaps he figured his youngest was simply too immature to handle such a weighty disclosure. Star and Jeremi had kept the family secret from their little brother. Years would pass before Nathan heard his dad's name uttered in the same breath as words like "spy" and "CIA."

4

A New Counterspy Collaboration

"Our investigative agencies seem to be more concerned with protecting their own bureaucratic turf than getting down to the business of catching spies. The nation cannot afford to let this situation continue."
—U.S. Senator Dennis DeConcini, May 3, 1994

Langley, Virginia, 1994

In May of 1994, Bill Clinton signed a presidential directive that reshaped the U.S. spy-catching apparatus. The administration, stupefied by sloth and missed opportunities in the Aldrich Ames case, ordered the FBI and CIA to share information to maximize the effectiveness of national counterintelligence efforts. Clinton's directive required CIA counterintelligence officers to permanently staff management positions in the FBI's National Security Division and possibly the bureau's field offices. The directive also ordered that a senior FBI executive permanently serve as chief of the counterespionage group within the CIA's Counterintelligence Center.

These changes came as a crisp slap in the face to the CIA, an acknowledgment by the executive branch that Langley couldn't be trusted to identify its own bad apples. The two agencies, notoriously competitive, would now be forced to work together to identify and catch spies in their own ranks.

For Ed Curran, the first FBI executive embedded as the CIA's counterespionage chief, the job was a bit like going to work each morning in the opposing team's locker room. He was given a blue CIA badge, a parking space, and a small office at the agency's headquarters, all of which gave him the appearance of being a senior agency man. But he was an outsider, a law enforcement guy, and his new position didn't make him popular at Langley. After just two days, he wondered what in the hell he'd gotten himself into. Some of his new colleagues loathed the presence of any FBI man trespassing in the hallowed halls of the CIA, and this went double for an agent willing to turn the place upside down in the hunt for turncoats.

"The bureau came in there, after Ames, like the Panzers into Poland," observed Paul J. Redmond, who supervised the CIA's investigation of Ames and was the agency's deputy director of counterintelligence during the Nicholson probe. "They were in charge. They were throwing their weight around. We were getting the shit kicked out of us. We were pretty defensive."

It's unlikely anyone hated the FBI's taking over the counterespionage section of the shop more than Redmond, who had no faith in the bureau's abilities to identify spies. He fully expected Curran and company to take residence at Langley, get a good look at how hard it was to commence spy-catching operations, and quit complaining, forever, about how the agency did things. Redmond secretly hoped the FBI would screw things up so royally that the bureau would permanently get out of his hair.

But Curran wasn't going anywhere. Early in the new job, he learned that from 1993 to 1994, about three hundred CIA officers—from first-tour spies to chiefs of station—had failed agency polygraph tests designed, in part, to unmask moles. Results of the tests were supposed to guide counterintelligence. But in the CIA's culture, Curran explained, you could fail a test and no one took action. So he and his colleagues in the counterespionage section ordered new polygraphs for those who blew their previous ones. Officers were hauled in from all over the world for their turns on the box. Curran went so far as to assign three CIA polygraph operators—the best in the agency—to conduct a precise, highly targeted line of questioning he called "my test."

Curran wasn't the kind of guy you'd want to find in your rearview mirror. He took a job as a clerk in the FBI in 1962 and clawed his way to agent and supervisor positions before breathing the rarer airs of the bureau's top management. Curran, who stood six-foot-two, was a blunt, imposing lawman. He spoke with a word-merging, consonant-swallowing New York accent, which he salted with colorful runs of profanity. He grew up on the Upper West Side of Manhattan, spitting distance from Harlem, the same Irish Catholic neighborhood that the comedian George Carlin dubbed "White Harlem." Curran followed Carlin by a few years at Corpus Christi School, where nuns kept order with an iron ruler. The FBI man was known to take just so much bullshit from any man, which was none at all.

At the CIA, Curran's new colleagues put the agency's officers through fresh rounds of polygraphs. They didn't give a rip whether CIA employees had beaten their wives or cheated on their taxes; being an asshole was perfectly acceptable, Curran said. They were hunting for spies. The wave of polygraphs caused a lot of grumbling at the agency. Supervisors berated Curran and Redmond. They complained that employees who failed their turns on the box fell under suspicion, their careers derailed, promotions denied, overseas assignments canceled.

"The CIA had screwed up so badly with Ames that it could no longer be trusted to clean its own house," former CIA man Bob Baer wrote in his 2003 memoir, *See No Evil.* Baer rotated through Langley the very month Curran showed up, and he, too, was put through two polygraphs in a half year. Baer complained that innocent officers under scrutiny were reassigned to security facilities in nearby Tysons Corner. "Everyone," Baer wrote, "had a friend or colleague tied up in the security purgatory."

Baer said in an interview that a colleague's desk had been yellow-taped as part of the morale-killing juggernaut of FBI agents, CIA security officers, and investigators from the Inspector General's Office rolling through Langley. "All the outsiders were looked at as being a hostile occupying force," he said. Operatives like Baer considered lie detection part of the dark arts, a fraud that scared people rather than establishing guilt or innocence. Putting the FBI in charge of counterespionage in the building was debilitating, he said. "It was like putting the fox in the chicken coop and saying, 'Find me a crime.'"

Curran acknowledged the paranoia wrought by the polygraphs. But he and Redmond knew secrets that Baer didn't. The CIA and FBI were quietly working to resolve several espionage cases in their own ranks, and the only CIA personnel who needed to fear their investigations were those moonlighting as spies for foreign powers. The onslaught of polygraphs cleared all but about 5 percent of those who had proved deceptive in previous rounds on the box. But Curran noted that the lie detectors were just one piece of the Counterintelligence Center's housecleaning strategy.

The CIA constantly worked its overseas contacts, including assets inside foreign intelligence services. It had developed information about leaks inside the agency that were far more ominous than the rank and file could have known. The CIA had turned up intriguing tidbits from a Russian intelligence officer about an agency man selling secrets to the SVR. The source didn't know the CIA officer's name, but knew he had worked in Asia, spoke a foreign language, and had spent time in the Middle East.

The tip was vague, but alarming to U.S. counterespionage officials.

New Delhi, India, December 1994

That summer Jim jotted a note in his journal, saying he had no regrets about his work at The Farm or his forthcoming flight to India.

"Both of them color my life experience," he wrote, "and give me satisfaction that I'm doing much to get the most from my time on Earth."

In Delhi, Jim posed as a tourist in the lobby of Le Meridien Hotel. As he'd been instructed, he held a shopping bag and wore his Rolex on the wrong wrist. The man who approached him was a hulking fellow with a broad face and dark hair thinning above his temples. Jim stood casually, waiting for the big man to amble over and run his half of their *parol*.

The stranger, pretending not to know Jim, asked if he were with a tour group, which he named. Jim played it out, telling him no, and that he was there with another group. That simple recognition dialogue commenced a lucrative bond between spy and handler. Jim would open the spigot of top-secret U.S. files and keep them flowing to the Russian Federation. In exchange, Moscow would pay Jim generously.

Sergei A. Polyakov (friends called him "Seryozha") introduced himself to Jim, who quietly handed over his shopping bag. The sack held a batch of CT dossiers straight off The Farm, which Jim had printed himself. Later that evening, a car collected Jim from the hotel and carried him to a commercial office, where Polyakov handed him a brown paper package. Jim looked inside and saw five bands of hundred-dollar bills. Fifty grand.

Jim and Polyakov spent the next couple of days in Delhi getting to know each other. The two men were close in age, but Polyakov had risen much further in his spy agency than had Jim. Polyakov was born into what passed as privilege in the old Soviet Union. His father had been a member of the Communist Party Central Committee. Polyakov was chief of the SVR's South Asia Division, a high-level position equivalent to that of a senior intelligence officer in the CIA.

Moscow had called in a serious player to handle Jim.

Russian spies took a long-term approach to running agents, and the U.S. could have learned a few things. When the CIA recruited foreign assets to spy for the United States, it almost always assigned their care and handling to a case officer in an overseas station. This meant that if the CIA handler was reassigned to a different city—as often they were—the foreign asset got a different handler. This required the new case officer to waste time boning up on the asset and forging a brand-new spy-and-handler relationship. The Russians labored to keep things simple. Typically one spy was assigned to one handler, forever. Polyakov would handle Jim as long as he was helpful to the SVR.

For the next couple of days, Polyakov and his fellow officers coached Jim on how to beat the inevitable polygraphs back at Langley. Jim and his SVR handler both knew the CIA would eventually run him through one of its routine lie-detector tests and ask him variations of the question most likely to trip him up: *Have you had unauthorized contact with foreigners?* Jim would have to learn how to lie without tripping the box. Polyakov's people prepared him to defeat the test without drugs.

For as long as police, government agencies, and private employers have used polygraphs, people have found ways to muddle the results. They have swallowed sedatives, counted backward in their heads, applied antiperspirant to their fingertips, and—to increase blood pressure readings early in the test—taken such measures as holding their breath, tightening their sphincters, or imagining wild sex. The polygraph test is, by most accounts, an interrogation tool backed by a modicum of science; the better the polygraph operator, the better the chance of getting to the truth.

The Russians hooked Jim up to the box and got him comfortable for practice runs. They threw him a curve by putting him through their own single-issue test to ask whether he had reported any of his illegal contacts with the Russians to anyone. Jim must have passed easily, because the Russians kept him on the payroll.

Before departing Delhi, Polyakov told Jim to buy a Toshiba Satellite T1960CT, a state-of-the-art laptop that ran Windows 3.1. The Russians were thinking ahead as they collected data from their agent. They hoped later to get Jim to download files to diskettes, which they would teach him to encrypt, minimizing his chances of getting caught with a satchel of top-secret documents.

With his kids spending Christmas with Laurie and his family, Jim passed through Kuala Lumpur, where he wired $9,000 to his credit union checking account and a $6,000 cash payment toward his American Express card. He flew home, stopping in Oregon to ring in the New Year with his parents. On Saturday, December 31, 1994, Jim walked into his credit union in Eugene, where he pulled out a wad of hundred-dollar bills. He put down $3,000 to pay off the loan on Laurie's Volkswagen and applied $10,019.35 toward his Visa card.

Camp Peary, Virginia, early 1995

By January, Jim's second group of students had completed their first full week of instruction. He wrote in his personal journal that he was impressed with his class, and pleased with the quality and nature of his life. "I have those who love me, plenty of things to keep me occupied, and am living a great adventure," he wrote. "I want this to continue to the end, getting better and better. I really should write an adventure book, or at least try to."

Jim surfed the CIA's computer system from his office at The Farm. His top-secret security clearance gave him access to cables pouring in from around the world, many of which were potentially valuable to the Russians. He printed out files and took them home, where he typed up summaries of the juicier tidbits and copied them to diskettes.

With summer approaching, Jim cabled his superiors at Langley with plans to take his annual vacation leave. After school ended he would pack the kids off for Oregon, where they would stay with Nick and Betty until Laurie completed a six-week field study program in the scrublands of eastern Oregon. Jim would then fly to Singapore, bound for Jakarta, Indonesia, and Kuala Lumpur, with a side trip to Hong Kong. In July, he mailed the Russians a postcard to the Zimbabwe accommodation site with a phony return address from their old friend Nevil R. Strachey, a signal their next meeting was on.

He met Polyakov in a park that July in Jakarta, where they exchanged pleasantries and another shopping bag of files that included reports about the exhaustive debriefings of Aldrich Ames. They met again later that day in a Russian housing complex, where Polyakov handed Jim a package that held another $50,000 in cash. It was there in Indonesia's capital city that Polyakov began to give Jim tasks. He wanted to know how the Clinton administration would react if Boris Yeltsin ramped up military operations against the Chechen guerrillas who had broken from the Russian Federation and were clashing on the border with Russia's troops. Polyakov also wanted Jim to learn more about the Ames debriefings; the SVR was desperate to know how much information the imprisoned former CIA man had coughed up about their dealings.

When spies like Ames were caught, the FBI and CIA were left to determine the extent of the damage they caused. They often debriefed the turncoats for many days, wringing every detail out of them, in what are called damage assessments. Ames' plea agreement required that he share every move he made, every secret he sold, during his decade of espionage on behalf of Moscow. For months, he had recalled the fine points of his staggering perfidy.

Ames had begun moonlighting as an agent of the KGB in 1985, serving nine years as its mole inside the CIA. He betrayed the names of dozens of operatives on the payrolls of Western spy agencies. The KGB reportedly killed at least ten of those assets, one of whom was a two-star general in Soviet military intelligence who had sold Moscow's secrets to the FBI for nearly twenty years. Congress would later rip the CIA for failing to determine early in its mole hunt that Ames was living awfully high on the hog for an agency man. He had never earned more than $69,843 a year, yet he had paid cash for for a $540,000 house. One of the Jaguars he drove during his work for Moscow was valued at $49,000. Ames' wife, Rosario, had expensive tastes.

The U.S. government had collected a massive pile of evidence against Ames to make sure he pleaded guilty. The specter of such a spy testifying at trial was nightmarish. Not only was the CIA red-faced that it took years to roll up one of its own, but the idea of watching such a diabolical turncoat take the witness stand gave them shivers. Ames literally knew too much. From the stand, he could have betrayed closely held secrets about ongoing spy operations, putting even more lives at risk.

To thwart such a move, prosecutors seized on Ames' key vulnerability—his concern for his wife, Rosario—and cut a deal that would ensure keeping sensitive information out of the news. Ames, acting out of love and sorrow, accepted a life prison term in exchange for a lenient sentence for Rosario. He would later come to believe he'd been snookered by the government.

"I think I made it clear at . . . my plea and sentencing hearing that my wife's involvement was limited to a year and a half of guilty knowledge at the source of my money," Ames wrote in his letter from Allenwood. "I was led to believe by her attorney and my own that she could receive a life sentence if found guilty at trial. It was therefore a no-brainer for me to forsake my defenses and my bargaining leverage. I have since learned, of course, that the threat of a life or 40-year sentence was an empty one."

While in Jakarta that July, Polyakov told Jim that it was too risky for him to keep copying and carrying paper documents into their meetings. Jim spent his final day there learning how to code his work with the Soviets' encryption program. Then he flew out of the Indonesian city, over the Java Sea, to Kuala Lumpur, and formally broke things off with Lily. He headed back to Camp Peary, where he penned a new entry in his journal: "I live my life in the rapids-head, afloat and sometimes in seeming control, but always in danger of drowning whether I recognize it or not."

It was about that time in 1995 that a squad of FBI counterintelligence agents based out of the Washington Metropolitan Field Office ramped up its investigation of several CIA officers suspected of leaking secrets to Russia. A supervisory agent named Tony Buckmeier, who worked at headquarters, drove over to the CIA's Directorate of Operations to get a list of CIA officers who might fit the bill supplied by the Russian source. The FBI team winnowed the list of suspects to about seven CIA officers, and Jim was at the top of their list. They wanted to put him under the full weight of the bureau's eavesdropping capabilities, a brand of surveillance bordering on the proctologic. But when Buckmeier took their evidence to Justice Department lawyers for review, they told him he didn't have enough evidence. Miffed but undeterred, Buckmeier carried his papers to Marion "Spike" Bowman, a senior FBI lawyer.

Bowman was an expert in the legal complexities of spy cases. He had served six years in Navy counterintelligence, then twenty-one as a JAG officer, before being recruited to work in the FBI's National Security Law Branch. His job was to keep the bureau's spy catchers on solid legal footing and, as he often put it, out of jail. Bowman and Larry Parkinson, the FBI's deputy general counsel, dug through the mound of papers outlining evidence against Jim and other CIA officers who might be spying for the Russians. Bowman and Parkinson spent days poring over the multitude of facts gathered by the investigative team, tapping evidence into a spreadsheet. They built a matrix around information provided by several sources—including the CIA's key Russian tipster—and matched it against the data on the group of CIA officers. The evidence wasn't conclusive, Bowman said many years later. But it pointed to Jim.

Their first option was to take the evidence to lawyers in the Department of Justice to open a criminal investigation. But that exposed them to questions about the Russian. The first thing Justice's lawyers would ask is how much money the CIA was paying him. Too little, and they would question the authenticity of his information; too much, and it sounded like bribery.

A better option, Bowman and Parkinson agreed, was to keep the inquiry under tight wraps and out of the hands of criminal investigators until necessary. They drafted an application to eavesdrop on Jim under the provisions of the Foreign Intelligence Surveillance Act of 1978. The law permitted government agents to set up wiretaps and other forms of surveillance against suspected spies or terrorists working for foreign powers on U.S. soil. The FBI lawyers got their application signed by

Louis J. Freeh, the bureau's director, and then, joined by Buckmeier, crossed Pennsylvania Avenue with a thick paper file stamped "Top Secret" to confer with the Department of Justice's national security team. Janet Reno or one of her top subordinates certified the application and allowed the FBI men to carry it upstairs to the Foreign Intelligence Surveillance Court.

The panel operated in the penthouse of the Justice Department, the most secretive court in the land. It was no conventional courtroom, but more of a windowless office behind a cipher-locked door, its walls impervious to electronic bugging. A lone judge, one of seven working on a regular rotation, sat behind a big desk poring over FISA applications. The judges had no room for a gallery, no need for a gavel. Their job was to look over applications by the FBI, CIA, or National Security Agency to physically or electronically eavesdrop on espionage or terrorism suspects. The panel's judges would review 697 government applications to snoop on targets that year, approving every one of them. At least two of the classified orders targeted Jim.

The FBI also sent national security letters to banks and credit institutions where Jim kept his money. A 1981 law allowed the FBI to collect Jim's financial records, and it forbade bankers from disclosing to Jim that they had handed them over. Agents pored through every penny that moved through Jim's credit cards, checking accounts, and savings. They matched his deposits against his overseas travels, and they found a pattern. Jim had deposited cash into all manner of bank accounts, including savings for his three children, immediately after his foreign travels. The amounts of those deposits were highly suspicious for a CIA man earning less than $80,000 a year.

On October 16, 1995, a CIA polygraph operator hooked Jim to the box, part of what he thought was a routine security update. Jim's answers, examined by computer, showed he was deceptive on two questions: Are you hiding involvement with a foreign intelligence service? Have you had unauthorized contact with a foreign intelligence service? Four days later, they put Jim through another polygraph. This time, his answer to one question—Are you concealing contact with any foreign nationals?—proved inconclusive.

When Jim came back for a third polygraph on December 4, 1995, the polygraph operator noticed that he took deep breaths and held them during the control questions—a clear attempt to elevate his heart rate and throw off the machine. The operator told him to knock it off. A computer analysis of Jim's lie-detector test showed there was an 88 percent chance he answered deceptively when asked two questions: Since 1990, have you had contact with a foreign intelligence service that you are trying to hide from the CIA? Are you trying to hide any contact with a foreign intelligence service since 1990?

Jim did not hear from Langley about the results of his latest bout with the box. No news was typically good news where CIA polygraphs were concerned.

Two weeks later, Jim boarded a plane for Zurich, Switzerland.

He rendezvoused with Polyakov in the lobby of the luxurious hotel Novotel, where he handed over diskettes he had encrypted himself. The storage devices, primitive by today's standards, were choked with the names of more CIA trainees and additional details about the government's debriefings of Ames. A grateful Polyakov handed him $125,000— Jim's standard $50,000 payment, plus the $75,000 Moscow had been holding for him. That evening, after Polyakov had digested the new information, he joined Jim for a dinner of sashimi and yakitori at a Japanese restaurant. The Russian told him that some of the information about Ames was new, which suggested to Jim that the SVR might have another mole inside the CIA.

While in Zurich, Jim paid a visit to Bank Leu, an institution built more than forty years before Napoleon Bonaparte conquered Switzerland. Swiss banks are spectacularly secretive, and a who's who of notorious crooks have used them to hide money. Bank Leu's good name had weathered some unfortunate publicity in the 1980s, having stored tens of millions of U.S. dollars acquired by the likes of Ivan Boesky, the arbitrageur who famously told business school graduates,

"I think greed is healthy. You can be greedy and still feel good about yourself."

Jim met with Roland Keller, a Bank Leu manager who handled private accounts. Keller was happy to deposit Jim's $61,000 in U.S. cash in an account bearing the name "Harold Nicholson." Jim jotted down his Swiss bank number on the back of Keller's business card and slipped it into his wallet, a tiny mistake that would come back to haunt him.

Back at Camp Peary, Jim continued blowing cash on the kids, who found life with their single dad a parade of adventures. They had toured Colonial Williamsburg and spent days at Busch Gardens Theme Park and Water Country USA. They ate out whenever they pleased. Their house had the latest big-screen TVs. Sometime in 1995, Jim bought Nathan a state-of-the-art Sega Saturn video console, allowing his boy to lose himself in the hit game *Virtua Fighter 2*. When the game system crashed, Jim sent it out for repairs and hightailed it to the store to buy a new one so Nathan wouldn't miss a beat.

With Christmas approaching, Russia's money in his pockets, his kids safely parked in Oregon with Laurie, and his relationship with Lily safely in the rearview mirror, Jim jetted off to Bangkok to visit his old love Kanokwan Lehliem. Jim had feelings for the quiet Thai for a decade, and while it's unknown how closely they kept in contact, their romance clearly was rekindling.

When Jim returned to the U.S., he made eleven bank transactions that put $26,900 into his accounts and mutual funds. The SVR had now paid him a quarter-million dollars, with promises of much more.

Langley, Virginia, early 1996

On March 17, an SVR officer reached out to the FBI for information that might help Moscow's efforts to combat terrorists in Chechnya. The SVR officer told the FBI that the request was part of a global accumulation of information on Chechen terrorists by Russia's foreign spy service. It wasn't an unusual request. The southwestern corner of Russia was embroiled in a bloody civil war that had been a long time coming, and Washington and Moscow had mutual interests in holding Chechnya's Islamic terrorists at bay.

Chechens had been itching to get out from under Moscow's thumb since the early 1920s, when they were dragged into the Soviet Union by the Red Army. As the U.S.S.R. disintegrated, they declared their patch of the Northern Caucasus, between the Caspian and Black Seas, a sovereign nation. But Mother Russia, whose oil and gas pipelines passed through Chechnya, wasn't having any of it.

In December 1994, Russian president Boris Yeltsin had sent troops into Chechnya to disarm the resistance in places like Grozny, which Chechens had declared their capital. The Russian military swept in with tanks and warplanes and artillery. But they were met with waves of protesters and heavily armed guerrilla forces in a city already teeming with crime bosses, gun-toting thugs, and a smattering of Muslim terrorists. Tens of thousands of people died in the fighting. The Russians left Grozny looking like a sepia photo of Oradour-sur-Glane at the end of World War II, a wasteland of rubble and twisted columns of metal.

On the afternoon of April 21, 1996, Yeltsin and President Clinton met in the Kremlin, where Yeltsin told reporters, "There are no military operations now under way" in Chechnya. But late that very evening, the key leader in Chechnya's war against Russia, General Dzhokhar Dudayev, was talking on a satellite phone in the western village of Gekhi-Chu when a Russian rocket hurtled earthward and killed him. Many observers believe Western intelligence—most likely the NSA—honed in on the phone to help knock off the Chechen leader, stabilize the region, and push Yeltsin to reelection over Communist Party challenger Gennadi A. Zyuganov. While the U.S. role may never be completely known, Yeltsin retained the presidency and prevented a communist resurgence, a major victory for the West.

Five days after Dudayev's death, Jim drove up from The Farm to CIA headquarters and went door to door asking colleagues to provide him with background information on Chechnya. He pretended to be collecting details about the troubled region's struggles as part of a training exercise for students at The Farm. He drove home with a package of papers.

Jim's request, juxtaposed against the SVR's interest in Chechnya, ramped up concerns that Jim might be a mole. CIA officials told FBI investigators they had not planned any training exercises at The Farm that involved Chechnya. Instructors at the covert training center had to submit curriculum changes well in advance of training exercises to a board of review. Jim hadn't taken any such steps.

Investigators now worried that Jim would poke through the daily churn of overseas cables at The Farm and print sensitive files for his Russian pals. Those leading the counterespionage probe decided they couldn't afford to let Jim operate out of their sight any longer. They talked CIA superiors into quietly canceling Jim's request to take a chief-of-station job in Addis Ababa, Ethiopia, where he could meet at will with Russian spies. Investigators cooked up a plan for the CIA to give Jim a promotion, installing him as a branch chief inside the Counterterrorist Center at Langley. They wanted Jim close enough to feel his pulse, a play right out of *The Godfather II*—"Keep your friends close, but your enemies closer."

Then came trouble.

As Jim readied to move to the town house in Burke with the kids, he cabled vacation plans to CIA superiors: Before starting in the new job at Langley, he wanted to take a trip to Singapore and Bangkok, where the SVR's spies were as thick as the local mosquitoes.

Jim's trip to Singapore marked a crossroads for the counterintelligence team at Langley. Investigators knew that if Jim really was leaking secrets to Moscow, he'd probably take the opportunity to meet with the SVR. They also knew that if they could tail Jim, catch him in the act, they'd be one step closer to rolling him up for espionage.

What kept investigators up at night was the possibility that Jim had figured out he was under investigation. If he was onto them, it was over: They were convinced Jim would travel overseas and bolt for the nearest Russian embassy. Once in Russian hands, Moscow would shuttle Jim off to the motherland, where intelligence officers would pluck him clean for every U.S. secret he kept in his skull. Maybe they'd send him off to a nice dacha on the Black Sea to live out his days on the dime of a grateful nation. Jim would never set foot in a U.S. court.

Curran and Redmond both knew they needed more evidence to make the case rock-solid. They would have to find a way to tail Jim in Singapore to see whom he was meeting.

Redmond was a tough, sharp-elbowed leader, a diminutive Harvard man given to bow ties and profanity. He grew up in Southborough, thirty miles west of Boston, one of those small, sweet, New England towns once surrounded by apple orchards and now—as Redmond often complains—choked with McMansions and annoying people from New Jersey. He grew up like most New Englanders with an aversion to Rs, a young man of privilege accustomed to cracking *lobsta* and running up sailboat sheets with *halya'ds*. Some of the friends Redmond sailed with in his youth had parents who worked in the CIA. The agency had attracted generations of well-bred Ivy Leaguers since World War II. Inspired by John F. Kennedy's famous words—"My fellow Americans, ask not what your country can do for you, ask what you can do for your country"—Redmond took the Foreign Service exam. But he bombed the oral. So he joined the Army, which shuttled him off to California to study Russian. It was a good language to learn at the midpoint of the Cold War, and it paid off for Redmond. On or about April Fools' Day 1965, he entered duty with the CIA.

Redmond and Curran rose to senior management positions in their respective agencies through grit and the power of their personalities. They were smart, cocky managers who had the good sense to build teams of talented investigators that produced results. Now, suddenly comingled as spy-catching allies, they pretended to like each other.

Curran didn't think the CIA knew the first thing about counter-intelligence. He knew they were great spies, highly trained at human intelligence gathering. But he considered them lousy spy catchers. In his opinion, Redmond's counterintelligence group had convincingly proved the point by bungling the Ames case. For his part, Redmond didn't want the FBI meddling in the agency's counterspy operations. The problem with the bureau guys, he said, was that they couldn't get it through their thick heads that working spy cases was far more nuanced than pinching drug dealers in Newark. There was nothing wrong with bringing the FBI in to make the collar in a spy case, Redmond figured. Let them take the credit and swagger, for all he cared. But in his opinion, the bureau didn't belong in his counterintelligence group.

To their credit, Redmond and Curran put their differences aside to confront a cold fact: Jim was flying to Singapore on personal business—most likely to meet his Russian handler. They knew Jim's travels corresponded with cash deposits way beyond his means into multiple bank accounts. They knew he was surfing the CIA's computers for information he didn't need. They knew he was friendly with the SVR *rezident* in Malaysia. And they knew Jim had a motive to sell his country's secrets: He was a single dad with expensive tastes, one son in college, two kids under his roof, and an ex-wife demanding money. But they would need a lot more evidence to prove Jim was selling the Russians secrets.

"We didn't have a case at that point," Curran said. "We could not prove an espionage case."

Redmond and Curran both knew Singapore presented them the best chance to catch Jim in the act. But they argued bitterly about whom they'd assign to put eyeballs on their target. Curran was steadfast in the FBI's capabilities. His agents were cops, after all, and surveillance was their bread and butter. Redmond was convinced the CIA knew the turf and was better equipped to keep eyes on Jim. As the clock ticked toward Jim's departure for Singapore, neither man would budge.

They decided to break the impasse by bringing in the CIA's chief of station in Singapore to ask him the smartest way to tail Jim on his turf. The timing was perfect, since Rich Smylie was at The Farm for the agency's annual chief-of-station conference. He'd be driving up from the training center to glad-hand with the bosses at headquarters and meet with other staffers. His boss, the chief of the East Asia Division, asked him to meet the following day to discuss "an issue." Smylie knew there was no such thing as a good "issue" in the agency.

"We need your help," his boss told him. "We need you to take a polygraph."

Smylie figured he'd pop into headquarters early for his turn on the box. But his boss asked him to report instead to an FBI office in Arlington. There Smylie found himself wired up for a standard counterintelligence polygraph to find out if he'd had unreported contacts with foreign intelligence officials. After he passed the test, agents briefed him on their case. They were investigating a CIA officer suspected of moonlighting for the Russians. Their target was heading to Singapore. His name was Jim Nicholson.

Smylie grimaced. He remembered Jim because they had served together in Manila back in the 1980s. Now Smylie's old friend was accused of espionage, a stunning turn of events that left him feeling betrayed and pissed off, but not altogether surprised.

"Jim," he told me, "was always out for himself."

Smylie made his way to Curran's office at Langley, where Redmond joined them to discuss surveillance options in Singapore. Curran liked Smylie right away. The CIA's man in Singapore seemed like a pro with a lot of self-confidence. Curran told his guest that he thought the joint FBI-CIA team should tell Singapore's intelligence service that the U.S. would be running surveillance operations in their backyard. Redmond thought it was a terrible idea to share information with the locals.

"What's your opinion?" Curran asked.

Smylie explained to the senior spy catchers that the CIA enjoyed an excellent relationship with Singapore's Internal Security Department. The ISD, as it was known, had been up and running at a high level since 1970, and Smylie had huge respect for its work. Its intelligence officers were smart, agile, and trustworthy. He recommended that investigators from the FBI and CIA sit this one out.

"If you do this on your own," Smylie told them, "you'll fuck it up."

The island nation of Singapore was just a little larger than the city of Chicago, with tightly restricted borders. The ISD knew every inch of the place, and could identify anyone who set foot in the country. Singapore was populated almost entirely by people of Chinese, Malay, and Indian descent. Smylie believed that putting tall, serious-looking white guys on the streets to tail Jim would draw attention they didn't want. He also knew that even if the CIA or FBI put together a surveillance team of Asian-Americans, they'd still look out of place, because Americans walked, talked, and dressed differently than the locals. Smylie was certain U.S. investigators, with only a superficial understanding of the venue, wouldn't have the skills to run such a complex eavesdropping operation on a professional spy.

Curran and Redmond both worried that Singapore's intelligence service might have been penetrated by the SVR. Moscow's foreign spy service had its eyes and ears in a lot of faraway places. Every man in the room knew that if the Russians had a contact inside the ISD, their case against Nicholson was toast. The Russians would alert their mole, and quicker than you could say "*Na zdorovie*," he'd be gone forever. They asked Smylie if he thought Singapore's intelligence service might leak news of the investigation to the Russians.

Negative, he said. He trusted the ISD.

When Smylie left Curran's office, Redmond blew up. He told Curran he wasn't going to risk the fate of the Nicholson case by putting a major surveillance operation in the hands of a foreign intelligence service that might include a Russian mole. Curran fought back, saying that if the CIA's own station chief in Singapore had confidence in the ISD, so did he. The two were just reaching a rolling boil when another man walked into the office.

They looked up to find George Tenet, the CIA's deputy director. Tenet was the number two man in the agency, a legend in the building.

He was an intense man with dark hair who was trying to break his cigar habit, an unlit stogie perpetually clamped between his lips. By year's end, President Clinton would appoint Tenet director of the CIA. But on that summer day, the deputy director turned mediator. He knew the clock was ticking. Decisions about how to eavesdrop on Jim Nicholson needed to be made.

Tenet asked Curran and Redmond to state their positions on the surveillance operation in Singapore, and he listened carefully to each. When they were done, he stood up.

"I agree with Curran," Tenet said. "We're gonna let the Singaporeans handle it."

He walked out. End of discussion.

Curran knew one thing: If they got this wrong, it would be his ass.

Singapore, summer 1996

On June 26, Jim checked into a $300-a-night room in the Shangri-La Hotel, a luxury high-rise that jutted out of a lush lawn full of banyan trees and koi ponds north of central downtown Singapore. The hotel, with its massive white columns, overlooked a bustling city and its famed Botanic Gardens. Jim's room was in the Garden Wing, which featured marble-floored bathrooms and personal balconies. The U.S. Embassy sat a few hundred yards away.

The ISD put a tail on Jim at 10:11 the next morning, a Thursday, when he strolled out of the Shangri-La past towering palms. They kept watch for the next four hours as Jim toured the Lion City, camera bag on his shoulder. The CIA man would walk down a street, appearing committed to a single course, then suddenly whirl around in the other direction. He stopped to stare into shop windows, using them as mirrors to look behind him. At one point, he traipsed down a set of stairs into the bowels of the subway and sprang back up in a moment, giving the appearance that he was a slightly confused tourist.

Singaporean intelligence watched Jim return to the Shangri-La
after about four hours, having shot nary a photo of his exotic surroundings. The ISD briefed Smylie on his moves. Smylie and a joint FBI-CIA
team in Singapore concluded that their target had taken a surveillance
detection route. Jim had practiced this "dry cleaning" all over the world.
For Smylie, this was the first clear indication his old friend might be
working for the Russians.

Back in D.C., FBI investigators tried to determine what Jim might
have brought with him to Singapore. Agents at Dulles had secretly
poked through Jim's checked bags, but found no sign of secret files.
They thought he might be carrying government papers in the camera
bag constantly tethered to his shoulder.

At 6:15 that night, Jim was on the move again, walking out of the
Shangri-La still carrying the camera bag. He followed the same route he
had taken that morning. Precisely three minutes after sunset, he stepped
into the subway station and stood on an elevated platform. He seemed to
be waiting for the rush-hour crowd to move downstairs to the trains that
would carry them home. When the bulk of the human traffic dispersed,
Jim caught an escalator down and sat on a stone bench. He waited for
a few moments before heading up to the main concourse.

There he found his old friend Polyakov.

The spy and his handler strolled out to the street, where a car pulled
up to a taxi stand and stopped. The lid of its trunk popped open; Jim
dropped his camera bag inside and pushed it shut. He climbed into
the backseat with Polyakov, and the car pulled away. The ISD took
note: The car bore diplomatic plates from the embassy of the Russian
Federation. The Singaporeans tailed Jim as the car headed northwest,
past the Shangri-La.

The ISD updated Smylie, who cabled headquarters, where Redmond, Curran, and management of the East Asia Division were on
the edge of their seats. When Smylie's phone rang a few minutes later,
it was one of his ISD contacts. Intelligence officers had just witnessed
the car that carried Jim drive through the gates of a white compound

at 51 Nassim Road, the Russian Embassy. Smylie phoned his division chief at Langley.

"Nicholson is with the Russians as we speak," he said.

"We jumped out of our chairs," Curran recalled. "We jumped out of our chairs!"

Smylie kept the updates flowing.

A senior ISD officer phoned him later that day to come see him immediately at the Ministry of Home Affairs in New Phoenix Park. Within fifteen minutes, Smylie found himself in a private meeting with several of his most trusted contacts. They told the station chief that Nicholson was still in his meeting with the Russian. The ISD officers wanted to know if Smylie should tell the FBI about this or let the CIA handle it on its own. It took Smylie a moment to grasp what they meant.

"They thought we'd go out and whack him," he recalled.

Smylie told the ISD officers he wanted the FBI looped in, assuring them that the American justice system would handle Jim.

That evening, Jim handed over the latest packet of secrets to Polyakov and walked away with a cool $50,000 in a plastic bag.

The following day, the Singaporeans, who'd stayed in covert lockstep with Jim for two days, watched discreetly as their target walked into an American Express Travel Services Center to pay $8,300 toward his well-used Amex card.

Jim had cabled Smylie before his trip to tell him about his plans to be in Singapore. CIA officers who travel abroad, even on vacations, are obliged to let the station chief in whatever nation they're visiting know they'll be in the country. The old friends talked on the phone and made plans for lunch. Both the CIA and FBI approved the meet. They didn't want to give Jim any hint that things were amiss.

Smylie's driver picked him up in the station's forest green Rover sedan and drove over to the Shangri-La. Jim climbed in carrying a plastic bag. Smylie had to wonder if it was the same bag Jim had used to carry his money from the Russians. They were seated together in the back when Jim reached into the bag and pulled out a four-inch-tall pewter figurine of a laughing Buddha.

"A present for you," Jim said. "Just my way of saying hello."

It was an odd gesture. Fellow officers rarely gave gifts to one another. This present was probably worth fifty bucks. Smylie thanked him and set the heavy figurine on the floor as they made their way toward the Singapore Island Country Club, an exclusive golf resort along the MacRitchie Reservoir. There they settled in for plates of Singaporean chicken rice. Smylie would later recall sitting outdoors across the white-linen table from Nicholson and feeling proud of himself for acting naturally and not betraying the fact that he'd just as soon shoot the sonofabitch. After lunch, they drove to the U.S. Embassy and settled into Smylie's private office in the station.

As Jim sat on the other side of Smylie's desk, he contemplated what biographical information to jot down on one of the agency's field reassignment questionnaires, known as FRQs. Jim was desperate to get an overseas job as a station chief. Smylie, unbeknownst to Jim, was cabling Langley from his desktop computer. He let the investigation team know their suspect was right there with him.

Jim asked his old friend what skills he might include on the FRQ to improve his chances.

Smylie couldn't help himself.

"Jim, how are you at countersurveillance?"

"I'm *good*," he said.

"Why don't you put that down?" Smylie suggested helpfully. "Have you worked against Russian or other Eastern bloc intel officers?"

Jim said he had.

"Put it down," Smylie said.

After the two men parted, Jim paid his tab at the Shangri-La with $1,679.59 in cash and stopped by the Overseas Union Bank, where he bought gold coins valued at $820.58.

Smylie turned over the laughing Buddha statuette to the FBI to be X-rayed for bugs. When it cleared the bureau's scrutiny, they gave it back. Only later would Smylie come to believe that Polyakov had given the Buddha to Jim, who had regifted it to him as a sick joke. It dug in Smylie's craw that his brother officer came to Singapore to commit espionage under his nose and expected to get away with it. Jim's ego, Smylie later explained, had exceeded his expertise.

Back in the U.S., FBI agents tuned in to Jim's hour-by-hour doings in Singapore were now certain they had a traitor in their sights. But they would still need more evidence.

"You'd lose your job for stepping into a limo of a foreign service, but you don't go to jail for that," said John E. McClurg, an FBI supervisor who worked under Curran at Langley. "You have a hard time passing a polygraph when you do things like that, but you don't go to jail. So from that moment on, we knew the horses were off and running. Now the task was to build a defensible criminal case against this guy."

The FBI and CIA wanted the Nicholson case dispatched quickly, by plea bargain. But to get there, they needed overwhelming evidence. Jim's secret meeting in Singapore wasn't the rock-solid evidence they needed.

Some of Jim's colleagues would later ridicule Jim for making the mistake of climbing into a car with Russian diplomatic plates. But the Russians had set things up that way, perhaps a calculated move to further assert dominion over their CIA man. They were showing their mole they owned him.

On July 1, 1996, after Jim's business in Singapore concluded, he flew to Bangkok. He retraced familiar ground, speeding across gentle green farmland abundant with Buddhist shrines toward Aranyaprathet to see Kanokwan. He headed back through time to the place, and the people, where their adventures began. The following day, they caught a plane to Hawaii for a short vacation.

Jim had already notified the CIA he intended to marry Kanokwan. She was thirty years old, fifteen years his junior, and her devotion to Jim and his government remained strong. Agency policy required thorough background checks of foreigners who intended to marry into the CIA. This was to ensure that a rival intelligence agency hadn't planted a spy—masquerading as a lover or potential spouse—in the bedroom of one of its own.

Kanokwan and Jim luxuriated for a few days at the sprawling Hanalei Bay Resort on Kauai before flying off to Oregon, where she would meet his family. Nick and Betty let Jim and his love stay with them in their little home in Eugene. They weren't bowled over by the demure Thai, but it was clear their oldest son was smitten with Kano-kwan, who was so much younger, and Buddhist. They wondered how Jim's kids would react.

The Nicholson kids, spending their summer in Oregon, were polite to their dad's love interest. Jim had often told his family that Kanokwan had saved his life a few times during his assignment on the border of Thailand and Cambodia. But the Nicholson children were still torn up by the divorce and their parents' lingering acrimony.

When Jim quietly drew the kids aside to announce his intentions to marry Kanokwan, Jeremi and Star balked. They refused to bless the union. Both thought the divorce, finalized only two years earlier, was too recent for their parents to consider remarrying.

"My sister and I selfishly believed that our family was *our* family," Jeremi recalled years after that conversation. "We wanted to keep it that way. We didn't want to bring outside sources in." Star, who would turn fifteen in the fall, understood that her dad wanted to start a new family with Kanokwan. But neither she nor Jeremi wanted half brothers or half sisters. Stubbornly, Jeremi said, they refused to yield to their dad's plans to bring Kanokwan into the family. Both he and Star turned two thumbs down.

Nathan, who would celebrate his twelfth birthday at the end of the month, thought his dad often seemed terribly lonely. He was happy to share him with someone who could light him up. He voted yes to the marriage, as he had with Lily, another demonstration of Nathan's fidelity to his dad.

By all accounts, Nathan was a whole lot like Jim. Both were charm-ing and possessed the perfect mix of left- and right-brain capabilities. They also bore an uncanny resemblance, with the same toothy smiles, strong brows and chins, and eyes as blue as an early summer sky. But it was Jim's and Nathan's temperaments that people noticed most. They were both so easygoing, very slow to anger. They were also risk takers with bold ambitions, and both placed high value on these qualities. They endeavored to move through life's adventures as charming gentlemen. The fundamental difference between Jim and his youngest was that Jim could be uncommonly self-centered, while Nathan—to a fault—thought of everyone else first.

Star was fiercely protective of Nathan, and smothered him with love. She was a classic middle child, brokering peace and serving as a human barometer of the family's moods. When things were going poorly, she was the first to break down and cry. But she was typically upbeat, kept a close circle of girlfriends, and treated the family cats as humans. Jeremi was intellectually curious, a student of the world who kept an eye on his siblings. In the years to come, he would take on an almost paternal role in dressing Star down for swearing or sneaking a beer. Nathan's siblings fought often.

On July 12, Jim gave Jeremi $12,377.50 to buy a new Dodge Neon. His oldest was headed to college that fall, to his parents' alma mater in nearby Corvallis. Two days later, Jim flew home to northern Virginia, paying a $120 parking tab at Dulles. It's unclear whether he took Kanokwan with him. What is clear is that they didn't make immediate plans to marry.

By now, the FBI had launched an investigative full-court press. Their orders from the Foreign Intelligence Surveillance Court allowed them to tail Jim wherever he went and electronically eavesdrop on every utterance he made. Investigators now believed Jim was selling out his country. But they met resistance at CIA headquarters, where a few senior officials bitched that the FBI was about to ruin the career of a promising officer. The bureau's investigators didn't give a rip about Jim's promising career.

Jim's Singapore trip foreclosed on virtually any chance the U.S. might spare him from criminal charges. U.S. intelligence officers caught in compromising situations with foreign spies were sometimes recycled as double agents. In Jim's case, senior CIA officials could have kept him on a short leash at Langley, allowing him to keep his regular meetings with the SVR. They could pass mildly interesting or phony information to Russia, giving Jim the chance to report to the CIA what kinds of information the SVR sought. But this was always risky business. Had the U.S. played that card, the CIA ran the risk of watching Jim defect to Moscow.

Government lawyers hoped to gather enough evidence to arrest Jim on an espionage charge potentially punishable by death. This would give prosecutors leverage to negotiate a quick guilty plea in exchange for a lesser sentence. But they had much work to do. On July 16, 1996, Jim took his first management position at CIA headquarters. He remained disappointed the agency turned him down for the station-chief job in Addis Ababa, where he and the kids could have had a housing allowance and a maid. But his new job as a branch chief inside Langley's vast Counterterrorist Center came with a promotion to GS-15, the highest civil service pay rating in U.S. government. By that fall, he would earn $78,385 a year.

Investigators now kept tabs on Jim around the clock. A July 19 audit of the CIA computer system showed that while working at The Farm, Jim had searched for cables and other reports using such keywords as "Russia" and "Chechnya." Jim's high clearance allowed him to access the Central Eurasia Division database, but he wasn't authorized to poke around in those files. His breach had triggered security alerts and caused CIA systems personnel to list him as a "surfer."

5

We Have Another Aldrich Ames

"We should begin by recognizing that spying is a fact of life . . .
We're in a long twilight struggle with an implacable foe of
freedom."
　　　　　—Ronald Wilson Reagan, presidential radio address,
　　　　　　　　　　　　　　　　　　　　June 19, 1985

Langley, Virginia, summer 1996

John Maguire sat in a cubicle village on the second floor of CIA headquarters, a clean, well-carpeted place full of file cabinets and misery. After
fourteen years of exciting spy work, he now labored in utter obscurity
in a pool of human resources mopes. Maguire had spent most of his
years in the agency on the front lines of the Cold War, although more
recently he labored as a counterterrorism operative in the Middle East.
He had served in such garden spots as El Salvador, Honduras, Lebanon,
and Iraq. But now it was abundantly clear that at forty-two, his once-
promising career in espionage was over.

　　Maguire had gotten crossways with his boss, the Near East Division
chief, for refusing to take an overseas posting in Karachi, Pakistan. His pen-
ance was a position in HR, in the bowels of the CIA's Original Headquarters
Building, part of the agency's sprawling, highly secured compound in the
Langley community of McLean, Virginia. There he drank sweetened coffee

and pushed pencils amid the agency's plebes, poring through the personnel files of other CIA officers to determine those worthy of promotions. He found it disheartening to labor through the applications of agency employees who, unlike himself, might actually be promoted.

Maguire's ennui was broken, from time to time, by the prank calls of colleagues still performing actual spy work. Some disguised their voices to ask about their promotions packets before busting a gut. Others phoned to make such helpful declarations as, "You're so fucked." One day, in the spring of 1996, Maguire's phone rang and he heard the voice of Anna, the secretary of the Near East Division.

Anna was a powerful figure in the division, something of an aging Miss Moneypenny, and as part of the senior secretarial pool, she enjoyed the oblique horsepower of her division chief. When Anna called, you paid attention. When you needed help, she was your oracle. Need to proof-check an official memo? She pored over it, caught your errors. Need to reach an overseas leader, a business figure, someone at the White House? She had the number. Screw up badly? She dressed you down, leaving you standing with your shoes smoking as if you'd been struck by lightning. Anna was a striking, statuesque woman with raven hair. All the senior secretaries in the CIA had juice. If they liked you, they could make your life easier. Anna seemed to like Maguire.

"How are you doing?" she asked.

"I'm trying not to kill myself in my seat," he said.

"Come upstairs," he heard her say. "Don't tell anybody where you're going. Just leave your desk and come up here to me right now."

"OK."

Like so many times in his career, Maguire could only imagine the fresh patch of hell in front of him. He had served seven years as a cop in his native Baltimore, then fourteen more as a spy. He understood the swift, decisive nature of upper-management bureaucrats, whose sudden decrees often fell into subordinates' laps like hot coals. Maguire hauled his six-foot-three, 195-pound frame out of his chair and slipped away quietly. He caught an elevator to the sixth floor, one level below the penthouse of power, where the Director of Central Intelligence runs the show. There, outside his boss's door, he found Anna at her desk. She steered him into the office, and the door closed.

He stood in front of a familiar wooden desk, behind which sat Steve Richter, whom he had never seen without a suit and tie. Richter, a key part of the Directorate of Operations, the CIA's clandestine wing, oversaw spy operations across the Middle East. Maguire thought his boss was one of the smartest and most talented of the agency's senior intelligence officers, and also one of the most vindictive.

The previous fall, Richter had flown to London to tell Maguire of his next assignment: Karachi. The move would have taken Maguire out of his work in northern Iraq, and he wanted none of it. He had run spy and paramilitary operations in the Middle East nation for five years, having first dropped into Iraq for the Persian Gulf War. Maguire felt invested in Iraq's future. It had taken years to wrap his head around the country's complicated, tribally based culture, its Ba'ath Party leadership, and the wickedness of Saddam Hussein and his power-sick sons, Uday and Qusay. He had hoped that his good work would be rewarded with a promotion to a leadership post in Amman or Abu Dhabi.

Maguire asked Richter to let him stay on in London. He was happy there, enjoying what is known in Foreign Service parlance as an "accompanied tour" with his wife and two daughters. Maguire told Richter he hoped to continue his vital work in Iraq, where he had developed locals—sometimes with trunks of cash—to gain secrets from inside Iraq's seats of power.

Richter hadn't flown to London to negotiate. He urged Maguire to take the assignment and report to the CIA station in Karachi. That's when Maguire played his last card. He told Richter that his wife, a registered nurse, had long told him there were only two countries on the planet so full of filth and disease that she refused to raise their girls in them: India and Pakistan. For those reasons, Maguire told his boss, he would have to politely decline the job in Karachi. Richter wasn't accustomed to being told no. He left Maguire in stony silence.

Soon after, Maguire got the cable letting him know he was being
called back to Langley to work in human resources, his requests for posts
in the Middle East denied.

Now he found himself standing in front of Richter's desk.

Maguire's boss, not known for warm and fuzzy moments with subordinates, didn't invite him to take a seat. It would be a short meeting.

"I have an assignment for you," Richter said. "I can't tell you anything about it." He told Maguire that he needed an answer then and
there, and that a yes would be good for his career. If he said no, all he
had to do was go back downstairs and never utter a word about the
conversation. "You have to give me an answer now," Richter said.

Maguire, flummoxed, glanced to his right. A stranger sat on the
couch. The man wore a nice suit and a blue badge denoting him as a
CIA staffer. Maguire figured he was a senior agency man. He planted
his eyes on Richter's face to read his reaction to his next words.

"Can I ask a question or two?"

Richter peered at Maguire sourly.

"You can ask," he said.

Maguire turned to the man on the couch.

"Who's this guy?"

"I'm Ed Curran," the stranger said. "I'm the highest-ranking FBI
agent assigned inside the CIA."

Fuck me, Maguire thought.

His mind flew back to Iraq and the troubles there. The FBI was
still investigating the CIA's role in organizing an unsuccessful coup that
March against Saddam Hussein by his own military. Maguire and his
team had rotated into northern Iraq during that covert action (code-
named DBACHILLES), which failed. Saddam executed at least eighty
of his officers involved in the attempted overthrow.

Maguire feared that the new "assignment" Richter was offering
might be a ham-handed setup for questioning by the FBI. The appearance of Curran only deepened his anxiety. Maguire's choices seemed
clear. He could turn down a potentially choice assignment, whatever

it was, and retreat to the cubicle dungeon and the slow immolation of his soul. Or he could do as the paratroopers say in that instant before leaping out of airplanes: Pull the cord, trust the Lord.

"Fuck it," he said. "I'll take it. Whatever it is, I'll do it."

"Wise choice," Richter said.

Maguire could sense by the tone of his boss's voice that the meeting was over.

Curran, no doubt amused by the exchange, gave Maguire orders: Go downstairs to the lobby. Do not talk to anyone, and tell no one where you've been. You'll meet a couple of FBI agents at the front door, who will give you instructions.

Maguire nodded along.

"OK," he said.

Outside Richter's office, he shot a glance at Anna.

She winked.

Moments later, Maguire walked off an elevator on the first floor, turned a corner, and trudged down a half-dozen steps, where he badged through the security turnstiles. He walked past the statue of William J. "Wild Bill" Donovan, a figure who stood literally and figuratively on a pedestal in the agency. Donovan had created the Office of Strategic Services, forerunner to the CIA, which helped win World War II. Maguire stepped across the agency's iconic lobby, with its massive seal—the head of an eagle atop a thirteen-point compass—laid into cold granite. There he found two men standing in business suits. They flashed their credentials and asked Maguire to follow them. All moved for the front doors.

Maguire found himself seated in the rear of a plain-Jane bureau car, which rolled out of the Langley compound into the northern Virginia suburbs. The ride was a blur of bright green tree canopies, the engine's drone, and a pair of FBI agents attempting to break the tension with small talk. Maguire heard one of them ask him, "Whattaya think?"

"Well," he said, "I'm not used to riding in the back of a police car. It doesn't fill me with confidence. But I'm not cuffed yet."

The agents told him to relax. But Maguire, who had served on some of America's most dangerous streets in Baltimore, didn't feel fine. When he was a cop, *he'd* been the one putting perps in squad cars for the free rides to jail.

Soon the car pulled up to a house deep in the suburbs, in a neighborhood Maguire didn't recognize. The FBI agents led him inside, where he spied a few others. Only then did he fully understand where he'd been taken. He was in a bureau safe house. Agents brought him to a bedroom, where he found an older man sitting behind a desk. The man hooked him up to a polygraph with a confidence that only contributed to Maguire's unease.

Maguire was accustomed to routine lie-detector tests. The agency wired its clandestine officers to the box every few years, usually when they rotated through headquarters, for single-issue polygraphs. Tests on the box were supposed to help the agency detect turncoats in their midst. But rarely, if ever, did they do anything of the kind.

Polygraph operators place their subjects on a pad that can sense the clenching of their sphincters, a device known by those who've sat on them as the "whoopee cushion." Maguire took his seat, his sphincter already tight enough to crush walnuts. There the older agent connected him to a series of wires that measured his breathing, blood pressure, pulse, and perspiration.

Polygraphers always begin with slam-dunk queries—"Is your name John R. Maguire?"—before asking the subject to respond with a deliberate lie or two. These are called control questions. For instance, the operator might tell a subject to deliberately lie to a question such as, "Have you ever stolen anything?" Few humans can honestly answer that with a no. When the respondent lies, the polygraph's stylus jiggles, giving the operator a benchmark for later deceptive answers. Relevant questions follow.

Maguire dreaded the first such query, which he imagined would go something like this: "Did you, or did you not, authorize or participate in an attempt to overthrow the regime in Iraq?"

He tried to think ahead. He knew he hadn't done anything illegal; the actions of CIA officers in the field assigned to wresting Saddam Hussein from power were fully authorized by senior agency officials like Richter. The White House was distancing itself, but officials in the Clinton administration had been briefed directly. Maguire decided that if the agent running the box posed even one question about Iraq, he'd politely ask to speak with his lawyer.

The genteel polygraph operator, perhaps sensing Maguire's inner tumult, told him to relax, everything was going to be OK. And sure enough, when the older man eventually got around to asking the moment-of-truth questions, they were all about Russia and Russian intelligence. Maguire breathed easier. He had no operational history with the Russians, and if Moscow's foreign intelligence officers had anything on him, it would have been thin, dated, and focused on his paramilitary past. As far as he knew, he'd never been a target of the KGB or the SVR.

The polygraph took about ninety minutes, and when the operator told him he'd passed, one of the FBI agents led Maguire into another room in the house, which clearly served as a hub for an investigation of some kind. They seated him at a desk, where he signed formal papers by which he swore not to divulge any of the classified information he was about to hear. The agents told him they were from Squad NS-34, a counterintelligence unit based in the Washington Metropolitan Field Office. They occupied a dilapidated building at the confluence of the Potomac and Anacostia Rivers, a gritty corner of D.C. known as Buzzard Point.

Maguire spied a photograph of a bearded man on the wall. It appeared to be an official CIA photo. He didn't recognize the face.

"You've been selected for this position," one of the agents told Maguire. "We have another Ames, and we have to catch him."

The FBI and CIA had handpicked Maguire to help catch this new mole. His background as a cop, and his experience testifying in court, made him a shoo-in as a candidate to help the bureau gather evidence inside CIA headquarters and neuter their suspect: Harold James "Jim" Nicholson.

Agents explained that Jim, whom Maguire had never met, was now in his sixteenth year as a CIA operations officer. He taught tradecraft at The Farm, a plum job given to spies who'd proven themselves in the field. Jim, he learned, was a single dad with primary custody of his three kids: Son Jeremi was headed to college; daughter Star and younger son Nathan lived in a two-story government house at Camp Peary, but were soon moving to the family town house in Burke, Virginia.

Maguire knew The Farm well. He had taken his five-month career trainee course and extensive paramilitary training on its grounds before being sent to a CIA demolition school in a covert redoubt in the mid-Atlantic tidewaters. There, he had learned how to build and dismantle all manner of explosives.

The agents had cooked up a scheme for senior CIA officials to call Jim back from The Farm and assign him as a branch chief in the Counter-terrorist Center, or CTC, in the Original Headquarters Building. (It was later renamed the Counterterrorism Center.) Maguire would apply to work as the deputy branch chief under Jim. FBI investigators hoped Jim would pick Maguire over other applicants for the position. If all went according to plan, Maguire would take the office next to Jim's. The FBI-CIA team would covertly supervise Maguire's undercover tilt against his own boss, a spy-versus-spy operation in the bosom of CIA headquarters.

No such investigation had ever been run under the roof at Langley.

Investigators knew Jim would interview several experienced CIA officers for the position of deputy branch chief, his top subordinate. But they secretly stacked the deck with Maguire, who had much stronger credentials than the others. Maguire was a founding member of the CTC, a distinction marking him as a "plank holder." He knew the territory, having worked against Middle East terrorists for years.

Maguire was a good spy, and the kind of guy you'd join for a few rounds of bourbon. But investigators looking to bring Jim to justice were more interested in the skills Maguire had acquired in his former life as a Baltimore City cop. He had worked long hours in the violent corners of Charm City's neighborhoods, streets later made famous in *The Wire*. Maguire worked well with prosecutors and logged countless hours on witness stands.

He walked into Room 6E2911 that summer for his interview with Jim. They took seats in Jim's office, which sat behind a heavy cipher-locked door on the far end of a bullpen of case officers and career trainees. Much was revealed to Maguire when he sneaked a glance at the I-love-me walls flanking his prospective boss's desk. Everywhere he looked there were framed photos of Jim, certificates, military awards, and other commendations. It was clear the guy was smart, and liked himself. A lot.

"He was a good interviewer," Maguire recalled. "He was looking for somebody who knew what they were doing, understood the target, somebody he could rely on—somebody he could use."

Maguire recited his bona fides to Jim, explaining that he was an experienced hand, good at cultivating assets, and was happy to put some of his best Middle East contacts back on the payroll. He said his assets could help Jim's branch identify and break up cells of Islamic fundamentalists bent on killing Americans or otherwise threatening U.S. security.

Jim wondered how a talented case officer had fallen so far, ending up in HR. So Maguire leveled with him. He'd pissed off Richter, who had cast him into the abyss. Maguire joked about wanting to jump out the window, but HR was on the second floor and he'd only break a bunch of bones. The two veteran spies shared a laugh. Jim knew Richter, and he'd certainly faced his own hassles with agency bureaucracy. But although he appreciated Maguire's dire predicament, he couldn't promise him anything.

Maguire walked out thinking he'd nailed the interview. But he knew Jim wasn't about to hire him until he'd worked the hallway file: the informal vetting of prospective employees in the corridors, back offices, and massive food court on the first floor of the agency's Original Headquarters Building. There were plenty of people inside who would vouch for Maguire's native talent as a spy, and a couple who could fuck things up with a mixed review.

Investigators crossed their fingers. Without somebody working for them inside Jim's locked office, there was no telling how many of the nation's most closely guarded secrets Jim would purloin and sell to the Russians during daylight duties in the CTC.

Weeks later, Maguire picked up an envelope addressed to him at work. Inside was a directive from the personnel division. The CIA bureaucracy was so big that if you moved from one part of the agency to another, even laterally, someone had to create paperwork to update your salary and benefits. The papers told Maguire to report immediately as deputy branch chief in the CTC under Jim Nicholson. This was his passport out of the Death Star, and a chance to try his spy skills against one of the shrewdest characters he'd ever met.

Not long after Maguire got word he would be working for Jim, Redmond called him for a meeting in one of the agency's "black rooms," offices with no descriptors on the door, just cipher locks. There he found himself buttonholed by the veteran counterintelligence supervisor who had headed the long-in-coming apprehension of Rick Ames. Redmond confided in Maguire that if he performed well in his undercover role, he'd serve his country admirably and notch a major milestone in his career.

"If you fuck it up," he said, "you're finished. So don't fuck it up."

On the first day of August, a warm, cloudy Sunday, Jim drove up to a row of blue mailboxes in an office complex in Tysons Corner, Virginia. The boxes sat along Greensboro Drive, a business park flanked by the Tysons Galleria and Tysons Corner Center shopping malls. Cars buzzed past as Jim dropped his envelope through the mail slot and eased away in his minivan.

FBI agents tailing Jim stopped to drop a marker in the box to help them find their target's envelope. The FBI often works with U.S. Postal Service inspectors to covertly retrieve evidence in criminal cases, and they soon found what appeared to be Jim's correspondence, a sealed Hallmark greeting-card envelope. It was addressed to a mail drop in Zimbabwe and bore oversized commemorative stamps with a face value of one dollar, more than necessary to fly the missive overseas. Agents opened the envelope and found a postcard with the words "Washington, D.C." printed on the front.

"Dear J.F.," Jim's note began. "Just want to let you know that unfortunately I will not be your neighbor as expected. Priorities at the home office resulted in my assignment to the management position there. Some travel to your general vicinity to visit field offices will occur, but not for more than a few days at a time. Still, the work at the home office should prove very beneficial. I know you would find it very attractive. I look forward to a possible ski vacation this winter. Will keep you informed. Until then, your friend, Nevil R. Strachey. P.S. I am fine."

It didn't require a team of code breakers to determine that Nicholson was alerting his handler through an accommodation address that he'd been turned down for the chief-of-station job in Addis Ababa and assigned instead to Langley. But the line about a ski vacation was vexing. Where would Jim meet his Russian friend?

Not long after Jim's mailbox drop, he flew to Beirut, Lebanon, on official CIA business. In the wee hours of Sunday, August 11, a team of FBI agents prepared to search Jim's minivan. Their target had left his 1994 Chevy Lumina sports van on an employee lot in the Langley compound. It was blue-gray with vanity license plates clearly picked by Jim: 8888BAT.

The supervisory FBI agent who set up the minivan search was John McClurg, who served as a liaison between Langley and teams of investigators spread across the D.C. metropolitan area. McClurg's job was to make sure that the FBI's technical agents made it onto the sprawling CIA compound, planted their bugging devices and other surveillance gear, and got out without being spotted by custodians, security teams, or agency employees working after hours. McClurg had covertly obtained these workers' schedules and studied their minute-by-minute movements on the 258-acre CIA compound, which hugs the western edge of the Potomac River.

McClurg was a handsome man with sandy blond hair and a dimple in the middle of his broad chin. But he wasn't just another FBI pretty boy. McClurg, one of Curran's trusted deputies, possessed a potent and precise mind. The two had become friends in the Los Angeles Field Office, where Curran had served as McClurg's "rabbi," bureau slang for mentor and benefactor. Curran, fourteen years older than his protégé, had been duly impressed with his success as a cybercrime expert.

McClurg's cyber career had begun, quite by accident, when one of his bosses in the FBI's counterespionage group yelled, "Who here knows anything about UNIX?" McClurg raised his hand, and his boss handed him a paper file. Get right on this, he said. Only after reading the document did McClurg realize his mistake. He thought his boss had said "eunuchs," something that he knew quite a lot about. Mc-Clurg had grown up in Libya hearing the story of an Egyptian pharaoh who defeated an invading army of Libyans and took as trophies the uncircumcised penises of more than six thousand enemies. Now his big mouth consigned him to the study of UNIX. McClurg saved himself by reaching out to Sun Microsystems, a company specializing in computer operating systems.

He later played a starring role in the takedown of Kevin Lee Poulsen, a black-hat hacker known as "Dark Dante." Poulsen famously cyber-swiped the unpublished phone numbers of Soviet officials in their San Francisco consulate. U.S. defense industry officials had given Poulsen a security clearance to identify their vulnerabilities. But Poulson's cheekiest crime came on June 1, 1990, when he hacked into KIIS-FM's "Win a Porsche by Friday" call-in promotion in Los Angeles, commandeering twenty-five phone lines to win a Porsche 944 S2 sports car. McClurg and his FBI colleagues put another hacker undercover to take Poulsen down.

Curran and McClurg made an odd pair. Curran was known to drink himself flannel-mouthed on occasion, and McClurg, a devout Mormon, never touched the stuff. They both had lived in the "FBI Ghetto" of Thousand Oaks, home to many agents. The town sat in the Conejo Valley, a brutal commute into the L.A. Field Office that Curran and McClurg often made together. They were riding into work on the morning of April 22, 1994, Curran behind the wheel of his Toyota, when news broke over the radio that the FBI had arrested Aldrich Ames.

Curran looked stricken, as if he were having a heart attack.

"What's the matter, Ed?"

"It's Rick," he said.

"Who?"

"They've arrested Rick Ames," Curran said. "I worked with him in New York."

Curran and Ames went back more than fifteen years, to the late 1970s, when the CIA assigned Ames to the Big Apple. Ames earned a reputation as a talented, if forgetful, spy. Once, on his way to meet a Soviet asset, he left a briefcase full of sensitive documents on a train. The FBI retrieved the case from a Polish émigré, and the CIA man got off with a reprimand.

Ames' 1994 espionage arrest had a strangely serendipitous result: The FBI assigned Curran to CIA headquarters to serve as counterespionage chief so that the agency never produced another turncoat like his old compatriot.

Curran pulled McClurg aside at his going away party. He explained that he was allowed to bring one agent of his choosing with him to the new assignment at Langley, and he wanted McClurg. The younger agent had just finished doctoral course work at UCLA in "Philosophical Hermeneutics," and he was planning to embed himself with Crips and Bloods to see if teaching them conflict resolution skills might curtail gang carnage. Instead, he took Curran up on the offer and became one of the deputy branch chiefs in the espionage group at Langley. McClurg's cover story was that he was working on Curran's polygraph program. Instead, he would secretly work counterspy cases, spending much of 1995 and 1996 setting up technical operations to collect evidence against the CIA's Batman.

The search of Jim's minivan in the parking lot at Langley wasn't your standard black-bag job. Getting inside the van would be the easiest part of the operation, requiring no burglar tools. All investigators needed was a key, which any FBI agent could get with a vehicle identification number and credentials. But hauling off the Lumina was fraught with obstacles. They couldn't drive the van off the lot because Jim might have jotted down the odometer reading before flying to Beirut. Also, they couldn't search the van on the CIA lot, because Jim's agency friends might see them and report the suspicious behavior—a potential case blower.

On top of that, investigators knew little about the innards of the minivan, and they didn't want to miss any hideaways during their search. So they bought another 1994 Chevy Lumina and took dry runs dismantling it. They had to find any cavity inside the vehicle that Jim might exploit to hide evidence of his espionage.

McClurg and his team picked the first hours of the second Sunday in August, with clouds muting a crescent moon, to make off with Jim's minivan. A flatbed truck equipped with a boom pulled into the parking lot of the CIA compound and lifted the 3,510-pound Lumina onto the flatbed. It was important to McClurg and other investigators that the van's wheels not turn an inch. The truck carried the Lumina to a shed that looked like a Quonset hut.

Only after agents pored through Jim's minivan did they get a glimpse at just how much damage he had done.

Agents snatched Jim's Toshiba laptop out of the van's rear cargo area and mirrored the hard drive, which confirmed the government's worst suspicions. Investigators found a letter of instructions from Jim's Russian handler. They also learned that Jim had copied a trove of classified files to the laptop. Some were merely sensitive, but others were marked "Secret," "Top Secret," and another classification known as "SCI"

(Sensitive Compartmented Information). Analysts determined that all the files from the program directories had been deleted, leading agents to conclude Jim had copied the information to diskettes and passed them to the Russians.

Fragments of the hard drive showed the computer once held a secret file about staffing inside the CIA's Moscow station, including the true identity of its new chief of station. Part of the chief's job was to assess the Kremlin's military preparedness and determine how much the Russians knew about U.S. defense plans. Those disclosures likely damaged U.S. intelligence-gathering operations in Russia and posed grave consequences—including possible execution—of assets cultivated there by spies supervised by the station chief.

The hard-drive fragments also yielded a secret document about a closed-door briefing concerning Russian spies' attempts to recruit CIA officers. In addition, analysts found summaries of the U.S. government's debriefings of Ames, a nearly verbatim copy of a secret report about Chechnya, and a secret report on the embarrassing expulsion of CIA officers caught spying in Paris. They also recovered a lengthy report, in Jim's own words, of one of his blown polygraphs at Langley. He included a detailed analysis of the questions posed to him about his contacts with a foreign intelligence service, and his insights into the polygraph examiner's reactions during his testing.

FBI agents also recovered a 3.5-inch diskette from the minivan, which held a CIA document on what are known as access agents. These agents are private citizens—some working for pay, others volunteering out of patriotism—whose travels and business relationships give them entree to information about foreign governments and companies that interest the CIA. The agency carefully guards the identities of those agents for their safety.

The diskette also held summaries of three CIA reports (all dated July 18, 1996) that revealed confidential intelligence gathered by agency assets on the Russian economy and banking system; high-frequency radar research; submarine weapons systems designs; and the efforts of a foreign government to obtain Russia's cruise missile technology. These summaries identified the sources' code names, positions, and points of access to the information, leaving countless people exposed to Moscow's reprisals.

All this information was devastating to U.S. interests across the globe. But the most damning data found on the skeletal remains of Jim's hard drive were the names, biographies, and assignments of hundreds of CTs, some of whom Jim trained during his two years at The Farm. Some of those trainees weren't much older than Jeremi.

The Russians wanted names and data on as many clandestine officers as Jim could muster. This information was precious to SVR officials. The Russians spent countless funds identifying and spying on the CIA's spies. Knowing the names of the officers they'd go up against gave them a huge advantage. Instead of wasting time and money to identify CIA officers and keeping tabs on whom they met, the SVR would already know their names and could quietly sabotage them.

Jim's move from The Farm had taken him away from easy-to-download files on career trainees. But now, in the heart of CIA headquarters, he would go headhunting in his own office.

6

Spy vs. Spy Under Langley's Roof

"Prescience cannot be gained from ghosts or gods, cannot be augured through signs, and cannot be proved through conjectures. It must be gained from what is learned by men."
—Sun Tzu, *The Art of War*

Langley, Virginia, late summer 1996

John Maguire felt like a captive. Spying on another highly trained case officer put him on a wake-at-dawn, collapse-at-night schedule. In only a few months, he had performed more acts of espionage inside the CIA compound than over the bulk of his career. He had piled up so many fourteen-hour days that he felt guilty about neglecting his wife and daughters, often reaching home just in time to tuck the girls into bed. He was blessed with a wife tolerant of his suddenly-insane work schedule.

Jahala Handy was accustomed to long hours. She had met Maguire during a shift change at The Horse You Came In On Saloon, a bar in Fells Point, on the Baltimore waterfront. She worked as a registered nurse in the Johns Hopkins Hospital trauma center. He worked on a bomb squad–sniper unit at a nearby pier, where the seventy-foot-high "Domino Sugars" sign cast an iconic neon reflection across the Inner Harbor brine. Both were battle-hardened by the nightly carnage on Charm City's streets, and it's amazing they met over cold beers, not a corpse. Handy was dating a buddy of Maguire's, a brother officer, which gave them time to get to know each other without sexual tension getting in the way. Eventually, as Maguire recalls things, they became each other's wingmen. She was perfect for a cop with a high threshold for mirth and a low tolerance for boredom, and it's no wonder they fell in love.

Handy supported Maguire's interest in joining the CIA. The agency took him on in 1982, and they married the following year. Their roots in a working-class town, and their shared sense of comic fatalism, bound them tighter as Maguire's employer bounced them around the world in what felt like long, exotic field trips. Maguire and Handy raised two girls, sharing the family secret with them only when they were old enough.

His elder daughter was eleven when she stumbled onto the truth. The Maguires were living in Amman, Jordan. It was 2 o'clock in the morning and Maguire was heading to a business meeting, although no one in attendance would be wearing Brooks Brothers. Maguire was standing in his bedroom in jeans, putting on a Kevlar vest. There was $100,000 in cash on the bed, along with a Kalashnikov rifle. He was talking with his wife, who was blowing the smoke of a clandestine cigarette out the window. Suddenly Handy began making slashing motions with the flat of her hand across her throat. Maguire looked up to find his older daughter in the doorway, a teddy bear under one arm, eyes wide as saucers. She stared at her dad, then at her mom. Her gaze shifted to the assault rifle and the money, then back to her surprised father.

"Daddy," she said. "Are you a bank robber?"

Maguire had prepared himself for this one. He and his wife had long ago agreed that lying to their kids about what he did for a living could emotionally damage them. They had kept his profession under wraps as long as they could, but now had come the moment of truth.

"Look, honey," Maguire told his daughter, "we'll talk about this tomorrow. I'm not a bank robber. But don't say anything in school about this. Mommy and I will talk to you tomorrow."

She went back to bed, and the Maguires told her the secret the next day.

Handy enjoyed a broad understanding of her husband's work without benefit of knowing precisely what he did for the agency. Early on in his CIA career, he had made it clear that he couldn't share details. But when he was read in earlier that summer in the Nicholson case, he had the good sense to tell his wife a true but unrevealing version of what lay ahead.

Maguire explained that he would be on a special assignment that would either spring him from his dead-end job in human resources or, if he failed, burn his career to the ground and salt the earth behind it. He said the operation involved a problem inside the agency, sort of like a city cop working an internal affairs case. He told her he'd be gone without explanation, work crazy, unpredictable hours, and wasn't having an affair. Also, he said, the situation was fluid and offered no clear view of the end zone.

"It can't last long," he told her, "because I'll be dead if it lasts too long. Just roll with it."

She did.

Maguire woke at 5 o'clock most weekday mornings to make the seventy-eight-mile commute to CIA headquarters from his home in the rolling farmland northeast of Baltimore. He badged in most days before 8 a.m. so he could duck into a basement black room or some other secretive hide to meet with his FBI handlers and plot the next move against Jim. Maguire's handlers treated him so well it surprised him. They understood the physical toll of a protracted counterspy operation, and the emotional strain of undercover work. They also knew the gut-sick guilt of building a case against one of their own.

His FBI handlers, top-shelf spy catchers, were excessively supportive. In their world, the best game plan was defense; it was their job to make sure Jim was caught before he could do grave damage to the nation's security. What they lacked was an insider's understanding of espionage, which is all about offense. That's where Maguire came in. He would have to learn Jim's motivations, think how he thought, and even befriend him. Maguire knew he and the investigators needed prescience to anticipate Jim's next move.

The FBI counterintelligence teams at Langley made Maguire an honorary member of the team. Together they would have to call the right countermeasures to make sure Jim didn't flee the country, and that he never met another Russian on their watch. Once Maguire entered his CTC office, he was the FBI's only eyeballs on Jim. The case was so highly compartmentalized that no one else in the center knew about it.

Maguire's primary marching orders, cast in stone by Curran, were to keep an eye on the materials Jim was accessing on his computer, and to make damn sure that if Jim so much as climbed out of his chair to stretch or hit the john, his FBI handlers knew about it. If Jim headed for the door of their branch, Maguire knew to pick up his green phone—a secure line inside the agency—to alert the FBI agents downstairs. A team of technical agents and analysts had set up a command post next door in the CIA's New Headquarters Building, which overlooked the lot where Jim parked. If he made an unexpected move for his minivan, a slew of FBI agents stood by to tail him.

The branch that Maguire and Jim supervised, dubbed "Other World Terrorism," wasn't created as a ruse to spy on Jim. It was a functioning office that performed real counterterrorism work. This forced Maguire to keep two jobs. He would spy on Jim while helping to supervise seven or eight other employees, including case officers and CTs, a few of them fluent in Arabic. The branch kept tabs on foreign terrorist groups, almost exclusively Sunni extremists who had taken up arms against the West. This played to Maguire's talents.

He had spent much of the previous decade cultivating assets from Beirut to Baghdad. Maguire made his bones as a case officer by helping to run covert operations against Nicaragua's ports to cripple the economy of its Soviet-backed government. Now he schooled Jim in the backgrounds of their dangerous Sunni targets, discovering that his boss was a quick study. But he could also see that Jim viewed his own job in the CTC as little more than an unpleasant layover on his way to another exotic chief-of-station job. Jim seemed resigned to cooling his heels until the next overseas assignment came along, one that would likely make things easier to communicate with his Russian pals.

Jim held the agency in contempt and often complained to Maguire about senior management. Maguire commiserated about some of the jerks in the Senior Intelligence Service, hoping their mutual resentments would draw them closer. But he sensed Jim was as cutthroat as any of them. Maguire sometimes joked about the special Kevlar worn inside the agency; its protective barrier only covered one's back from the knives of backstabbing colleagues. It galled Maguire that Jim burnished his image as a minivan-driving, Boy Scout–shuttling, father-of-the-year type. It seemed that Jim, much like a professional actor, had lost himself in the deceit of a role—just another cover in a career full of them.

Maguire also saw Jim as rootless, with few if any close confidants in the building. Jim had forsworn allegiances to the Mormons, and was now attending Christian worship services. But he maintained friendships with brother officers in what has often been called the CIA's "Mormon Mafia." Maguire wondered what Jim's Latter-day Saints pals might think if they knew he was bird-dogging women with abandon, earning a repu-tation as quite the pole vaulter. He was smitten with a gorgeous Lebanese subordinate. So much so that Maguire feared his boss would be accused of sexual harassment before they could indict him for espionage. While Jim wasn't the best-looking boy in the building, he was prettier than a lot of the schlubs in the agency, and generous with his money.

Jim held Friday evening beer parties in the office that subordinates dubbed "Vespers." Jim liked to kick back with a few beers, preferring Beck's and other imports. They drank and shared laughs and told stories. Nobody was supposed to be drinking in the building. But Jim's branch sat behind a heavy door with a cipher lock, and the agency's security officers weren't exactly busting shoelaces to nail spies for blowing off a little steam after a hard week of work.

Maguire watched Jim work the room.

One of the skills that spies acquire on the job is elicitation, the art of asking questions and gathering intelligence without targets knowing they are being plied. Maguire seethed as he saw Jim subtly pulling the life stories out of his own employees. It was clear that Jim was taking mental notes, which he could later jot down and sell to the Russians, along with their colleagues' names, ranks, specialties, skills, dates of birth, previous assignments, and even photographs. Jim's subordinates trusted Jim with their lives. Maguire could only sit in silence as he watched Jim's headhunting. Hundreds of thousands of dollars had gone into training each of these young officers, and his duplicitous boss was probably going to eighty-six their careers by exposing them to Russia's spy network.

Jim's Other World Terrorism branch was created to cut fanatical jihadists off at the knees. No one knew it at the time, but the Sunni extremists on whom they were gathering intelligence—most of them from the Salafi and Wahabi sects—would pioneer an Islamic terrorist movement that would later come together under an umbrella organization that called itself al-Qaeda.

"We were on the front end of the spear," Maguire recalled, "and we have a spy that's the boss." He laughed so hard at the irony that I thought he might choke.

That year, veteran CIA officer Michael F. Scheuer launched a specialized counterterrorism unit outside the Langley compound to track an emerging but little-known terrorist figure named Osama bin Laden. This was a pivotal moment for the agency—too early to connect the dots between the wealthy Saudi, a series of radical Islamic bombings, and the movement that morphed into al-Qaeda. But Maguire believes coupling Jim's branch with Scheuer's that year would have greatly improved the CIA's odds of crippling bin Laden before al-Qaeda's suicide pilots could kill 2,977 innocent people on American soil. Instead, key officials at the CIA—including Director of Central Intelligence John M. Deutch—crippled the CTC.

President Clinton had appointed Deutch as CIA director in the late spring of 1995, but the cabinet-level position wasn't Deutch's first choice. The Massachusetts Institute of Technology–trained chemist wanted to be U.S. secretary of defense and took over the CIA somewhat grudgingly. It's never good when the agency's number one guy considers the job on the top floor at Langley his second choice, and by all accounts, Deutch never much cared for the place. He was variously described as blunt, brilliant, and a short-tempered "bull-in-a-china-shop bureaucrat." As a professor at MIT, he had earned the nickname "Shoot-ready-aim," and Pentagon officials dubbed him the "unguided missile." Deutch made decisions that threw barriers in front of the CTC's efforts to identify terrorists who later declared war on the U.S.

Insiders say Deutch's greatest mistake was hiring Nora R. Slatkin as executive director of the CIA, the number three spot in the agency. Slatkin was a little blonde from Long Island who caught Deutch's attention while working as the Pentagon's chief of acquisitions. Deutch essentially handed the day-to-day operations of a $3 billion, 17,000-employee spy agency to a woman described in news accounts as a data-driven, Diet Coke–guzzling career bureaucrat with no experience in the intelligence field. Slatkin worked sixty-hour weeks at the $122,688 job, trying to improve morale at an agency still in the dumps over the Ames affair.

Slatkin and Deutch swiftly instituted a prohibition against the recruitment and payment of foreign assets who violated human rights. These dirty assets, many of whom were extraordinarily helpful to U.S. counterterrorism efforts in the Middle East, were considered politically incorrect because they were criminals and nihilistic thugs. Scrubbing them from the payroll was part of Deutch's "clean hands policy."

Maguire was incensed that Slatkin, whom CIA insiders nicknamed "Tora Tora Nora," systematically jettisoned some of the best Middle East assets run by his branch, some of whom he knew personally. He explained that these dirty sources—working out of such strategic locales as Lebanon, Syria, and Cyprus—helped the CTC detect, deter, and dismantle Islamic terrorist cells. Jim's branch had about twenty-five sources on the payroll in various stages of development, almost all of whom were thoroughly vetted. They were great assets, Maguire said, risking their necks for the U.S.

"They were bad people," he said. "They were murderers. Terrorists. That was the problem we had with this whole asset scrub thing. There are not a lot of Franciscan monks that work in this organizational structure. If you're gonna find out about radical Sunni Salafists in Lebanon, you can't go to the Christian community and get that information."

The Clinton administration had deep concerns about putting violent wing-nuts on the payroll to spy on what appeared to be disparate groups of terrorists. The agency downsized its overseas spy operations, and Deutch ordered his minions at headquarters to focus on quality of foreign assets over quantity. This begat what has been called the "asset validation scrub" of 1995 and 1996, which put guys like Jim and Maguire in the business of rating their foreign assets check-box style. Deutch allowed Slatkin to cut all but about 20 percent of the assets working for Jim's team.

"That sowed the seeds for 9/11," Maguire said. "We scrubbed our best cases."

Langley, Virginia, late 1996

McClurg and his FBI technical team crept into Jim's office one summer night to put another eye on Jim. They planted a pinhole camera above his desk, setting the lens in one of the thousands of tiny holes in the acoustic ceiling tiles. This would give investigators a real-time video feed of their target. McClurg and the technical agents had run countless yards of fiber-optic T3 lines above the ceiling. Now they painstakingly glued down each panel so their clever suspect would have to destroy the ceiling to determine whether he was under surveillance. They made sure to leave no particles or heel prints on Jim's desk.

Over the next few months, agents occasionally crept into Jim's office, dodging shifts of custodians and security staffers, to shoot photos and look for evidence. These were quick sneak and peeks designed to find evidence that Jim was preparing files for the Russians. They skulked through the CTC late at night, avoiding contact with agency employees who could catch them in the act. Their biggest fear was that one of Jim's CIA buddies would tip him off, and it'd be game over.

McClurg was poking through Jim's office one evening, watching the clock, when security guards approached unexpectedly. He slipped into Jim's office and quietly closed the door behind him. He stood in darkness, heart racing, and waited out the guards. He tried to imagine what he might say if discovered. Minutes passed, an eternity each, and finally he heard the guards depart. When his breathing returned to normal, McClurg crept out and into an elevator.

As investigators kept their surveillance under wraps, Jim seemed to grow more brazen.

Kathleen Hunt spied Maguire one day as he made his way through the branch and motioned him to her cubicle. Hunt was thirty-six years old, a veteran case officer recruited right out of college by the CIA during the early Reagan years. The agency's headhunters must have been dazzled when they sat her down at Bay Path College, a small women's school in Longmeadow, Massachusetts. She was the whole package, a stone-cold knockout with Celtic skin, cobalt eyes, and dark hair with a hint of chestnut. She had an inquisitive personality and a laugh so powerful it could rattle your coffee cup. The agency hired and trained Hunt, then sent her straight to Eastern Europe, the front lines of the Cold War.

Maguire could see there was something serious on her mind.

In a low voice, she confided to Maguire that Jim had requisitioned gadgets completely unnecessary for the branch's work. He had sent CTs to fetch him a camera and a portable printer.

Maguire tried not to betray his emotions. She was sniffing Jim out, and he'd have to throw her off the scent. Hunt, of course, was spot-on. There was positively no reason for Jim or anyone else in the branch to have a spy camera or a portable printer. The office was supposed to operate like the vault of closely held secrets that it was.

The room sat behind a heavy wooden door with a spin-dial combination lock. Inside was a bullpen of workstations. Every desk had locking drawers, and it was mandatory to button up tight before leaving each night. Computers were designed for internal use only; they had no ports for diskettes, and the e-mail system was internal and didn't reach beyond the CIA compound. It was verboten to shoot photos inside or carry documents out. An electronic security crew swept the office for bugs. Jim and Maguire, both supervisors, had private offices at the back of the room, each with keypad locks.

Hunt looked at Maguire imploringly. She wanted assurances about Jim's peculiar requisitions.

"What's he need them for?"

"That's just Jim," he told her, explaining that Jim was a gadget nut. "He's quirky."

Maguire knew that Hunt had worked under Rick Ames during a headquarters assignment in the Soviet/East European Division. He knew Ames' betrayals had left her feeling betrayed, and angry. Her inquiries about Jim showed she was following her training; she was properly skeptical and vigilant. Ordinarily, Maguire would have welcomed such concerns. But since their boss was a suspected traitor, and Maguire was secretly helping to catch Jim, he had to figure out a way to calm her down. His immediate fear was that Hunt would take her concerns to someone else in the building, perhaps even to Jim. He worried she might raise such a fuss that she'd derail the case, turning Redmond's motivational speech—"If you fuck it up, you're finished"—into prophecy. Maguire looked Hunt in the eyes and calmly suggested she let it go.

When he left the office that night, Maguire considered signaling a meeting with his FBI handlers. He thought they might consider reading Hunt in on the case; her instincts were clearly valuable. But Maguire knew it was unlikely the FBI or the agency would include her. Investigators were doing their best to keep a soft footprint in the CIA, where Jim still had friends, fearing someone might spill the secret. He kept his worries to himself.

Mercifully, Hunt didn't pass her concerns higher up the food chain. She trusted Maguire implicitly and believed his tale of Jim's eccentricities. From the moment Hunt first stepped into Jim's office to interview for the CTC job, she had found him an odd duck. He was a bit like a bearded Mr. Rogers, but vain. His whiskers were always perfectly trimmed, and he hit the tanning beds. Every time she popped in to talk to Jim, an adornment on his wall caught her attention: a round web of string and feathers big as your forearm. One day she had to ask what it was.

"It's a dream catcher," Jim told her.

Nathan had told his dad about the Native American webs, which were supposed to ward off nightmares. They had made it together at home.

"Would you like one?" Jim asked.

Hunt declined, politely, thinking it all so new agey. She had to wonder if Jim's ex, whom he had described as a kind of "Miss Moonbeam" character out in the sticks, might have been behind the dream catcher.

Mystical totems and vanity aside, Hunt found much to like about Jim. For one thing, he had an exceptional military background, which she admired. He was easygoing, too, not at all the mercurial sort that often ascended to management positions in the agency. He also was bright and effortlessly competent, and seemed to have a life outside the office. Many clandestine officers in supervisory positions worked long hours and glared over their glasses at underlings who didn't follow suit. Jim seemed just as happy to work a normal day and join the crush of rush-hour commuters in his minivan, another Superdad racing home to the kids.

On September 23, a Monday, investigators watching the video feed from Jim's office saw their target set papers on his lap and reach into a desk drawer. Jim pulled out the spy camera he had requisitioned and began shooting photos of documents on his lap.

Eleven days later, Jim booked flights to Europe with two of his subordinates to meet with friendly foreign intelligence services on an official counterterrorism mission. They were headed to New York, South Africa, and Italy. But Jim also made plans to peel away from the group for a personal vacation. He planned to see Polyakov in Switzerland.

On Wednesday, October 9, Maguire joined Jim for a drive down to Georgetown for what turned out to be a liquid lunch at one of the D.C. neighborhood's trendy bistros. They lingered over a few beers before Jim picked up the tab, as usual, and then piled back into his minivan for the drive over the Potomac River to the CIA compound. Inside the van, the two officers opened fresh beers. Maguire soon noted that instead of hooking north along the Potomac, Jim drove westward on Interstate 66. He said nothing as Jim kept driving out of their way, beyond the western stretch of the I-495 loop. This detour took them through northern Virginia suburbs several miles from Jim's town house. They drank beer in broad daylight and kvetched about the usual stuff—the office, the assholes they worked for, women.

Suddenly Jim jerked the wheel and swerved through traffic, speeding up and darting into the far right lane where overloaded truckers and blue hairs slowed everybody down. Maguire knew instantly what Jim was doing. His provocative maneuvers were intended to expose anyone who might be tailing. The agency had taught him well. But not well enough. Maguire stole a glance in the rearview mirror, relieved that the FBI's tails covered them constantly.

They were a full twenty minutes outside of downtown D.C. when Jim pulled up to a U.S. Post Office across the street from a 7-Eleven in Dunn Loring, Virginia. The brick building sat on the corner of Gallows Road and Electric Avenue, an intersection in the outer burbs. The FBI stayed close as Jim parked the minivan on an L-shaped lot. Jim announced that he had to buy some stamps and that he'd be right back. He left Maguire in the van.

When Jim returned, Maguire asked why they had driven way out to bumfuck to buy stamps they could have picked up at headquarters.

"I collect stamps," Jim said. The Dunn Loring post office, he explained, had quite a collection of unique overseas postage.

Back at Langley, Maguire signaled his FBI handlers for a meet. Later that day, he talked things over with one of the agents, explaining that it's common practice for spies and their handlers to signal rendezvous by mailing letters with unique stamps or combinations of them.

"You should smother him tonight," Maguire told his handler. "I think he's going to do something operational."

Dozens of agents tailed Jim that night as he drove the minivan toward his town house in Burke. Agents were pulled off other assignments and told—on a need-to-know basis—that they had to stay glued to a high-priority target driving a late-model Chevy Lumina, license plate 8888BAT.

They observed their target ease his minivan up to a row of blue mailboxes that hug the east side of the Dunn Loring post office, where Jim had stopped that very day to buy the stamps. Agents saw him drop a parcel into one of the boxes and drive off. They waited until Jim was well down the road before calling in a team to pore through the belly of the blue box to find what they were looking for, a sealed airmail envelope that held a postcard. Stuck to both the card and the envelope were the same oversized commemorative stamps, each with a face value of one dollar.

"Hello Old Friend," the postcard read. "I hope it is possible that you will be my guest for a ski holiday this year on 23-24 November. A bit early but it would fit my schedule nicely. I am fine and all is well. Hope you are the same and can accept my invitation. Best Regards, Nevil R. Strachey. P.S. The snow should be fine by then."

Maguire scarcely slept that night. He hoped he hadn't wasted the FBI's time with his tip about the stamps. The work was wearing him down, and he caught himself fretting over things he couldn't control. They'd all been working long hours.

He stumbled into work the next day, sleep-deprived and hoping for good news. When Maguire's green phone rang, he heard triumph in his handler's voice.

"You scored a touchdown last night."

Maguire's handlers now gave him high-risk tasks to collect evidence against Jim. The FBI needed him to come up with a sample of Jim's DNA, along with the key to his town house, without arousing his suspicions.

The FBI camera mounted in Jim's office ceiling spied the perfect repository for a sample of his DNA: a paper coffee cup from a stand on the agency's first floor.

Maguire waited for Jim to leave the office before sweeping in. He saw that Jim's cup was partway full and dashed downstairs to grab an identical one. On the way back, he poured out some of the fresh coffee, letting the rest cool for a few minutes before carrying it into Jim's office and swapping it for his boss's java. He then carried Jim's cup downstairs into a distant corridor, where a female FBI agent was striding toward him with an identical cup in her hand. They pulled a classic brush-pass, exchanging the cups so quickly no one noticed.

The FBI bagged and tagged Jim's cup and its contents and sent it to the lab for testing. His saliva would provide investigators all the DNA they needed to match Jim to evidence of his crimes, including the postage stamps he licked to signal his meeting with Polyakov.

Maguire's next task was to help the FBI get a copy of Jim's house key. Jim gave him an opening one day when they headed for lunch at one of Jim's favorite restaurants in Georgetown, one of those Thai or Vietnamese places where the peppers ranged from blistering hot to napalm. On the way back to the office, riding shotgun in Jim's minivan, Maguire quietly pulled out his wallet and dropped it to the floor between the seat and door. Later, in the CTC, Maguire walked into Jim's office looking a bit sheepish, saying he lost his wallet.

"I think I might of left it in your van," he said.

Jim didn't blink. He tossed him the keys.

A few moments later, Maguire pulled open the minivan's passenger door and plucked his wallet off the floor. He lifted from his pocket a compact key impression kit, a plastic folding model with casting material that left no trace on keys. Maguire quickly made an imprint of the house key and badged back into the building through a side entrance.

He made his way to a basement black area, where he dropped off the impression kit with a brush-pass.

FBI surveillance teams studied the layout of Jim's three-bedroom town house in Burke, Virginia. The cream-colored dwelling had tiny lawns, fore and aft, and a sturdy back deck with a privacy fence. The property sat on the lower end of a seventy-home condo complex that hugged a curving cul-de-sac called Burke Towne Court, one of many such developments cut into stands of maples and oaks west of Washington. Jim's bedroom windows overlooked a short, steep hill topped with brambles at the edge of a thick wood and a view across a grassy easement to another unit in the complex.

FBI investigators were delighted to learn the town house next door was for sale. Jim's bedroom sat less than seventy-five feet away.

Agents Steve Hooper and Bernie Cerra went undercover to meet with a real-estate agent on the parking lot of a nearby supermarket. Cerra, using a cover name, had set up the meeting to arrange a tour of the property. The agents had just begun talking with the Realtor when Hooper heard a familiar voice calling from across the lot.

"Excuse me, sir, are you following me?"

Hooper turned to see a woman he knew, a family friend. Their sons went to school together, and she knew that Hooper and his wife were both FBI agents. Hooper's friend was just playing around, not realizing he was on the job. He whirled and pulled eyeball to eyeball with his neighbor.

"Don't talk to me," he said in a low voice. "You don't know me."

"OK," she said cheerily, "I'm going now."

The FBI bought the house next door to Jim's and installed two agents, posing as husband and wife, to run surveillance operations on the Nicholson home. They would see Star and Nathan leaving the house on weekday mornings, returning like other latchkey kids after school. Their microphones would pick up the sounds of mysterious tapping, late at night, from Jim's bedroom.

On a Wednesday morning in late October, Hooper and two other FBI agents, including Tom Almon, one of the primary agents in the Nicholson investigation, pulled into a parking space in front of Jim's town house. An agent running surveillance in the neighborhood told them through their earpieces that the coast was clear, and they climbed out of their car. Agents casually hiked Jim's concrete steps to the front door as if they belonged there.

They had timed their entry so that no one was home: Jim was under watch at the CIA compound, and Nathan and Star were off at school. The agents stood on the landing in front of a grayish brown door affixed with a cheap brass knocker and let themselves in with a key made from Maguire's key-impression kit.

They stepped into the narrow foyer, where they were confronted by two sets of stairs. One dropped into a den. The other climbed to a kitchen, which faced the front of the house, and a living space that opened to a back deck. Another flight of stairs led to the top floor, which served as sleeping quarters for Jim, Star, and Nathan. The agents were extremely careful not to let either of the Nicholson kids' cats—Megacin and Maxina—flee through the front door. (There is an old story in the bureau about agents who accidentally freed a cat during a covert entry. After a frantic effort, they recaptured the fugitive feline and put it back inside before they left, only later to learn—the hard way—that it wasn't the right cat.)

The agents had just enough time for a sneak and peek, their task specific. They needed to discover the origin of the tapping noises in Jim's bedroom. The agents had been in the house a few minutes when their outside man alerted them through earpieces that someone was approaching. Whoever it was had walked into the backyard and was now approaching the door.

One of the hazards federal agents face in their daylight entries are amateur snoops, such as cranky condo board members and neighborhood-watch nazis, whose observations might be reported to their target. Agents knew that if a neighbor spied a stranger inside the Nicholson home, and Jim heard about it, he would realize he was under investigation.

"It might be a neighbor," Hooper heard the surveillance agent say.

He glared wide-eyed at Almon and the other agent.

They froze in place, waiting for more details. A long moment passed.

"It's the gas man," they heard the surveillance agent say. He was there to read the meter.

In the master bedroom, the agents found Jim's Toshiba laptop, the source of the tapping. They also turned up a document scanner. The agents were careful not to touch or move anything as they snapped photographs and prepared to exit. When the coast was clear, they slipped out as if they'd never been there.

One weekday that fall, the phone rang in Maguire's office. He picked up the receiver to find one of the FBI guys on the line.

"What the fuck is he doing? He's standing on his chair!"

Maguire leaped up and walked to Jim's office, giving a perfunctory rap on the door before barging through. There he found Jim still standing on his chair, staring at the ceiling.

"What're you doing?" Maguire asked. "Redecorating?"

Jim stammered and stepped down.

On November 3, a Sunday, FBI agents sneaked into the Other World Terrorism branch. They moved slowly toward Jim's office and stopped, studying the lines between his door and door frame to make certain Jim hadn't applied a tiny sliver of clear tape or some other marker that would show someone had secretly entered his office.

Once inside, they shot photos to document a "before" picture, including images of the item they'd come to search, a black folder atop Jim's desk. They peeked inside and saw that it was choked with papers about Russia. There were roughly forty files in the folder and a few other spots in Jim's desk, none of which had anything to do with counterterrorism. They photographed every page and put the documents back as they'd found them. They shot a few "after" photos before quietly slipping away.

The following Saturday, one week before he would leave for Europe, Jim drove up to Langley to prepare documents for Polyakov. The computers in his branch, unlike the ones at The Farm and CIA stations around the globe, had no disk drives. So there was no easy way to copy, edit, or transfer documents. Jim went old-school. He pulled files out of the black folder and took scissors to the tops and bottoms of each page, shearing away classification stamps. Documents about Russia, which had been clearly marked "Secret" and "Top Secret," were now devoid of any classification.

That Tuesday, CIA employees from the Office of Technical Service appeared in Jim's office.

The OTS, part of the Directorate of Science and Technology, is one of the least-heralded but coolest subdivisions of the agency. Its personnel serve up real-life gadgets, much like the fictional character "Q" in the James Bond movies. The OTS helped develop the U-2 spy plane; played a critical role in developing safe but extremely high-energy lithium carbon monofluoride batteries; and, through expert disguise, helped to sneak six American diplomats out of Tehran, Iran, after protesters overran the U.S. Embassy in 1980. The CIA also credits OTS scientists with engineering the first ultra-miniature camera.

This time, OTS employees were delivering Jim a document camera built into a briefcase. The case was designed so that when you opened it, the camera—bolted to a folding frame—lifted over a document platform. When the OTS folks left, Jim closed his office door and opened the case under his desk. He grabbed papers out of his black folder and knelt on the carpet, setting documents on the platform to photograph. Jim spent a half hour on the floor that day, and returned to shoot more of the documents later that night. He was at it again the following morning. The watchful eye of the video camera mounted in the ceiling captured every click.

Maguire watched the FBI's video of Jim copying top-secret documents for what was clearly a planned intel dump for the Russians. It had been one thing to imagine he was a turncoat, quite another to watch him prepare his next betrayal of his brother officers. Maguire now wanted the prick behind bars. His career in espionage had put him elbow to elbow with dirty men all over the world, duplicitous souls guided by greed. But Jim had taken it to a new level. He was the mercenary's mercenary, a purely destructive personality.

Armed with the latest tapes, the FBI took charge. Everyone involved in the investigation now knew they had enough evidence to charge Jim with espionage. For the first time Curran could remember, the FBI and CIA were in complete concurrence about their target. It was time to roll him up.

The question was where. Government prosecutors needed to prove that Jim was in play, taking overt actions to spy for the Russians. One way to catch him in motion was to let him take the flight to Europe for a meeting with the SVR. The Department of Justice considered getting the CIA to create a fictional crisis that demanded Jim's urgent attention in Paris or London; there he could be summoned to a U.S. embassy in either city. Once they had him inside either diplomatic station, the FBI could sweep in and arrest him—possibly with top-secret documents in his bag. The trouble with that plan was that Jim might realize he was being set up. If so, he might rabbit and they would lose him forever.

Investigators devised a different plan. But it, too, carried risks.

That Friday night, November 15, Jim picked up his half brother, Rob Nicholson, at the airport and brought him back to the town house. Rob, who was thirty years old, had agreed to watch Star and Nathan while Jim was away on business. He missed his niece and nephew, having not seen them since their summer visit with their mom, and was happy that Jim paid his way to Virginia to see them. By the time they reached Burke Towne Court, the kids were already asleep. Rob caught up with his big brother before turning in.

They would all rise early the next morning to see Jim off.

7

FBI Takedown at Dulles

"In Guarani, a language spoken in Paraguay, 'nye-eh' has two meanings. It is the word for 'word' and the word for 'soul.' The Guarani Indians say those who lie betray the soul."

—George Papagiannis

Sterling, Virginia, November 16, 1996

Jim steered his minivan to a stop in front of Dulles International Airport and stepped into the brisk sun of a Saturday morning. Rob climbed behind the wheel as his big brother threw his arms around the kids for one last hug. Then Jim was on the move again, striding toward the iconic terminal building with its beveled wall of concrete pillars and glass. Jim turned for an instant and shot them all a grin. He had a way of smiling through his eyes, a glint of pure mirth. He looked like a middle-aged college professor, bearded and bespectacled, dressed in white slacks and a dark turquoise button-down shirt. He carried a suitcase in each hand, and a brown leather satchel hung from his shoulder. His kids returned enthusiastic waves as their dad moved for the bank of glass doors.

Nathan had turned twelve on the last day of July. He had never stayed put in one home longer than three years, accepting Jim's travels and new assignments without question. He was adaptable, cheerful, never tired of adventure. When he grew up, he hoped to be just like his dad.

He reminded himself this was a short trip. A week or so and his dad would be on his way home with funny tales of foreign travels. The old man had spent less time overseas since taking the new job at headquarters, and Nathan had taken advantage of his dad's presence during those two years in Virginia. They had drawn immensely close. With Jeremi off at college, Nathan was pushing out of his big brother's shadow, asserting himself as Jim's main man.

As Rob steered for home in the minivan, he made an announcement to distract the kids from their father's departure: "We're gonna have an adventure this week." But nothing could prepare them for the adventure that lay ahead.

Jim planned to rendezvous in the terminal with the two subordinates in his CTC branch who were joining him on the trip. They were set to hop on a thirty-two-seat American Eagle puddle jumper to New York, then jet off to South Africa and Rome on official counterterrorism business. At the end of the business trip, Jim planned to break away for a short vacation in Switzerland to meet with Polyakov.

One of Jim's suitcases held nothing more than a pair of tan money belts; one he would wear under a pant leg, the other around his waist. Polyakov had promised $50,000 for the new haul. In his camera bag were ten rolls of exposed but undeveloped film. They held the images of seventy-four classified documents, some of them stamped "Top Secret." He also carried two computer diskettes choked with a dozen classified files and an encrypted message for his Russian handler. Jim's wallet held the business card of Roland Keller, his Swiss banker.

Jim strode to the American Airlines ticket window and checked his suitcases, then headed through security. He joined his two CIA subordinates in the main terminal and climbed aboard one of the airport's big boxcar-on-wheels contraptions known as "people movers." Moments later the vehicle pulled to a halt at the mid-field terminal, where they debarked.

FBI agents dressed as travelers folded into the crowd, eyes on Jim's every move.

As Jim and his CIA companions neared Gate 24, the woman in their party—an Arabic language specialist—suddenly walked off to hit the ladies' room. Up ahead, at the mouth of the gangway, stood a pair of undercover FBI agents posing as husband and wife. Their objective was to wait until the CIA officers entered the passageway and follow them downstairs to the tarmac. But suddenly they were the last people standing at the gate; all the other passengers had made their way to the airstrip. They couldn't appear to be waiting for Jim, which might spook him. So they launched into an improvised marital spat that rang in the ears of every agent on the investigation team. The improvisation seemed to work. Jim and his colleagues walked past, and the agents shut down their vitriol to quietly fold behind them.

Agent Steve Hooper had walked onto the tarmac a few moments earlier wearing an American Airlines jacket and a blue ball cap with the Dallas Stars hockey logo on it. He had nonchalantly taken a position on one end of a blue metal baggage cart, where a real luggage handler, a lean blond woman also wearing an airline jacket, stared at Hooper as if he had just stepped off a spaceship. Hooper, a former hockey player from Boston with one of those thick Tom Selleck mustaches, shot her a reassuring look.

"Don't worry," he told her. "I won't be here long."

As Jim reached the ragged queue of passengers on the cold tarmac, he heard a voice.

"Hey!" Hooper called. "Jim Nicholson!"

Jim grinned and took a step toward Hooper. Perhaps he thought the stranger in the American Airlines jacket knew him from somewhere, or needed to talk to him about his luggage. He was still smiling when Hooper got close enough to flash his credentials.

"Jim, FBI," he said. "It's over."

Jim tensed and balled his fists, looking furtively past Hooper.

"Don't try it," Hooper said. "It's over."

Dave Raymond, a baby-faced FBI tech agent in jeans and an identical American Airlines jacket, stepped behind Jim and locked hands around his suspect's right arm.

Hooper tightened his grip around Jim's other arm. He had arrested all kinds of people in his career, having worked organized crime and Russian mob cases. Most of his targets knew the day was coming, probably even expected it. But Hooper had never seen anyone look quite the way Jim did just then: stone-frozen paralyzed. His eyes were vacant. He seemed unable to utter a word.

Jim unclenched his fists. There would be no fight, no footrace.

Above the action, a member of the FBI surveillance team photographed the moment, frame after frame documenting the takedown with such clarity you could see that the crown of Jim's head had grown a little threadbare. One of Jim's CIA subordinates began to protest as agents guided his boss away from the plane. The officer explained that they were supposed to be taking an overseas business trip.

"Canceled," an agent said, presenting his creds.

Hooper and Raymond handed Jim over to several of the key Squad NS-34 investigators behind the day's collar. "The Three Mikes," as they were known—Lonergan, Donner, and Anderson—received their suspect like a group of hunters accepting a pheasant from a floppy-eared springer spaniel. They had been hiding nearby, watching Jim hike to a plane they knew he would never board.

Lonergan, being a counterintelligence guy, was a little rusty cuffing suspects. But Hooper had agreed to take Jim into custody only if Lonergan agreed to do the honors and cuff his ass. As Jim assumed the position, hands behind his back, Lonergan swung the cuffs around his wrists expertly.

McClurg and others on the investigation team gathered at Buzzard Point, the FBI's metro D.C. headquarters, watching the takedown on a closed-circuit video feed. He was delighted to see Dave Raymond taking part in the collar. Raymond was a key member of McClurg's technical team, the guy who had covertly pulled what seemed like miles of fiber-optic cable through the ceiling at Langley to collect videotaped evidence of

Jim's espionage. Tech agents carry guns just like street agents, but their behind-the-scenes work, too often unheralded, plays a critical role in major cases. This time, the very hands that installed the camera above Jim's desk had also taken custody of his suspect, affirming the bureau's appreciation for his literal high-wire operations at Langley.

Maguire stood in the British Airways' executive lounge, the only CIA man invited by the FBI to attend the arrest operation. Several other agency officers were deeply involved in the case, but none worked longer hours than their spy-versus-spy guy. During his previous life as a cop, Maguire had paid grudging respect to the FBI. The agents always carried themselves with a little more polish than city police. They even had a little more swagger, if that was possible. They also seemed to bring limitless enthusiasm, and huge government resources, to joint investigations with local law enforcement agencies.

Maguire knew he would never be a part of the FBI brotherhood. Those bonds were forged at the FBI Academy in Quantico, Virginia, tempered in field-office bullpens around the country, cemented on grueling overnight surveillance operations, and celebrated—often with strong drink—after they cuffed the bad guys. But for just a moment on that chilly Saturday, the ex-cop from Baltimore felt like one of them. They stood shoulder to shoulder, staring through a big picture window, all waiting for the money shot.

It came fast.

Agents bent Jim over the trunk of the car, spreading his legs and frisking him. They stripped him of his wallet and Rolex and shoulder bag. Those watching Jim saw his characteristic élan had evaporated, his eyes telegraphing the cold truth that he was now at the mercy of the government he betrayed.

To his credit, Jim never shed a tear.

Maguire made his way to a holding room, where agents guarded Jim's two shell-shocked subordinates. "Look," he told them, "you just witnessed something really bad. You're not in any trouble. You're not part of this. You'll be interviewed by the FBI. This is all under control. We'll talk about it when you get back to the office." The officers stared back, still not comprehending Maguire's role in this. He felt sorry for them, and he knew things were only going to get worse. The FBI would drive the officers to a nearby hotel for questioning. They would be sequestered overnight, unable to phone their families. The FBI would subject them to hostile interrogations, demanding to be told what they knew about Jim's work for the Russians and how they might have helped him. The CIA had prepared them for such events in simulated interrogations. But this time, it was real.

FBI agents would interview all the CIA personnel in Jim's branch after the bureau and agency made Jim's arrest public the following Monday. They would drill down to the marrow, extracting every detail to make sure Jim had acted alone.

Investigators sat with Jim in a separate room and formally read him his Miranda rights. They asked if he might have anything he'd like to say.

"I'd like to see a lawyer," he said.

Nathan heard loud raps on thick wood.

Whoever was at the front door had forgone the light tap of the brass knocker in favor of big, hard fists. From his bedroom window upstairs, which overlooked the front door, he parted the curtains for a peek. He saw a man and a woman he didn't recognize on the stoop. He lingered for a moment, looking at the tops of their heads, thinking Uncle Rob would take care of it. But Rob was back in the den watching a college football game on TV, and probably couldn't hear the knocking.

Nathan thumped down two flights of stairs.

On the other side of the door lay a cataclysm.

Nathan twisted the doorknob and pulled. He found a pair of unsmiling adults. They were asking for Mr. Nicholson.

"He's not here right now," Nathan told them. "He's on a business trip."

The man explained they needed to speak with Robert Nicholson.

Nathan called for Rob, who came down from the den to greet their visitors. Nathan passed him on the way back upstairs to resume his video game. When Rob reached the door, the strangers on the stoop flashed FBI credentials. He glanced over his shoulder and stepped outside, closing the door behind him. They had his undivided attention.

"Jim's been arrested," he heard one of them say, "for espionage."

Rob thought they were playing a joke on him. He now figured the strangers were a couple of Jim's cronies pranking the bumpkin from Oregon. But Rob was no bumpkin, and he wasn't buying the stiff-faced strangers' story.

The agents told him they had a warrant to search Jim's house.

"Well," Rob told them, "you're not coming in till I see the warrant."

He watched one of the agents, the woman, retrieve papers from their car and hand them to him. One of the FBI's key investigators had written the document, signed by a federal magistrate, that gave the bureau the right to search 5764 Burke Towne Court for "fruits, evidence, and instrumentalities of crimes against the United States, to wit: espionage . . ." That was as far as Rob needed to read. The words put him on his heels, and it took him a moment to get his bearings. Suddenly this was real, and his first thought was about the kids. How was he going to tell Star and Nathan?

The agents explained to Rob that investigators would take many hours to search the town house, and they needed to clear the Nicholsons out. The bureau had booked them two hotel rooms nearby, where they could stay for the night. What the agents didn't say was that an FBI team would turn the home upside down. They would slice open Jim's mattress, cut through the popcorn ceiling in his bedroom, look behind every light socket, peer into every inch of his crawl space, and explore a basement storage closet that the kids sometimes played in. They would haul out any shred of evidence that Jim sold classified files to the Russian Federation.

Rob's face went ashen. He turned somberly for the stairs and climbed toward the kids' bedrooms. In his heart, he felt the FBI had it all wrong. There was no way he could believe his big brother, the guy he'd idolized since birth, was guilty of spying against the U.S. No way. In Rob's mind, Jim was a patriot, a "Screaming Eagle" in the Army's 101st Airborne, a globe-trotting government servant who helped his country win the Cold War.

When Rob reached the landing at the top of the stairs, he called to Nathan and Star. He told them to pack bags for the night and not ask any questions, he would explain everything later. Dutifully, the kids packed without a word.

The FBI checked the Nicholsons into a nearby hotel. There, Rob sat down with Nathan and Star. With a leaden heart, he broke the news to his niece and nephew that their father had been arrested for espionage.

Star began to bawl, begging her uncle through sobs to tell her that her dad would be OK.

"They're not going to hurt him, are they?"

Rob told Star no one was going to hurt her dad.

Nathan wept quietly. His suspicion that his dad was a government spy had finally been confirmed. Unbeknownst to him, Jeremi and Star had learned the family secret by the time they reached their early teens. Jim had never had the talk with his youngest son. Nathan now pored through the sounds and images of his past. Whispers between his mom and dad. Jim's long absences. All the foreign travel. Demonstrations at The Farm. Nathan's mind looped over the word his uncle had used to describe his dad's arrest: "espionage." How could that be a crime?

"Uncle Rob," Nathan said, "that's what they *pay* my dad to do."

This was complicated business for a twelve-year-old. But Rob, too, was bewildered by the turn of events. He figured Jim had fallen so deeply into his work for the agency that someone had set him up.

Agents drew Rob into another room, leaving the kids alone to watch TV and fret. They told him it was time for him to phone his mom and dad. But Rob balked, telling them he simply couldn't be the one to break the news to his parents, that it would shatter them. The agents assured him that the FBI had already made contact with Nick and Betty. So Rob picked up the phone and dialed his parents in Eugene. His mom answered.

"I guess you've heard the news about Jim," Rob said.

"No," Betty gasped.

Rob could have killed the FBI for doing this to him. Now he had no choice but to break the news that her firstborn was in jail.

Betty was standing in the kitchen of their little house in the Woodland Park Estates, bracing herself for the worst possible news. The tone of Rob's voice was grave, and she feared he was about to tell her that Jim's plane had gone down.

"He's been arrested," Rob told her, "for espionage."

"Arrested? Jim? Are you sure?"

Yes, Rob told her. By the FBI.

A couple of hours later, a pair of FBI agents, both women, pulled up to Nick and Betty's home to confirm the news and take statements.

Laurie was deep in the Siskiyou Mountains of southwestern Oregon that Saturday, where she was interning as a seasonal field ranger for the Oregon Caves National Monument. She lived a spare, bohemian life that gave her time to appreciate the magic of the natural world. The kids had been gone since the end of summer. She lost herself in her work on the mountain by day, and retired to her bedroom and her books in an old lodge by night.

The place was nirvana for an earthy forty-two-year-old geologist. A quarter-billion years before, an ocean basin collided with a massive reef, causing limestone to cook into marble that rose four thousand feet into mountains. Rain had poured off trees, seeping through acid-rich earth to dissolve tunnels, creating one of the nation's rare marble caves.

Laurie had spent that Saturday on the south side of the caves, where she was helping a moth expert with his research on the many species that wintered there. With sunset closing in, they hightailed it over a creek crisscrossed by deadfall timber, reaching the ranger station after dark. A message awaited Laurie.

One of her brothers had phoned, leaving an urgent message to call him. When she got him on the line, he said Jim had been arrested on spy charges, and that the FBI needed to talk with her in Eugene.

Laurie drove three-and-a-half hours through hard rain to reach her hometown. She spoke for about ninety minutes that night with a pair of agents, candidly sharing her impressions of her ex. She told them he was a control freak, and that he squandered money on himself while constantly griping to their kids that he was short on cash. The agents slid some photos in front of her—Russians she didn't recognize. Laurie knew from their years together that Jim had frequently been targeted for recruitment by Moscow's spy services. But she didn't think they would ever succeed in turning him. Now it appeared Jim, who had wrongly accused her of betraying their country to the Romanians, was getting a criminal comeuppance.

Later, Laurie recalled how the FBI's news had struck her: "Serves him right, the bastard. Sooner or later, a person shows his true colors."

Laurie filed a motion for full custody of her kids, which was granted almost immediately.

Jim spent that Sunday, his forty-sixth birthday, in jail.

The FBI took Nathan, Star, and Rob back to the town house to pack clothes and a few of their other belongings. The kids rounded up their cats and put them in pet carriers. They were heading to new lodging, a motel closer to the airport, and it was unclear whether pets were allowed. So the agents draped blankets over the carriers and helped the kids smuggle the cats into their room.

In Oregon, Jeremi arranged to redeem frequent flier miles to fly his brother and sister back to their family. He feared that if he didn't get them on a plane right away, the Commonwealth of Virginia would split them up, put them in foster care, and he would never see them again.

Jeremi prepared to withdraw from his freshman year at Oregon State. His mom's job didn't pay enough to support them all, so he would get work to help out. It wasn't immediately clear where they would live. But Jeremi took control as the man of the house. One way or the other, he would keep the family together.

The FBI waited until Monday to publicly announce Jim's arrest.

Nathan and Star were sitting in their hotel room that morning, watching TV as the hours ticked down to their flight to Oregon. Suddenly their dad's face appeared on the screen. They heard a voice saying Harold James Nicholson had been charged with espionage, and that he potentially faced the death penalty.

Star began to sob, and Nathan tried to calm her down. But she was beyond consolable. The FBI had jailed their dad, torn up their home, and sent them packing with little more than their cats and the clothes on their backs. Nathan had never seen his sister more anguished, and he would never forget her next words, a declaration that bared the sudden, terrible upheaval in their young lives.

"I don't believe in God anymore!"

8

Forsaken All Allegiance to His Homeland

"The guy in After the Fall says, 'Why is betrayal the only truth that sticks?' I can't answer that altogether, but after all, the Bible begins with a betrayal, doesn't it?"
—Arthur Miller, interview in the *Paris Review*

Langley, Virginia, November 1996

Something caught Kathleen Hunt's eye when she walked into the branch office on the Monday morning of November 18. She peered across the bullpen to the back of the room. Strands of canary yellow crime-scene tape crisscrossed Jim's door, which was covered with the human silhouette of a target straight off a shooting range. She stood gawking. It was the most bizarre thing she'd ever seen in a CIA office.

A few of Hunt's colleagues were already in the room, including Maguire, who crossed the carpet to see her.

"Jim's been arrested for espionage," he said.

Hunt's jaw dropped.

"I was so worried that you had figured it out," Maguire said, reminding her of their conversation about Jim's requisitions for the camera and printer. "You were asking all these questions."

But she hadn't figured it out. Who goes to work in a secure office—the CIA, for God's sake—thinking one of her coworkers is a mole?

First Ames, now Jim. Ames was precisely the kind of guy she could imagine switching teams. He was a sour, embittered bureaucrat who chain-smoked, drank excessively, and was prone to occasional bursts of anger. Jim was the mirror opposite. He was easygoing, seemingly self-assured, sober. But as she thought about it, she realized that Ames and Nicholson had a common bond.

"Each in their own way," she said, "were very insecure men."

Hunt took a closer look at the target taped across Jim's door. She noticed that someone had fired at least one slug through the forehead of the silhouette, the FBI's not-so-subtle way of counting coup. As Hunt recalls the moment, the hole symbolized what everyone in the building was thinking of the CIA's latest betrayer: *We want to kill you.* She asked Maguire if she could take a peek at the crime scene, and he obliged her by tearing through the mess in Jim's doorway. Hunt saw that his office had been picked clean. Agents had slashed through a leather side chair in their inch-by-inch hunt for evidence. Cushion stuffing littered the floor.

CIA and FBI officials spent that day interviewing Hunt and others in the branch about Jim and his arrest. During an hour-long talk with FBI agents, Hunt told them about Jim's peculiar requisitions. She also told them about another of Jim's unorthodox moves, which suddenly struck her as noteworthy. Jim had been pushing the notion of greater collaboration with Russian intelligence on counterterrorism. He seemed to be angling to shoehorn the Russians into the CIA's working model, she told them. Now it was clear why.

John Deutch hobbled into the branch office later that day with the wooden cane he sometimes used when an old leg injury flared up. It had been a grueling forty-eight hours for the CIA director. Deutch had flown out to L.A. to assure a hostile crowd in Watts that the CIA had not taken part in a plot to push crack cocaine into the U.S. to finance the Nicaraguan contras in their 1980s war against Managua's Soviet-backed government. Now Deutch was back in the agency's headquarters to put a good face on the unmasking of another CIA man as a Russian spy. He took a seat just inside the door of the branch and told Hunt and their colleagues to relax, they had caught their betrayer. Later that year, Deutch would leave the agency amid controversy after he made the rookie mistake of opening classified files on an unsecured home computer.

Jim appeared that gray Monday before a federal magistrate in the Albert V. Bryan U.S. Courthouse in Alexandria, Virginia. He was still in the turquoise shirt and white pants he wore onto the tarmac at Dulles. The magistrate formally read Jim's spy charges. Prosecutors sought forfeiture of $180,000 in illegal proceeds from the Russians.

Americans are granted by birth the right to a speedy trial, and few halls of justice demonstrate that inalienable right more emphatically than those in the Eastern District of Virginia. Its judges preside over a court calendar that moves so swiftly it is widely known as the Rocket Docket. The new courthouse, a postmodern building that opened eleven months before Jim walked in wearing cuffs, was accoutered with a statue above its entryway that seemed to personify the proceedings inside. The statue of Blind Justice stood twelve feet, six inches tall, eyes blindfolded, robe billowing, arms outstretched. One of her massive bronze feet was planted on a pedestal, another extended behind her as if she were breaking into a sprint. Her hands clutched the scales of justice as if they were track batons. The statue was inscribed, "Justice Delayed, Justice Denied."

Jim signed a financial affidavit stating he netted $2,900 a month, $1,360 of which went toward his town house mortgage and $160 in payment on his minivan. He acknowledged that he had $4,000 cash on hand. The affidavit asked if he had received payments from another profession or source. Jim checked no. The document publicly acknowledged what had been all over the news that morning: Jim's employer was the CIA.

He was the sixth American charged that year with spying. Two others—Phillip Tyler Seldon, sentenced ten days earlier with wrongly giving military documents to El Salvador, and Robert Chaegun Kim, accused in a conspiracy to steal U.S. military secrets for his native South Korea—had come through the same Alexandria courthouse. Jim's GS-15 rank put him a notch above Ames in the Central Intelligence Agency's hall of shame. He was the highest-ranking CIA official ever arrested for espionage. News agencies ate it up.

"Good evening," Peter Jennings said as he opened *ABC World News Tonight.* "We begin tonight with another American accused of selling out his country to the Russians." Jennings' segment quoted one outraged government official after another. U.S. Attorney Helen Fahey: "Mr. Nicholson betrayed his country for money. He was not motivated by ideology, but by greed." FBI director Louis J. Freeh: "The passing of such information placed those officers' lives, as well as the lives of these foreign contacts, in danger." Deutch predicted there would be more such arrests.

The FBI would in fact arrest one of its own, Earl Edwin Pitts, one month later. The forty-three-year-old supervisory agent and lawyer had been selling the bureau's secrets to Moscow's foreign intelligence services for nearly a decade. Much like Jim, Pitts sold the dossiers of colleagues and was betrayed by a Russian cooperating with U.S. counterintelligence personnel for money. The FBI had made its case against Pitts by sending in undercover agents posing as SVR officers to talk him into parting with U.S. secrets. They arrested him at the FBI Academy at Quantico, the bureau's holy land.

Top officials in the FBI and CIA trumpeted Jim's arrest, with Deutch acknowledging in a quip to ABC newsman Sam Donaldson the rarity of their joint counterespionage investigation: "It used to be that directors of the FBI and directors of the CIA only met at one or the other's funeral."

Paul Redmond, behind the scenes, quietly gagged at the Kumbaya moment. He soon got a call that would worsen matters. A Pentagon reporter for one of the TV networks missed the press conference, and Deutch now wanted Redmond to give an on-camera interview about the Nicholson case. It was late in the day, and Redmond had worked a slew of thirteen-hour days while supervising simultaneous counterintelligence operations. He passed word up the chain of command that he would only do the interview if what he called the "Federal Bureau of Curiosity" put one of its agents on camera with him. Curran got dragooned into doing the FBI's part.

Redmond and Curran were interviewed together that night inside the Langley compound. A producer then got the two of them to walk down the hall, side by side, so the cameraman could shoot B roll— footage to fill in visual gaps in the reporter's narration. The producer didn't like what she saw.

"You didn't talk enough," she told them.

So they did it again. This time, as Redmond and Curran strode down the hallway conversing, Redmond said to the much taller FBI man, "Eddie, every FBI guy I ever met is a fuckin' asshole." And Curran happily noted that Redmond and all his CIA buddies were assholes, too. Both men hoped there were no attentive lip-readers in the viewing audience.

Jim made a brief appearance before U.S. Magistrate Judge Thomas R. Jones Jr. that Wednesday wearing a jumpsuit stenciled "Alexandria Jail." Jim's lead attorney, Jonathan Shapiro, later told reporters his client would vigorously fight the accusations. The following day, November 21, a federal grand jury handed up an indictment charging Jim with a single crime: conspiracy to commit espionage.

Shapiro, who had never tried a spy case, would soon be joined by two other court-appointed attorneys, Michael W. Lieberman and Liam O'Grady. The defense team later filed papers asking the judge to prevent the government from talking out of turn about Jim:

"Counsel is shocked at the daily deluge of extraordinarily prejudicial comment, speculation and innuendo coming from the mouths of high law enforcement officials who seem bent on putting the best spin possible on their embarrassment about alleged security breaches at the CIA so close on the heals [sic] of the Ames case," they wrote. "Senior CIA and FBI officials are almost gleeful in their attacks on Mr. Nicholson, telling the world of the 'overwhelming evidence of guilt' and the 'ironclad case' they have developed against him, and disclosing alleged facts laced with speculation about Mr. Nicholson's motives, all with devastating effect on this defendant's right to a fair trial."

Jim's defense team spent a week preparing for a November 25 hearing before Judge Jones to spring Jim from the Alexandria jail. Detention hearings are key junctures for any defense team. Jim's lawyers hoped to persuade Jones that he posed no danger to society and wouldn't flee if the judge granted him pretrial release. It would pay big dividends later, assuming he didn't bolt for Moscow. The defense wanted to present Jim as the all-American boy, the guy who made the Commandant's List in Army officer training and helped Jeremi earn his Eagle Scout medal.

The government's top lawyer in the case, Robert C. Chesnut, had served as chief prosecutor in the Ames case just ten years after graduating cum laude from Harvard Law. Chesnut had recently played roles in the Seldon and Kim spy cases. The government had collected huge mounds of evidence in those cases and dispatched them with pleas.

Chesnut opened Jim's detention hearing by calling the agent who ran the arrest operation at Dulles, Steve Hooper, to the witness stand.

"After you arrested him," Chesnut asked, "did you take custody of his wallet?"

"Yes."

"And, later, did you have an opportunity to go through the contents of the wallet?"

"Yes."

"Did you find anything in that wallet that would relate to a foreign bank account?"

"Yes. There was a business card in there bearing the name of Roland Keller, and it had foreign language printing on it, other than the name, and an account number on the back."

"Was the account number printed or handwritten?"

"It was handwritten," Hooper said.

"And in what country was this bank located?"

"It appeared by the writing to be a Swiss bank."

Hooper testified that during the search of Jim's town house, agents found a payment sheet that showed Jim had deposited $61,000 into Bank Leu. The funds were still in the account, he said, but bank officials had frozen it. Jim hadn't bothered to mention the matter of a Swiss bank account on his financial disclosure form.

Shapiro took up cross-examination.

"Are you aware of any information that the defendant was leading a lavish lifestyle here in the United States?"

"No," Hooper said.

"Or that he drove, for example, a Jaguar?"

This was a wink to Ames, who had bought two Jags with Moscow's money.

"I'm not aware."

"Or paid for cash—paid for his house in cash?"

"No," Hooper said, "I'm not aware of that."

Shapiro asked the agent whether Jim would be tailed by the FBI or allowed to leave the United States if he was released while awaiting trial.

The judge ruled that Hooper didn't have to answer the question.

Everyone in the room knew that if the judge was boneheaded enough to let Jim free on bail while awaiting trial, the FBI would stick to him like a sea of barnacles.

Rob Nicholson took the stand as a character witness for his brother. He testified as to the bona fides of his patriot clan. Every member of his family could recite *The Star-Spangled Banner*. Nick, their father, had retired from the military in 1971 after combat tours in Korea and Vietnam, and he had taken part in the Berlin airlift, one of the early skirmishes of the Cold War. Rob had served in Germany in the U.S. Army Signal Corps. He held top-secret clearance. But he told the court he only joined the service after getting his big brother's blessing.

"I was apprehensive about whether or not he would like me to have joined the Army," Rob testified. "And he wrote me a letter back. I still remember to this day. He told me that it was a noble decision, an honorable decision, and that serving in the U.S. Army was one of the greatest privileges that I could—that I could have."

Rob gushed about Jim's parenting skills.

"He always, always took time for his kids. He'd tuck them in at night, read to them constantly," Rob testified. "If they needed help with their homework, he was always there for them." Rob told the court that Jim had flown him out twice to watch his niece and nephews when Jim left the country on government business, and that Jim felt better knowing the kids were being watched by family.

"Have you talked to the children about his arrest?" Shapiro asked.

"Yes, I have," Rob said.

"And what have they told you about it?"

"They do not believe that their dad could have done this, and they are behind their dad one hundred percent."

Under cross-examination, Rob admitted it was news to him that Jim was engaged to Kanokwan. Rob said he knew nothing of his brother's double life in the CIA, his aliases, or his meetings with foreign spies, and that he wasn't sophisticated about code names, mail drops, or electronic communication gear.

Shapiro grew agitated. He wanted to put an end to the notion that Jim might make a James Bond escape from the bosom of his own family.

"Mr. Nicholson," he said, "how much sophisticated electronic equipment do you have in your house in Eugene, Oregon?"

"We have a telephone and a fax machine."

"Do you have a mail drop in your house?"

"No, sir."

"If it meant your brother was going to be released, would you squawk if the FBI set up camp outside your house?"

"No, sir."

Shapiro then called Len Beystrum—Jim's boyhood pal and best man at his wedding—to the witness stand.

"Is he a man of his word, in your opinion?" Shapiro asked.

"Yes, he is," Beystrum said. "He's stuck behind me all my life and he's interested in seeing this through. I don't think he'll flee."

"All right," Shapiro said. "You have a son yourself?"

"Yes, I have a twelve-year-old son who was born on the same day as Jim's younger son, Nathan. We told our wives we had it planned since high school."

"And what is his middle name?"

Beystrum said Nathan's middle name was James, as was his own son's.

"We didn't communicate our plans," he explained. "So we both named them after Jim."

Chesnut cross-examined Beystrum about Jim's failure to disclose outside income to the CIA.

"Would your opinion as to Mr. Nicholson change at all if you learned during the course of the last, let's say, two years, he received over $180,000 from outside income and didn't report that on his disclosure [affidavit]?"

"That wouldn't change my mind."

"If it had been a million dollars, would it change your mind?"

"No, sir."

"So virtually nothing that Mr. Nicholson would have done, whether it broke a rule or not, would change your mind as to his . . . character. Is that correct?"

"I would say that the business that he's in, there are rules that not everybody is aware of."

Betty Nicholson, on the witness stand in a light blue pants suit, pledged the equity in her house as collateral to assure Jim would appear in court. Under questioning by Shapiro, she recalled her last chat with Jim.

"I think his last comment to me on the phone was to be sure that his children received plenty of hugs because he's concerned that they won't get enough without being with him," Betty said.

While Shapiro worked to build up Jim's character, Chesnut took the position that he was a dangerous man with nothing left to lose: The government had taken his house, minivan, and bank accounts. He faced life imprisonment. His fiancée lived in Thailand.

"Espionage, by definition," Chesnut said, "gives someone like Mr. Nicholson a place to go, a safe haven from prosecution where they cannot be retrieved by any form of extradition. By definition, there is a place in the world—Russia—that would welcome Mr. Nicholson, provide him with financial support and give him a safe haven from the serious charges in this case. . . . The evidence has shown that he has passed a significant amount of this information already, but what is of such great concern to the United States in a case like this is not what he's already passed, but what he has up here in his head, from sixteen years of working in so many different places through the agency, working with so many different people. . . . He has already ruined careers, your honor, of a number of people who wanted to dedicate their life to government service. . . . This is an individual who speaks a number of foreign languages. This is an individual who is truly very familiar and comfortable moving in and out of the world because of his work."

Chesnut said Jim had a track record of deception, violated his oath of office, disclosed classified information, and lied about his assets. For that reason, he argued, he needed to stay in jail while awaiting trial.

Defense lawyer Liam O'Grady stood.

"It's an interesting weave of an argument, your honor," he began. "The director of the CIA, director of the FBI get on CNN last week and say they've had Mr. Nicholson under investigation, observation, for years, looking in his house, looking in his office, looking in his car, tracking him across the world. And today we hear that there is all kinds of secrets that he may release to the community at some time in the future if he's permitted to. Well, your honor, that's just disingenuous. The government knows everything that Mr. Nicholson has done for the last two years, and it knows that he is not a future danger to this community on that basis."

O'Grady, who was Jim's age, told the magistrate that the client sitting next to him—if freed on pretrial release—had nowhere to go. The government's extensive pretrial publicity over the last week, he said, might have given Jim as much public visibility as O. J. Simpson, the former NFL star acquitted of murder in 1995. He pointed out that the FBI had already seized his client's passport and all his money, and that Jim was willing to live under house arrest, wear an electronic monitor, and allow his phones to be tapped.

"And we have an absolutely legitimate explanation for the $61,000 in that Swiss account," he said. "My goodness, why would a spy who thinks he's secreting money use his own name on a bank account, put the number of the account on a card in his . . . wallet and leave the receipt for the money in his home. That doesn't make any sense at all. He is very anxious to prove his innocence on these charges in a court of law where guilt and innocence properly should be determined and go get back to his children, your honor."

Judge Jones had the final word.

"Espionage is by its nature an offense which, in many cases, can be committed only by somebody with the sort of background that this defendant has." While Jim posed little danger of getting his hands on new U.S. secrets, the judge feared Jim might hold secrets in his head that were valuable to foreign governments. "Accordingly," he said, "Mr. Nicholson will be held without conditions of release until trial and is remanded to the marshal's custody."

Len Beystrum joined Jim's family—Nick and Betty, and half siblings Rob and Tammie—for the drive over to the town house in Burke. The FBI had carted off everything of value, and would eventually sell it all as proceeds of espionage. But they had left a few things—an empty cabinet, a cap-and-ball frontier rifle, and a couple of dozen paintings, which the family boxed up and shipped home to Oregon for safekeeping.

Judge Jones issued a gag order preventing both legal teams—along with the FBI, CIA, and Justice Department—from commenting on the Nicholson case.

Jim's defense team took another stab at getting Jim out of jail while he awaited trial. They took a novel tack, saying that the FBI had proven it could keep eyes on espionage suspects. They used the example of Felix Bloch, a U.S. diplomat suspected in 1989 of selling government secrets to the KGB. The FBI wiretapped Bloch's phones and performed "bumper-lock" surveillance wherever he went, sticking a circus-like entourage on him for seven months. In the end, Bloch faced no charges.

Prosecutors fought back, filing court papers of their own. They pointed out that a superseding indictment accused Jim of three espionage charges and that he faced the possibility of life in prison. The government, they wrote, was still reviewing evidence to determine whether it would seek the death penalty against him.

Chief U.S. District Judge James C. Cacheris was assigned as Jim's trial judge. As a young defense lawyer in the late 1960s, he and his big brother, Plato Cacheris, had served as defense counsel in the espionage case of Air Force cryptographer Herbert Boeckenhaupt, a Pentagon-based staff sergeant who had apparently seen one too many Bond movies. Boeckenhaupt sold secrets to the Soviets to buy himself Avanti sports cars and was sentenced to thirty years in prison. Plato Cacheris later negotiated Aldrich Ames' plea in that very courthouse.

"One who commits espionage has forsaken all allegiance to his homeland," Judge Cacheris wrote in an order denying Jim's pretrial release. He noted that it would be in Russia's best interest to help Jim conceal his crimes. "Finally, in this case, the defendant faces life in prison, or perhaps even execution, if ultimately convicted. These factors compel the court to find that the crimes with which Mr. Nicholson has been charged create an unusually high risk of flight, and a tremendous incentive on the part of a defendant and his or her co-conspirators to procure that defendant's escape."

Cacheris also served as one of the seven judges rotating through the Foreign Intelligence Surveillance Court. Five days before Christmas, the judge dropped a bombshell: He acknowledged that he had signed two FISA orders that allowed the FBI to electronically eavesdrop on Jim. Cacheris said he didn't feel that approving those orders as a member of the highly secretive court disqualified him from the case. But he said Jim's lawyers were free to file a motion for his recusal in the Nicholson case if they wished.

Members of the defense team were taken aback. The judge assigned to hear Jim's espionage case had just admitted in open court that he had approved secret orders to snoop on him. The defense wasn't allowed to view those papers, because they were protected from disclosure by the Foreign Intelligence Surveillance Act. This meant that if they challenged the constitutionality of FISA, Cacheris would have to consider the legality of the very orders he had approved.

Shapiro sought the assistance of Jonathan Turley, a George Washington University Law School professor who was one of the nation's leading critics of the surveillance court and the law that created it. Turley had long argued that the panel served as little more than a rubber stamp for the FBI's snooping. He was convinced FISA violated Americans' constitutional rights against unreasonable eavesdropping on their homes and belongings. Worsening matters, as Turley saw it, the government had gained additional powers under FISA in 1995, when President Clinton signed an executive order that allowed government agents to physically search homes, autos, and other property.

Turley joined Jim's defense team, which by early 1997 included eight lawyers. On January 30, they filed a motion asking Cacheris to recuse himself from the Nicholson case: "Under the unique circumstances presented in this case and in the absence of recusal, the same judge who authorized the FISA warrants against Mr. Nicholson will be called upon to assess the validity of the warrants—quite possibly without any substantive input or argument by the defense. . . . The appearance of partiality is raised by the possibility that Judge Cacheris—during his approval of the FISA warrant applications—received confidential information from the government concerning allegations against Mr. Nicholson beyond what will be used at trial; information that, due to the nature of FISA, will be unknown to the defense."

At a hearing on February 3, Jim's lawyers told Cacheris they were mounting a groundbreaking challenge to FISA—the first to attack the constitutionality of the surveillance court's authority to permit physical searches of targets. If Jim's lawyers prevailed in such a challenge, prosecutors might have to throw out a mountain of evidence gathered in searches of Jim's town house, minivan, and CIA office—a potential game changer for the defense. But at the end of the thirty-minute hearing, Cacheris said he wasn't disqualifying himself. He set trial for April 14.

Turley told the judge he needed more time to mount a proper challenge of FISA's constitutionality. He wanted to collect friend-of-the-court briefs from a half-dozen legal and civil liberties groups. Turley, a bold lawyer reviled by many national security lawyers, believed the surveillance court trampled civil liberties in the quest for national security. (Sixteen years later, Edward Snowden, an ex–National Security Agency contractor, took Turley's argument public by leaking a FISA court order that permitted the NSA to vacuum up the phone records of millions of ordinary Americans as it hunted down foreign terrorists.) Turley knew the outcome of his FISA challenge would have a major impact on Jim's trial strategy.

Cacheris, unbowed, told him he had seventy days to prepare for trial.

"I knew the Nicholson case was the best vehicle for challenging the FISA court," Turley later said. He had been looking for a test cast to put the law on trial before the U.S. Supreme Court, and he believed Jim's case was the ideal vehicle to demonstrate the law's unconstitutionality. "We made it clear we were going to take this FISA challenge all the way."

Lawyers spent much of February 1997 arguing the legality of the FBI's electronic snooping on Jim. Turley filed a motion to suppress the evidence obtained by the surveillance of Jim's home, office, minivan, safe-deposit box, and personal effects. He wrote that FISA had been denounced for nearly twenty years for failing to meet probable cause standards of the Fourth Amendment, which established that Americans had the right to be secure in their homes. Turley now sought copies of the Justice Department's applications to the surveillance court and the orders signed by Cacheris (and perhaps others).

Prosecutors in response acknowledged that searching Jim's home violated his privacy, but that the sneak and peeks were no more intrusive than, say, bugging his house, including bedrooms—which was legal under FISA. Attorney General Janet Reno signed an affidavit saying the release of the surveillance court documents would harm national security. Reno submitted, for the judge's eyes only, an affidavit from FBI director Louis Freeh, stamped "Top Secret," which she said set out the facts for her claim. She wrote that releasing this information in open court, or to the defense, would reveal FBI methods and sources that would undermine U.S. counterintelligence operations.

The FBI's applications to eavesdrop on Jim almost certainly held highly classified information about the Russian who helped the FBI pinpoint Jim as the leaker of CIA secrets. If Cacheris ruled that the defense had the right to know that information, Jim's lawyers would have carried a huge bargaining chip into plea negotiations. Reno and the U.S. government would go to almost any length to protect its sources—so much so that government prosecutors might have found themselves offering Jim a light sentence for espionage rather than risk public exposure of the Russian's identity.

The defense, meanwhile, filed a peculiar motion that appeared to be grasping at straws. Jim's lawyers asked the court to pay for him to join them in a flight to Singapore, where they would retrace his steps to prepare for trial. Prosecutors rightly pointed out that espionage wasn't an extraditable offense in Singapore, meaning that once Jim set foot there, he'd be a free man.

Cacheris denied Turley's FISA challenge on Valentine's Day, writing that while lawyers had attacked the constitutionality of the surveillance law since its inception in 1978, judges had upheld it every time.

This essentially crushed Jim's defense.

His lawyers would soon schedule meetings with government prosecutors and key FBI agents to hammer out a plea agreement. These gatherings offered Jim the chance to confess all his spy work for Russia in exchange for a more lenient sentence than life in prison. The government would not have to disclose its Russian source, and they would succeed in putting Jim behind bars.

But for how long?

*   *   *

On the last day of February 1997, Jim signed a plea agreement admitting that he was guilty of conspiracy to commit espionage. Part of the contract required him to tell government intelligence officials every detail of his betrayals to Russia before he gave interviews to news organizations. He also agreed to submit to polygraph examinations as part of those debriefings and turn over to the government any money he might earn by writing a book about his life or selling movie rights to his story.

A few days later, Jim forfeited his assets to the United States. This included the $180,000 he had stashed in banks (including the Swiss account, and savings set aside for Nathan, Star, and Jeremi), his minivan and Toshiba laptop, plus his town house and every stick of furniture in it. Jim also gave up all the interest in his Army and CIA retirement funds, although Laurie's divorce decree gave her half of his pension from the time they married until she left him in Bucharest. The government seized Jim's stamp and coin collections, including a couple of one-ounce Krugerrands, his Rolex, jewelry, an Olympus 35mm camera, books—including his collection of James Bond novels by Ian Fleming—a Technics CD player and sound system, and a handful of firearms that included a .40-caliber Glock 23 pistol (the preferred handgun of countless federal agents). The FBI even hauled off Jim's king bed frame, a brass model with baked enamel inscribed, "Especially handcrafted for Batman."

Jim relinquished rights to any money traceable to his spying for Russia. Moscow had a time-honored tradition of holding open accounts for spies imprisoned for the motherland. History is replete with examples of Western spies, facing espionage charges in their own countries, who defected to the Soviet Union and lived on Moscow's dime until they died, some of them by drinking themselves to death. The U.S. intelligence apparatus similarly remained loyal to Russians they bankrolled to spy on their country.

Jim also agreed in writing that if Russia ever paid money or some other benefit to him or his family, he would notify the CIA and assign those proceeds to the United States.

Jim spent much of that spring in a series of debriefings with FBI agents and teams of CIA officials. He acknowledged that the SVR had paid him $300,000—not the $180,000 investigators had identified—and he recounted in detail the secrets he handed to Polyakov. These informational downloads went on for ten weeks, sometimes three times a week. Jim walked his interrogators step by step through his meetings with his Russian handler in India, Indonesia, Switzerland, and Singapore. The sins Jim confessed helped the government assess the damage he'd done and prevent another Jim Nicholson. Agents independently corroborated much of what Jim told them.

When the debriefings ended, Jim took a polygraph. He easily passed questions about his contacts with the SVR, and whether he had been truthful about the money he made. But when he was asked whether he was withholding any secrets he'd passed to the Russians, Jim's answers came up on the box as deceptive. At the time, the FBI saw no reason to believe he was lying, perhaps attributing the deception to the vagaries of the polygraph. Agents had no evidence of further crimes. They had wrung him dry for details of his espionage, forced him to give up his money and property, and now would see him off to federal prison.

Prosecutors gave Jim credit for helping the government determine the damage he caused. But in a memo filed a few days before his sentencing, they noted that he betrayed his colleagues and his nation out of greed. They said he deserved 283 months in prison. George Tenet, now serving as the CIA's acting director, wrote that Jim put the lives of friends and colleagues at risk:

"Mr. Nicholson revealed, or planned to reveal, the names and positions of a large number of CIA officers whose jobs depend on their ability to work clandestinely. Some of these officers can no longer perform certain important assignments for which they were trained. Several other officers, who were working under our deepest cover program, had to be withdrawn because their missions, as well as their lives, were at risk. Still other officers whose identities were revealed to the Russians by Mr. Nicholson were our young Career Trainees, many of whom were his own students. The course of many of these young officers' careers has been affected by Mr. Nicholson's treachery."

Jim's giving up the names of NOCs—bona fide secret agents with nonofficial cover—killed the careers for which they had trained. The government had spent a lot of money putting them in some of the most dangerous spots on earth, and they had gone deep undercover to plumb the secrets of hostile governments and their militaries. Now they would be called back to Langley, where they would take desk jobs or quit the agency altogether. In all, Jim had given up the identities of several classes at The Farm—blowing the covers of hundreds of officers.

Tenet acknowledged that the U.S. spy apparatus might never know the full extent of the losses Jim caused. But the agency would have to assume the worst possible outcome. To that end, he wrote, the agency had no choice but to cancel promising spy operations, and had already recalled spies from overseas assignments back to the United States.

On the first Thursday in June, John Maguire lumbered into Cacheris' courtroom and took a seat in the front row, squeezing in with a few of the FBI agents he'd worked so closely with on the Nicholson investigation. Maguire had come to Jim's sentencing to hear what he would say for himself.

Jim walked in a moment later wearing a blue double-breasted blazer. Maguire caught his former boss's eye for an instant as he walked past. They exchanged a short glance, and Jim's face registered abject confusion. Maguire needed that. He wanted Jim to understand *he* had been the inside man. They had gone spy-versus-spy under the roof at Langley, both playing a brutal game of betrayal. But only one of them would go home to his family that night.

Judge Cacheris, still in his chambers, had read handwritten letters from both of Jim's sons, neither of whom could afford to fly back to Virginia for their dad's sentencing. Nathan had sounded like a little boy asking the all-powerful Oz to send his dad home.

"Dear Judge," he wrote, "As you know, my Dad is in jail. Please let him out as soon as possible because I miss him very much. My Dad did what he did out of his love for us. . . . We are going through a tough time right now and releasing my Dad would help a lot. Please don't make me wait for a long time. . . . I don't know if this will let you set my Dad free early, but I might as well try to do this for my Dad because I love him." He closed with these words: "My Dad's Son, Nathan Nicholson."

Jeremi's letter was raw and revealing. He wrote that his father was always capable and caring, a generous man whose work had so often taken him far from home. In Thailand, his dad was gone eleven out of fourteen days. But over the last four years, they had seen much more of him; his dad had served as mother and father.

"My father has always done everything in his power to have us live comfortably," Jeremi wrote. "Unfortunately my father showed his love by material means. He enjoyed buying things for us. Though, now I think about it, what parent who truly loves his/her children wouldn't wish to give them every comfort they can and as many of the items they desire (merely) to provide some physical proof that they care. I don't say that is the best method, but it seems to have been the only way my father felt comfortable trying to ensure that his kids knew he loved us."

When Cacheris took the bench, prosecutors told the judge what he already knew: The government had worked out a plea with Jim and his legal team. The United States sought a twenty-three year, seven-month sentence. The defense sought a couple of years less, with credit for time already served in jail.

Shapiro and O'Grady once again built up their client as a patriot who had given twenty years to his country, serving on the front lines of the Cold War, risking his life in the Middle East and Cambodia. "Mr. Nicholson established contacts nobody else could get," Shapiro said. "He personally penetrated communist groups himself." Shapiro recited the words of Jim's superiors across the globe, who had given him rave reviews. "No weaknesses. . . . Mr. Nicholson can do it all. . . . His future is bright."

When it was Jim's turn to speak, he stood somberly. Those in the front row of the gallery could see he wore dress shoes with no socks. Jim told Cacheris he had lost everything that was ever dear and important to him, except his faith in God and his endless love for his children. His actions, he acknowledged, had blotted out all the good things he had done for himself and his colleagues.

"I won't ask for the forgiveness of my colleagues and countrymen, for I know they cannot give it," he said. "I will ask for the forgiveness of my family and children, because I know they will. . . . I reasoned I was doing this for my children—to make up for putting my country's needs above my family's needs and for failing to keep my marriage together by having done so. I am, in so many ways, so very sorry."

Government lawyers and the federal agents who took part in the investigation were flabbergasted by Jim's I-did-it-for-the-kids speech. Some would recall his words years later as the most destructive guilt trip a dad ever laid on his children.

Cacheris sentenced Jim to the full twenty-three years, seven months. With time off for good behavior, Jim could be out by the time he reached retirement age. The judge recommended that the U.S. Bureau of Prisons (BOP), Jim's new keeper, let him serve his time in Oregon. Perhaps there, in the bosom of his family, Jim would make good on the declaration he made to a court officer before his sentencing: "I would greatly appreciate the opportunity to offer some positive example to my children before I die."

9

A New Cellblock Celebrity

"In prison, you get the chance to see who really loves you. That little buck gives you a lot of time to think."

—Suge Knight

Sheridan, Oregon, summer 1997

The U.S. Bureau of Prisons complex in Sheridan, Oregon, with its white concrete walls and red Spanish-style roofs, looks like a small college campus in the tropics. The compound spreads across 182 acres on the northern end of the Willamette Valley, just south of the little farm town of Sheridan, and is separated from its neighbors by twelve-foot chain-link fences topped with coils of gleaming razor wire. From the air, the grounds appear to be an island flanked by working fields and a large pond, a patchwork of agronomy in hues of camelback tan, olive, and emerald green. The soil on the eastern edge of Oregon's mossy coastal mountains can grow pretty near anything, from pears to pinot noir grapes to grass seed. But one of the town's leading employers is the prison.

The complex, formally known as the Federal Correctional Institution Sheridan, holds the majority of its inmates in a medium-security lockup, with others in a work camp and a detention center. Sheridan is the only federal prison in Oregon and employs several hundred people from the nearby countryside, their gray uniforms ubiquitous in the town's cafés and groceries. Their workplace was built on political pork and powerful influence. U.S. Senator Mark O. Hatfield, the prison's chief benefactor, served two stretches as chairman of the Senate Appropriations Committee, and few politicians were capable of steering more pet projects to their states than the maverick Republican. The government spent $52 million to build the prison complex, which houses inmates in dormitory-style units designed to foster rehabilitation. Today it holds a little more than eighteen hundred inmates, about four hundred over capacity, owing largely to prisoners of the decades-long war on drugs.

Jim passed through the gates for the first time at 3:13 p.m. on a warm Thursday in late July, one week before Nathan's thirteenth birthday. In a way, Jim had finally returned home. His birthplace in Woodburn sat just twenty-seven miles from the prison complex. Jim's overseers gave him a bright orange prison uniform that identified him as a new fish and a handbook that established the rules of conduct in the medium-security facility. He was almost immediately put to work in a 47,000-square-foot factory that produced oak and walnut executive desks and plastic office chairs. Jim's job with the prison industries program, UNICOR, eventually led to a position as a product control manager. The pay topped out at a little more than $1 an hour, but through longevity and overtime hours, Jim would eventually earn a few hundred dollars a month. UNICOR's furniture business was a national leader, and its captive workforce, laboring at prisons across the nation, brought in hundreds of millions of dollars.

Sheridan had a reputation as easy time—not quite the Club Fed depicted in movies, but a soft landing for the federal prisoners lucky enough to land there. The place teemed with white-collar crooks serving short stretches, and a few well-behaved badasses serving the final years of long ones. What set Sheridan apart was the number of cellblock celebrities on the compound. By the time Jim clocked in, two front-page news figures were sharing a cell. Jeffrey MacDonald, the Green Beret doctor who stabbed his pregnant wife and two daughters to death with a knife and ice pick, had just passed his sixth anniversary at the prison.

His crime had been chronicled in a book and a movie, both titled *Fatal Vision*. MacDonald, known as "Doc," shared a cell with the Cold War spy Jim Harper, serving life with the possibility of parole for selling U.S. missile defense secrets to the Soviet bloc.

Harper obtained American defense secrets from his girlfriend (and later wife) Ruby Louise Schuler, an executive secretary at Systems Control, Inc., a Palo Alto, California, Army contractor. SCI's research focused on highly secretive studies on such things as how to make Minuteman missiles less susceptible to Soviet intercepts. Schuler smuggled documents out of SCI in her purse, and Harper carried them to Poland's spy service, the Służba Bezpieczeństwa. They paid Harper $100,000 in 1980 for a trove of documents, which a team of KGB officers picked through in the Russian Embassy in Warsaw. A CIA source later provided clues that led to Harper's 1983 arrest.

Six days a week, Harper manned the desk in the prison law library, which sat between the chow hall and a recreation room. Inside were hundreds of law books and several rows of Swintec 7000 electric typewriters. Prisoners sat in private cubicles, tapping out legal papers, pro se appeals, and lawsuits that accused their overseers of missteps ranging from illegal beatdowns to bad food. It wasn't long after Jim reached Sheridan that Harper looked up to find Jim walking into the library.

Harper had tried for years to prove that the damage he caused the U.S. was minimal, and that he should be paroled. Through the U.S. Freedom of Information Act, he had obtained a redacted summary of his official damage assessment, which suggested the ballistic missile defense programs he compromised had been canceled before he passed secret papers to the Poles. He hoped Jim would glance at the documents and offer insights that might help him win parole. But when Harper stood to greet the new spy in town and ask if he might peek through the Department of Defense summary, Jim recoiled and said he could be of no help.

"It was just obvious the guy didn't want to have anything to do with me," Harper said in an interview years later from Lompoc Penitentiary. "I think it was the only time I tried to talk to him."

Harper would observe Jim over the next several years as he walked into the library in the evenings, took a seat at a typewriter, and banged feverishly. Jim kept entirely to himself, guarding what appeared to be a growing stack of papers from prying eyes. While many inmates share their latest strategies to get out of prison early or sue the Bureau of Prisons, Jim worked in utter secrecy. Harper figured that Jim was drafting a document to provide the U.S. government additional information to shave time from his sentence.

Jim's celebrity preceded him at Sheridan. He had spent much of June and July 1997 entertaining national TV journalists, positing a staggering array of rationalizations for his betrayals. He told ABC's *Nightline* correspondent Dave Marash, "The primary reason for my decision to work with the Russians was my need to take care of my children back in the United States. . . . I just found myself in an untenable situation and I didn't know how to get out of it. . . . No one was killed. No one was tortured and the only person that was arrested as a result of my action was me." Jim conveniently failed to mention to *Nightline* that had he not been caught, some of the spies he compromised might have been tortured or killed.

Jim told NBC's Katie Couric that by the time he became a walk-in for the Russian Federation, he thought Moscow was struggling to come to grips with democracy, and that assisting Russia's efforts was not a bad thing. Couric asked, "Do you think that way now?" To which Jim answered, "No, I don't think that way now. . . . It flew in the face of everything that I believe, everything that was important to me." An ABC crew shot footage of Jim talking with Nathan on the phone. Jim's youngest, who had not seen his dad since the morning of his arrest, offered this to an interviewer: "We don't have a whole lot to talk to him about, but it's nice to hear his voice every once in a while."

Jim's family soon trekked up to Sheridan to visit. Nick and Betty still refused to believe he had done anything terribly wrong. They had watched CNN's report on Jim the day he was sentenced to prison, and they just weren't buying the government line. They gave an interview to *The Oregonian* that day, saying they felt the CIA had somehow set up their son. "As far as I'm concerned," Nick told the newspaper, "the CIA and FBI are very capable of doing that."

Once Jim landed in Oregon, many of his family members drove to see him—his parents and siblings and children, even his aging uncle Harold. But he felt he wasn't getting enough time with his kids. So he carved out a plan so that he could share exclusive visits every other Saturday with Jeremi, Star, and Nathan. It was during one of those private meetings with the kids that Jim cleared the air about his crime.

Nathan vividly remembers that moment, his dad leaning forward in his chair, the faces of his children pushed close to hear his words. Jim began by saying how sorry and embarrassed he was for them to see him in such a place. He told them how proud they all had made him, holding things together without him. He was happy Star and Nathan had kept up their grades. And he was glad to know Jeremi, deeply hurt by his dad's arrest, planned to return to Oregon State. Jim grew bitter as he spoke of his blind devotion to the agency, his long absences from them, and the ruins he had left of his family since the divorce.

The next part Nathan would never forget. Jim somberly admitted he had indeed sold secrets to the Russians for money.

"I just wanted to help you kids out," he said.

Jim's children mobbed him with hugs, professing their love and vowing to stand by their father no matter what. Star cried. Jeremi launched into a lecture, and Nathan recalled his brother breaking the tension by telling his dad he was forgiven, adding in jest, "Just don't do it again."

Nathan never let go of the memory of that painful heart-to-heart. Seeing his dad so sorrowful, head literally hung low, churned in his young mind. He convinced himself that the government must have pressured him to confess—even to his own kids—that he spied for Russia. Nathan came to a conclusion about his dad's confession that day, a belief he would cling to for many years.

He didn't believe a word of it.

*   *   *

In letters to Nathan that fall and into the spring of 1998, Jim reminded his son how much he loved and missed him. How he longed for their next adventures together.

"I have spoken to Jesus about this," he wrote. "Apparently it is only the will of men that I be in prison—not of God. Since God's power is so much greater than man's, I've asked God to set me free." In a letter two months before Nathan's fourteenth birthday, Jim acknowledged that one of his character flaws—always trying to make people like him—had been an asset in the CIA. "In fact," Jim wrote, "my job demanded that and I really was into it. Now, I understand that it involved compromising my true beliefs in many cases. What was always the most important to me was my children."

Jim hosted evening prayers in his cell and made new friends. One of his kindred was Steven Paul Meyers, who walked into Sheridan twenty-nine days after him. Meyers had been a talented sculptor before taking part in an audacious series of bank robberies that ended in a shoot-out with police. Jim and Meyers, both born in 1950, were arrested the same month. Both were bright, adventurous, equipped with healthy egos, and hated that they were forced to follow their kids' lives through the filter of letters and phone calls.

In late January 1999, Meyers opened an envelope with a return address he didn't recognize. Inside was a letter from a San Francisco woman who worked as a paralegal for an international law firm. She was writing to say she'd read about him in a new book by true-crime writer Ann Rule. *The End of the Dream: The Golden Boy Who Never Grew Up* chronicled Meyers' exploits with Scott Scurlock, dubbed "The Hollywood Bandit." Scurlock's gang—given to guns, theatrical makeup, and prosthetic faces—pulled more than a dozen successful bank jobs. But on November 27, 1996, things went badly when Scurlock, Meyers, and another man hit a north Seattle bank during a light rain. They made off with a duffel bag full of cash, more than $1 million, but got into a running gun battle with police. Scurlock escaped, then took his own life as the cops moved in. Meyers, wounded, later drew a twenty-one-year prison term.

The paralegal writing to Meyers in 1999 explained that she had once been held up while working as a bank teller. She was fascinated by his personal story, and she hoped he would write back. Meyers responded in February, saying he was happy to trade correspondence. His note concluded with an odd postscript: "Is it a problem to write you at your work address as legal mail?" As a matter of policy, prison officials don't open mail that appeared to be attorney-client correspondence. The paralegal soon received a pair of letters marked "legal mail" from Meyers, including a screenplay Meyers wrote about his exploits as a bank robber.

The San Francisco woman, perhaps infatuated with the bad boy, made her way to Oregon in June 2000 to meet him in person. She and Meyers' brother, Randall, spent the better part of four days in Sheridan's visiting room, a space about the size of a high school cafeteria. Steve Meyers leaned forward in his seat during one of their visits and pointed across the floor to another inmate. In a hushed voice, he told his guests that the man was not only a friend, but a Russian spy. He didn't tell them Jim's name. But it would come up later.

It had taken Jim two years to figure out a way to circumvent the CIA's snooping on his mail. He wanted Meyers to send the paralegal a document he had prepared for the SVR, making sure to mark it "legal mail" so that no one at the prison read it. Jim intended for Meyers' friend to forward it to the Russian Federation, which had a consolate in San Francisco.

Nathan was deep into his teens, a time when most children pull away from their parents to spend time with friends. He lived with his mom, and they were close, but he clung to his dad. And who could blame him? He'd gone the first eight years of his life feeling almost fatherless before getting a four-year window in Malaysia and Virginia to cast Jim as the hero of his life. Suddenly he could spend every other Saturday quizzing the old man about his life in the Army and the CIA. Nathan thrilled at Jim's stories of parachute jumps in the Rangers, daydreaming of following in his dad's boot steps. Jim also shared tales of his days as the CIA's Batman, including the daring escapes, with sidekick Robin, from armed gunmen on the streets of Manila.

Jim's boy never considered him a traitor. After his dad's sentencing, a TV news crew had come out to Laurie's home in Oregon for interviews. They put Nathan on camera, asking the same question many different ways: *What did your dad do?* It was clear they wanted him to say his dad betrayed his country and was a turncoat, but Nathan never budged. He wanted to tell them his dad gave his life to the CIA, sacrificing time with his own family to protect America. But he let it go.

Jim always made Nathan feel like the center of his universe, and now his boy told him everything about the world outside the razor wire. Nathan painted vivid accounts of his life and times at Crescent Valley High School, just north of downtown Corvallis, where he earned As and Bs, ran a season of track—middling performances in the 200- and 400-meter sprints—and loafed around with a handful of straitlaced friends. They were a geeky bunch that gathered after the final bell to play cards, mostly Egyptian Rat Screw, and talk about the girls they secretly adored. They set up a closed computer network to do battle in Quake 3, a popular shoot-'em-up game. Eventually Nathan went punk, spiking his hair into a mild Mohawk, and got deep into hard-core music, thrashing to bands such as Disturbed. Nathan would later tell me his dad hung on every word, never appearing judgmental or uninterested.

Jim's fatherly guilt ran deep. He was gut-sick that he couldn't be there for his kids. He confided to other prisoners in his prayer circle the deep humiliation he felt in not providing material support to his own children. He wept openly about this with at least one cellmate. But in the presence of his kids, Jim tried not to let on how these shortcomings crushed him. It must have been punishing to live vicariously through his children's stories, knowing they were coming of age in a world that, by the sound of things, moved at the speed of light.

Nathan didn't want his dad to fall too far behind when he got out of prison in his sixties, so he constantly apprised the old man of developments in electronic gadgetry. He regaled his dad with news from the front lines of the expanding digital universe, from iTunes to Halo 2, Nintendo Wii to XBox 360, and the confounding iterations of Microsoft operating systems, from Windows 98 to Windows Vista. Even cellular phones had shifted beyond Jim's comprehension. When he was arrested, Nokia's top-of-the-line cells still had antennas. Now they were smaller, lighter, carried longer charges, and came with color displays.

Jim was ending his fourth year of confinement on September 11, 2001, when terrorists struck the United States. He wrote two letters to the CIA that offered his help in finding the terrorists who planned the jetliner strikes on U.S. soil. Those letters have never been publicly disclosed. But it's a good bet Jim reminded his former employer that his branch in the CTC had labored to draw beads on the likes of the Islamic fundamentalists now accused of mass murder. The CIA apparently never responded.

The attacks of 9/11 deeply wounded Nathan. He recalled standing at a bus stop near his mom's home north of Corvallis, on a clear morning, when a classmate asked if he had heard the news about an attack on the Twin Towers. Nathan misunderstood her. The only Twin Towers that came to mind were the Petronas Towers in Kuala Lumpur. The spires were still under construction when he left Malaysia, and now stood as the tallest buildings in the world. When he reached Crescent Valley High, every TV in the place was lit up with live TV coverage of the horrors three time zones away. Nathan sat and watched, boiling mad.

Since turning seventeen that summer, he had quietly made plans to join the Army. He had no money for college, no girlfriend to tie him down, and he was desperate to prove himself as a combat soldier. Now there was a righteous cause. His country was under attack, and it was soon clear the U.S. was headed to war in the Middle East. Nathan figured young men would swarm military recruiting offices, and he wanted to be one of them. He knew his enlistment would freak out his family. So, for the time being, he kept his plans a secret. Even from his dad.

Several months later, on February 2, 2002, the paralegal from San Francisco paid another visit to Steve Meyers at Sheridan. While waiting for him in the visiting room, she found herself talking to a slender six-foot-three prisoner with a New Jersey accent so strong he sounded like a character out of central casting, "Wise Guy No. 3." Phil Quackenbush was a bank robber and recovering crackhead who celled with Jim. He told the paralegal that his cellie was a convicted spy, and gave his name.

The paralegal put it together that Jim was the very guy Meyers had mentioned, the one trying to sneak messages to the Russians. When she got home to the Bay Area, she did a little research on Jim and phoned the FBI. Agents took a statement from her about the visits to Sheridan and her concerns that Jim was trying to pass messages to Russia. The FBI's San Francisco's Field Office had a sizable counterintelligence squad. Agents had much to protect from Russian spying in the tech-rich Silicon Valley, where defense contractors were plentiful. The squad kept a close watch on the Russian Consulate, a den of SVR spies.

The FBI has never disclosed what its agents did, if anything, to look further into the allegations against Jim. But in time, it would become clear they hadn't lost interest.

Summer 2003

On July 29, 2003, an FBI agent from San Francisco dropped in on Steve Meyers, who was living easy in a low-security prison in Big Spring, Texas. The Bureau of Prisons had moved Meyers out to the West Texas lockup a few months earlier, possibly at the behest of the FBI. Agents knew Jim had come up with a muddy polygraph during his 1997 debriefings, perhaps withholding information he gave the SVR. Now they worried he might have reestablished contact with Moscow. The FBI man wanted Meyers to tell him about Jim's scheme to contact the Russians.

Meyers told the agent what he knew. He had shared a cell with Jim before his transfer to Texas and was aware of Jim's work in the CIA and his espionage conviction. He said Jim had confided in him that he still held agency secrets in his head, secrets that were slowly going stale and would one day lose any value to Russia. Meyers also told the agent that after his release Jim planned to move to Russia, where Moscow was still holding his "pension."

The FBI sometimes rewards prisoners by recommending reductions in the sentences of those who cooperate with them. Meyers, perhaps sensing he could get time whittled off his punishment, continued his betrayals of Jim. He told the agent that one of Jim's plans was to sneak a letter to the Russian Embassy in Rome. Jim's impression, Meyers told the FBI, was that the U.S. did a poor job covering Russia's spy operations in Italy, making it easier for an American to pass a letter from Jim to the SVR there. Meyers explained to the agent that Jim had tried to rope his brother Randall into carrying a document out of the prison during a 2002 visit. But Randall had rejected it out of hand.

Meyers then dropped Quackenbush in the grease. He told the FBI agent that when Quackenbush was freed from Sheridan, he carried out a manila envelope full of Jim's papers.

Seven weeks later, on September 16, Quackenbush took a call from his probation officer in Las Vegas, Nevada.

"Listen," he heard his PO say, "I need to meet you at your house tomorrow night. Two gentlemen need to speak to you."

This wasn't good news.

By appearances, things had been looking up for Quackenbush. He was working full-time as a roofing foreman, going to school four nights a week at the Community College of Southern Nevada. He had a nice place in the Desert Park Apartments just ten minutes from the Vegas Strip. But he was smoking crack again. The last person he wanted to see was his PO. If he found out Quackenbush was on the pipe, he'd violate him and send him back to prison.

"Whattaya mean two gentlemen wanna talk to me?"

The PO told him two FBI agents needed information about a former cellmate. Quackenbush wasn't in a position to say no.

The next day, he entertained the agents at his apartment as the sun slowly dropped over the rocky red shoulders of Charleston Peak. Quackenbush was probably what the agents expected. He was thirty-nine, grew up in the Jersey suburbs west of Manhattan, and worked most of his life as a union plasterer before moving to Vegas, where at age thirty-five he met and fell in love with crack cocaine. He worked a second job as a serial bank robber to keep the rocks coming. But the law caught up to him, and he was sent to Sheridan on a fifty-one-month stretch in the spring of 2000.

He told the FBI agents he first met Jim in the prison chapel. They had both been raised as Christians and made friends with the chapel's music director, Shadley Wiegman, and her husband, Glenn, a prison volunteer. The deeply religious couple served as parental figures for many of the inmates, who often called Mrs. Wiegman "Mama Shadley." The Wiegmans worked in the prison ministry because it made them feel good to lift the spirits of prisoners clinging to life's bottom rungs, but also because the testimonies of these caged men lifted them, too. They were especially fond of Jim, a natural leader who served as a kind of chapel toastmaster, introducing preachers and speakers. He also wrote Christmas passion plays, organized evening Bible studies, and prayed with his brothers behind bars before bunking in each night.

Quackenbush looked up to Jim, who was thirteen years older. The former CIA man seemed unflappable, always under control. Quackenbush saw Jim as bright, personable, even lovable. But there was a vanity about him. Jim hated that he was growing gray, losing hair, showing his age. When later they agreed to share a "house"—prison slang for a cell—Jim took the top bunk. Quackenbush, sitting on the bottom rack on Saturday mornings, teased Jim mercilessly about using an old toothbrush to comb shoe polish into his beard to look younger for his kids. His cellie also was exceedingly fastidious about his prison khakis. While some prisoners wore them dirty or wrinkled, Jim kept his uniform tidy, the buckle of his fabric web belt dead center, and carried himself with a military bearing. It was almost as if Jim were proud of the number over his left shirt pocket.

Jim fancied himself a writer. Not long after reaching Sheridan, he had penned a 176-page novella titled *Welcome to Paradisio* under the pen name H. J. Nicholson. It's the story of a young San Francisco business-man who goes to work on a Caribbean island, where he is recruited by CIA operatives to cover for their work against drug cartels, terrorists, and revolutionaries. It was an imaginative narrative, with a romance built in. But he couldn't find a publisher.

Quackenbush recalled that during the time they celled together, Jim had taken piles of notes on pads and tapped them into a typewriter on loan from the unit secretary. Jim had referred to the manuscript as his memoir. As Jim clacked away at the new document, carefully stacking its pages, he tore his paper notes to confetti. As typewriter cartridges went out, Jim lifted them from the machine and yanked out the ribbons until they looked like a fly fisherman's nightmare. He tore them into tiny plastic pieces and flushed them down the toilet, Quackenbush told the FBI. Once, he said, the paper and plastic clogged the bowl, forcing him to reach into the soggy muck, haul it out, and feed it back through the porcelain mouth flush by flush until it disappeared.

Jim knew that Quackenbush would soon "kill his number"— prison slang for getting out—and he asked his cellmate to smuggle the document out with his gear. Quackenbush admitted to the FBI that he carried the papers—a sheaf two inches thick and stuffed into a manila envelope—when he flew home to Las Vegas. He told the agents he honored a promise he made to Jim that he not read it. Six weeks after reaching Vegas, Quackenbush said, he mailed the package to Nick and Betty Nicholson, just as Jim had asked him.

FBI agents returned to Quackenbush's apartment on a Friday morning in mid-October. They took him for breakfast and said they wanted to put him through a polygraph. Quackenbush had never taken one, and the thought of answering the FBI's questions while wired up to the machine put him about a screwdriver's turn from coming unglued.

"They pull up to a hotel casino," he recalled. "I was like, 'Oh my God, this is crazy.' Straight-up feds shit, right?" The agents led him into a suite, where he found a man with a polygraph box. The operator tried to put him at ease, explaining how the machine worked and that they were just going to ask him a few questions. It didn't take long to get to the moment-of-truth queries. Did Jim ask him to take classified information out of the prison? Did Jim ask him to mail a package to a foreign government? Quackenbush answered no to both questions, and he passed the polygraph.

Agents believed Quackenbush had indeed mailed Jim's envelope to Nick and Betty, just as he said. But they didn't want to confront Jim's parents about this until they had more to go on. Questioning the retirees about their son's mail would only tip Jim that he was under investigation. The FBI would wait until it had more evidence.

The bureau's case appears to have stalled about that time. But agents kept tabs on Quackenbush, knowing they might need him as a material witness if they gathered enough evidence to arrest Jim for further espionage. On February 17, 2004, their boy approached a teller in a Bank of America in Vegas and said, "Let me get some hundreds." The teller, failing to catch on, asked if he meant large bills. So Quackenbush, with crisp diction, helpfully cleared things up. "This is a bank robbery," he said. "Let me have all your hundreds." For this transgression, swiftly remedied by police, Quackenbush was sent to a penitentiary in eastern California to begin a fifty-seven-month sentence.

At least the FBI would know where to find him.

10

A Fall into Blackness

"And out of darkness came the hands
That reach thro' nature, moulding men."
—Alfred, Lord Tennyson, *In Memoriam*

Fort Bragg, North Carolina, early 2004

On the evening of June 14, 2004, Nathan and his fellow soldiers piled into the cargo hold of a sixty-five-ton C-130 airplane. The air smelled of rain. They took seats on benches along the walls of the flying boxcar, backs pressed into red nylon webs, diesel exhaust wafting past their noses as the hydraulic cargo door lifted noisily. The stocky four-prop plane rumbled down the runway, soldiers' guts shifting as she lifted into the North Carolina sky toward a waning moon. The C-130 Hercules is the U.S. Army's primary airlifter, a beloved aircraft. God and everybody flies it. The ninety-eight-foot plane was put into wide use after the Korean War to transport troops and gear into battle zones with short runways. The Herc can land on anything—sand, mud, snow, doesn't matter—and stop on a dime. That night, the C-130 carrying Nathan and his fellow soldiers in woodland-camouflage battle dress uniforms was headed for the "Normandy" drop zone at Fort Bragg.

Jim had written Nathan earlier in the year to say how proud he felt about this training. "The anxiety I experience over what you are doing is,

I suspect, my punishment for having infected you with the insanity gene," he wrote. "But, I am bursting with pride and gratitude when I know you are safe and have endured some new adventure. I know you can't avoid getting hard—it's necessary to do what you do. I just hope you will never grow so hard you won't enjoy a good McManus story with me."

In another letter, Jim recalled how infantry soldiers often talked about how fun it might be to jump out of perfectly good aircraft, but never took the plunge: "What they don't understand is what it's like to leap out into thin air from the back of a screaming aircraft into a place you can only pray is not going to hurt too much—provided, of course, that your chute opens, you don't get tangled up with someone else and the wind doesn't slam you down so hard you can taste the leather of your jump boots."

Jim had given Nathan a Bible on his eighteenth birthday, the final day of July 2002, perhaps knowing it marked a crossroads. Nathan had moved into an apartment with his siblings after Laurie remarried, nudging him out of the nest. He was passionate about joining the Army, but Jim hoped he would first go to Oregon State, as Star and Jeremi had. Jim counseled his youngest not to enlist, but to enroll at OSU and—just as he had done—take officer training in the ROTC.

For the first time in his adulthood, Nathan bucked his dad. He did take out a student loan and trooped off to Oregon State, and he even took an ROTC class. But he never joined the Officers' Training Corps, firmly believing he'd be a better leader by learning first what it was like to be led. His plan was to finish a semester of college and, unless he was completely blown away by the experience, enlist in the Army without telling a soul. When the fall term ended just before Christmas, he walked into an Army recruitment office fifteen minutes from campus and signed up for the delayed-entry program. He would soon drive to Portland to swear his enlistment oath. Nathan waited until after the holidays to tell his family.

Jim was wounded that his boy hadn't taken the ROTC track. Jeremi scolded his little brother, telling him he was an idiot because the U.S.

government would never let him rise through the ranks after their dad's crime. Nathan's mom and sister were stricken by Nathan's enlistment. Not a week went by that soldiers weren't brought home in body bags from the Middle East. Laurie and Star, he recalled, began to treat him as if he had already died in combat.

Nathan had hoped they would applaud his bold move to serve his country, as an enlisted man or otherwise. But they didn't. So he left his orange cat Megacin with Star and Jeremi and flew off to begin his Army career.

In 2003, Nathan graduated from basic infantry training and airborne qualification at Fort Benning, Georgia, the same muggy hellhole where Jim had begun his Army career as a newlywed. When Nathan earned his light blue infantry cord, Jim's best friend and boyhood pal, Len Beystrum, flew to Fort Bragg to cheer his accomplishment. Beystrum, who had parachuted from perfectly good aircraft a couple of times himself, bought Nathan a celebratory dinner at the LongHorn Steakhouse.

Nathan's legs had taken such a pounding during jump training that he suffered terrible shin splints and missed his chance to take part in Ranger initiation, a requirement to join the elite force. The Army sent Nathan to Fort Bragg that fall to try out for a Long Range Surveillance assignment, which would set him up to apply for Ranger school. He was one of five soldiers selected for the tryout. They were put through punishing combat survival tests, forced to jump off diving boards blindfolded and tread water with rifles over their heads. They were pushed to run mile after mile, and perform land navigation tests through swamps.

In the early winter of 2004, Nathan was sent into a frozen forest near Bragg as part of a Special Forces exercise. He took part in a mock ambush of an enemy force and was assigned to man a border surveillance post for several hours. Nathan, already exhausted from the operation, found himself alone in a shallow foxhole in the snow, where he tried to stay alert. His instructors had been known to sneak up and chuck Whistling Petes, noisy fireworks intended to simulate incoming mortar rounds. But many hours passed and Nathan's replacement hadn't shown.

He'd had enough MREs to stay fed for a day, but the food was now gone, and he was hungry and shivering. More than twenty-four hours passed before those running the operation realized they had mistakenly failed to replace young Nicholson. When they found him, his eyes were dry and bloodshot, his throat parched from lack of water. They seemed surprised Nathan had done as they ordered: He never left his post.

Nathan and another soldier passed the tryout. He earned the rank of private first class and was put on a list of soldiers scheduled for deployment to Iraq at the end of the year. Nathan looked forward to his second shot at making the Rangers. He was desperate to match his dad's accomplishments in the fraternity whose code of ethics dictates, "I will never leave a fallen comrade to fall into the hands of the enemy and under no circumstances will I ever embarrass my country."

The jump over Bragg's Normandy drop zone was Nathan's thirteenth. He had parachuted from C-130s five times at Fort Benning to earn his airborne qualification. Since then, assigned to Fox Company of the 51st Infantry Division, part of the 519th Military Intelligence Battalion, Nathan had jumped out of Hercs, twin-rotor Chinook helicopters, and a C-17 jet transport. On that night, he pushed the pain of his shin splints away, donning full combat gear—including Kevlar helmet, M-4 assault rifle, and parachute—to take part in a mass tactical jump off a static line. A jump intended to prepare him for combat.

The plane was cruising at seventeen hundred feet when one of the Herc's side doors opened just behind the bulkhead. Nathan and his fellow soldiers stood and took their positions. They had a saying in Army Infantry, which decorated the uniforms of its soldiers with a blue braided cord: "Why is the sky blue? Because God *loves* the infantry." Nathan did love the infantry, but there was not a shred of blue in this sky.

Nathan felt the rush of air as he reached the door on the right side of the plane and took that final stride into the ink of night, kicking his knees up, heavy rucksack riding on his lap. He waited for that instant when the chute popped and billowed, taking that big gulp of air. But his chute didn't fully open. He felt himself hurtling toward the ground, chute tangled above him into what parachutists call a "cigarette roll." The nylon dome filled with just enough air to slow him down but not enough to give him the lift he needed for a safe landing. Nathan cursed as he pedaled frantically to untangle the mess above him. He managed to give himself a little more lift, but the dark came too fast. He scanned the horizon to see if he had enough altitude to pull his reserve chute.

Now he saw treetops—too low—and gritted his teeth.

The ground came hard and fast, and Nathan released the fifteen-foot lowering line that tethered his rucksack to his left hip. The line is like the string on a heavy teabag: It keeps the pack from landing on a soldier and crushing his legs on impact. Nathan's pack weighed well over one hundred pounds, including radio gear, an AT4 antitank weapon, a Claymore land mine, two grenades, a stack of fully loaded rifle magazines, and a brick of simulated C-4 explosive, along with food and personal gear to last for two weeks. In the mad scramble to fix his chute, he had mistimed his landing, dropping the pack too soon, a mistake that sent him oscillating as he plummeted to the ground. He landed with his legs straight out, his butt and shoulder striking the earth, his useless parachute now pulling him like a plow as he skipped across the rocky field cursing . . . *fuck* . . . *fuck* . . . *fuck* . . . until suddenly, mercifully, it was over. He would learn later that soldiers back at the base had packed his chute improperly.

Nathan lay on the ground moaning and cursing, muscle memory sending his hands diving for his rifle to lock and load. He pulled a red ChemLight stick out of a pocket and popped it in the darkness. The rest was a blur: soldiers huddled over him, a stretcher, a neck brace and IV line, a ride in a Humvee, a doctor telling him he had fractured a bone in the curve of his spine just above the tailbone. Nathan would need assistance to walk. There was no way to splint or put a cast on the break. So the docs gave him crutches, a little rubber donut to sit on, and a bottle of pain pills.

His back, slow to heal, was murder. He hobbled down forty stairs from his barracks to make the daily formation, but his superiors sent him back every time. Nathan was scheduled to go to Ranger school for his

second and final tryout, but his injuries prevented him from participat-
ing. His dreams of becoming a Ranger were over, forever, a failure more
painful than his wounded back. Now he worried his medical problems
would sabotage his deployment to Iraq as his outfit readied for war.
Depressed, he flew home to Oregon on leave to decompress.

He stayed with Laurie, who was living in Salem with her husband.
Bill Billera was a former Oregon State Police trooper, a large, imposing
man who ran a tight ship on the home front and guarded his wife's
meager savings from her three broke kids. During a previous leave,
Billera had asked Nathan when he planned to pay back the $1,400 his
mother had loaned him for his car, a baby blue 1992 Eagle Summit.
Nathan explained to his stepfather that his mother bought him the car
as a high school graduation present. But Billera saw things differently,
sparking an angry quarrel over the money. Worsening matters, Laurie
took her husband's side in the dispute.

It was a tense time for Nathan, preoccupied with thoughts of either
dodging bullets in Iraq or washing out of the Army with a bad back. He
suffered in the riddle of his future, wondering how he would bear up
under fire and how he might handle himself if he never got the chance
to test himself in combat. He also feared death. Any combat veteran
could have told him his fears were natural, even a good thing; no rational
human enters a war zone without fear. But Nathan's greatest fear was
failing to take part, to prove himself.

Laurie secretly felt relieved. She had long worried Nathan would
go off to war and come back in a body bag. More than forty men with
ties to Oregon had already been killed in Iraq and Afghanistan. But her
boy, always the family daredevil, was smitten with the notion of military
glory. She understood how passionately men could behave in the service
of their country; she had watched Jim prepare for war in a peacetime
Army, then vanish into the violence of conflict on Cambodia's border
with Thailand in the 1980s.

At the end of his leave, Laurie drove Nathan to the airport for the
trip to Bragg and they got into an argument about the tension at the

house. In the heat of the moment, Nathan heard her say, "Maybe it would be better if you didn't come back." He took this to mean that maybe he should just go ahead and die and get it over with. Laurie hadn't meant it that way. She just didn't want Nathan to come back and fight with Bill.

Laurie's words destroyed her son. He flew to Bragg, diving deeper into depression with each passing time zone. By the time he returned to the base, with none of his close friends to confide in, he thought about punching his own ticket. Nathan's mind played tricks on him; maybe he really was better off dead. He was alone that weekend in his barracks bedroom. He sat on his rack for a long time, contemplating an end to his torment. He found the answer in a folding knife, pulling out the blade and surveying his wrists. He visualized a series of cuts up and across his veins. He would slice deeply, sit back on his bed, and let the warm blood drain him cold.

His phone rang with a jolt.

When he answered, he was greeted with a woman's recorded voice: "This call is from a federal inmate. . . ."

"Hey, son."

"Hey, Pa."

There were times when the only person in the world capable of pulling Nathan's ruined spirits out of his boots was his dad. Jim knew his son was depressed. But the timing of his call was pure prescience.

"I just called to tell you how much I love you," Jim said.

Nathan's throat tightened, tears running down his cheeks.

"I love you, too, Pa."

Nathan was too ashamed to tell Jim what he was about to do. But when he hung up, he was armed with new resolve. He put the knife away.

Oregon, late 2004

Nathan settled into an apartment in Springfield, just across Interstate 5 from Eugene, and took a job as a Pizza Hut deliveryman. Nathan missed the camaraderie of his friends back at Bragg, who were readying for Iraq, and considered them battle buddies. But for him, there would be no battles. He had flown home that fall with an honorable discharge and a duffel bag of despair.

Depression shadowed him like a bill collector. The night of his near suicide attempt at Bragg, with his father's voice still fresh in his ear, Nathan phoned his sergeant for help. The call set in motion a chain of events that began with the intervention of a mental health counselor, his acknowledgment of suicidal thoughts, and the end of his military career. His counselor, a man with thick glasses and a bow tie, prescribed Zoloft, little oval pills that were supposed to cushion emotional bumps. But Nathan never filled the prescription.

He had always powered through the obstacles thrown his way by counting his blessings. He carried the golden rule into life's trickier corners, treating others better than he expected them to treat him. Some of those he invited into his world saw these qualities as exploitable weaknesses.

Dustin Rogers, Nathan's cousin and confidant, was wary of his cousin's new love interest. Nathan had met the lady in his life in an online chat room during his Army days. After his discharge, he had driven way out to the scrublands of eastern Oregon to meet her family and bring her home to live with him in his second-floor walk-up in Springfield. Dustin thought his cousin's girlfriend was clingy and weird. She was several years older than Nathan and had an annoying habit of launching into loud, raunchy stories about their sex life, which left Nathan with crimson cheeks, sputtering to change the subject. From time to time, Dustin later explained, he could see a whole lot of crazy camped out in her eyes.

Nathan recalled that his girl had confessed early to him that she had overcome a drug problem. Her teeth were in terrible shape, and when a dentist discovered a pocket of toxins in her mouth that threatened to flow into her bloodstream and potentially kill her, Nathan maxed out his Citi card to pay for emergency dental care. His monthly income—a combination of his Veterans Affairs disability compensation and his tips and earnings from Pizza Hut—came to about $1,600. Now, in addition to rent and car payments, he faced the additional costs of paying for her dental work.

In early 2005, he enrolled at nearby Lane Community College to study drafting and architecture. Uncle Sam would later pick up the cost of his books and tuition. But as Nathan poured himself into his studies, his girlfriend remained jobless and relapsed into drugs. He offered to help her if she was committed to staying straight. When she was non-committal, he drove her back to her family for good.

Nathan focused on his studies that fall. He was a lonely single man still grieving over lost opportunities in the Army and wondering how much different his life might have been had a parachute opened correctly over Fort Bragg. When Veterans Day rolled around that November, he broke out his dress uniform and set the self timer on his camera. Nathan stood at attention and threw a crisp salute, his beret pulled down snugly, infantry cord hanging just right, lips pinched tight. He still believed that God loved the infantry. And, by God, he still loved the infantry and the Army buddies who had flown off for Iraq. But he was a broken man.

He felt blessed to have his dad to lean on. Every other Saturday, Nathan drove up to Sheridan to see him.

In prison, they call it killing birds. You serve a long stretch one day at a time, killing your sentence by working hard and earning extra time off by keeping your head above the fray of gangs and potential hostilities. Friends inside, real ones anyway, help you cope. They're the ones wishing each other a good day. Because a bad day in the joint is a very bad day indeed. A great cellmate can make the time go faster. An ideal cellie is a good conversationalist who knows when to shut up, tidies up after himself, doesn't hang out in the cell all day, and gives you enough privacy to think or beat off.

Many prisoners find faith behind bars, but Jim walked into prison with his. Confronted by a minimum two decades inside, Jim immersed himself in Christianity. Rob Tillitz, once a high-seas drug smuggler, served time with Jim in Unit 4B and recalled that his friend had a bit of a Jesus aura about him—he wore a beard and long hair, and he seemed to be the only inmate in the place wearing moccasins. Tillitz thought Jim seemed utterly placid and in control of himself, which he attributed to Jim's religious beliefs.

Jim struck out in his attempts to persuade Star and Jeremi to attend church. Star's faith evaporated the day of his arrest, and Jeremi had followed Laurie into a new-age religion that teaches its followers they are particles of God sent to Earth for spiritual experience. Adherents of Eckankar, a faith dating all the way back to 1965, study the "Light and Sound of God," believe in the concept of Soul Travel, and seek guidance from a spiritual leader known as the Living Eck Master. Jim was proud to hear that Nathan had become a regular at The Door, a nondenominational Christian congregation in Eugene. He thought it was a good place to get right with God, and maybe meet a nice woman.

Nathan and Jim connected in Christianity, reaching deep into the pockets of their faith. They sometimes prayed so hard in the visiting room that Nathan could practically feel God reaching through the wood-slat roof to hold them in his hand. He loved the steady, instructive timbre of his dad's voice in those moments. The old man was very close to God, Nathan told me, and it was easy to see how his dad's deep prayers sometimes transported him out of his felony tank.

Jim soothed his son's angst about not making it into the Rangers, and believed God had a different plan for Nathan. Jim told him that faith would carry him through life's roughest passages and into missions far greater than those undertaken by men and their militaries.

One Saturday in the spring of 2006, Nathan drove to Sheridan earlier than usual. He moved through the checkpoints and metal detectors as part of the weekend herd, reaching the visiting room well ahead of Star. He and the old man greeted each other with their customary bear hug.

Jim's kids were going through rough patches in their finances. Jeremi, who had enlisted in the Air Force in 2003 because he hated working at McDonald's, was $25,000 in debt. Star's student loans totaled $50,000, and her car was in and out of the shop. Nathan scarcely made a dent in his two maxed-out credit cards, including the one he'd used to fix his ex-girlfriend's teeth; also, he had bought himself a 2005 Chevy Cavalier and still owed $8,000 on the note. Jim's UNICOR earnings, even in a month choked with overtime, topped at about $400, scarcely enough to help his kids out financially.

"I have an idea," he shared in a whisper, "to help you kids."

Nathan perked up.

"Would you be willing to help?"

"Of course."

Jim asked his boy to do a little research on the Internet when he got back to his apartment. He wanted to find out the location of the nearest Russian consulate. Jim explained that his old friends in Moscow were holding an account open in his name, and that together they might be able to make some early withdrawals. Jim had lost his freedom in service to the Russian Federation, and now he felt it was Russia's turn to help support his kids while he was away. He wanted to know if Nathan was willing to serve in his stead on the outside.

The old man was preaching to the converted. Nathan agreed on the spot to offer his assistance. He drove home feeling glorious. The dry season had come to the valley, sunshine bleaching the daytime sky into an Andrew Wyeth painting, with heart-stopping sunsets that streaked the sky pink and purple. They were magical days that could make a broken man feel positively invincible.

Two Saturdays later, Nathan pulled into Sheridan earlier than usual and parked in his customary spot near a helipad just outside the main gate. He was happy to see that Star's decrepit hatchback wasn't in the lot. He moved among the crowd through metal detectors and other indignities before a corrections officer stamped his hand with invisible ink.

He followed uniformed staffers through the bowels of the institution, a journey punctuated by the crackling of radio traffic and the slamming of metal doors. Eventually he took his seat in the visiting room.

When Jim appeared, Nathan quickly filled him in on what he had learned: There was a Russian diplomatic station in Seattle, less than a five-hour drive north of his apartment, and a consulate in San Francisco, nearly nine hours to the south. Over their next few visits, Jim outlined his plan. He wanted Nathan to drive to San Francisco and walk into the Russian Consulate and ask for the director of security. Jim told his son he would prepare some notes that would introduce the two of them.

When Jim volunteered as a mole for the SVR in 1994, he was fully informed of possible consequences. Now he planned to send Nathan into the breach with the weakest possible grasp of the perils ahead. Perhaps Jim thought his son's naïveté would protect everyone's interests, including his own. What he surely knew—and failed to tell Nathan—was that the SVR had a huge presence in the big brick building in San Francisco, a den of spies likely to recognize the Nicholson name. He knew that once Nathan volunteered to serve as his agent, they would likely be happy to help his family. The Russians were sure to have questions for their long-lost asset, questions that Nathan could courier back to him in prison.

Nathan radiated in the glow of his dad's confidence in him. He asked few questions, intoxicated at the very idea of dipping an exploratory toe into his father's clandestine world. The old man's career had been peppered with such élan, and Nathan was excited to play a supporting role. He was thrilled to help Jim make contact with the Russians, delighted to help his family, and unaware of any consequences.

"It's risky," Jim said. But he assured his boy there was nothing illegal about an American walking into a Russian diplomatic station. Indeed there wasn't. But Jim didn't tell Nathan that it's a well-established fact in U.S. intelligence circles that FBI agents watched the consulate, and that the bureau gathered intelligence on suspicious visitors. If the bureau's counterintelligence agents spotted Nathan at the consulate, and identified him as Jim's son, it would have triggered a brisk and thorough inquiry.

Nathan was eager to take a road trip to San Francisco. He had passed through the town just once, on a trip to Disneyland with his dad. The notion that the Russians might give him money for his dad's previously rendered services was merely a bonus. "I didn't think I was starting up any trouble," Nathan would recall years later. It seemed only right to him that the Russian Federation, now a democratic nation with improving diplomatic ties to the U.S., would quietly lend a hand. He figured the Russians owed the Nicholsons, because it was his dad's service to the SVR that had torn his family apart.

One Saturday several weeks later, Jim told Nathan to wear a shirt with a breast pocket the next time he visited. His boy did as instructed. When Jim walked into the visiting room, they hugged and sat for a few moments, talking casually as surveillance cameras snooped the seating area. With spy-like sleight of hand, Jim plucked a note out of his khakis.

"Don't look down," he said.

Jim put his arm around Nathan's shoulders and pulled him close, palming a folded square of composition paper sealed with plastic tape. Then, making sure no guards were looking, Jim slid the note into his son's breast pocket.

"Don't open it," he said. He explained that if anyone ever questioned him about the note, he could say with all honesty that he hadn't read it.

Visitors weren't supposed to accept anything from prisoners. The institution's regulations forbade couples from exchanging so much as an overly long kiss. But Jim, who had learned the art of the brush-pass at the agency, had perfected it early in his incarceration. In the past, he had occasionally slipped folded Christmas wish lists into Nathan's pockets. Prison staffers never caught them.

Jim told Nathan he was mailing him a letter that included a photo of the two of them and that he was to carry that note to the Russian Consulate. The postmarked letter and father-son photo taken inside the prison would serve as evidence they were related.

As summer gave way to fall, Jim waited for one of their Saturday visits to slip an unsealed note under the food wrappers and napkins piled up on the snack tray between them. Nathan casually palmed it into his pocket. Jim told him to hand the note to the receptionist in Russia's San Francisco consulate, and to be sure to wear his black business suit. He asked Nathan to carry the sealed note, along with the mailed letter and photo, to the head of security. The Russians would take it from there. Jim cautioned his boy to keep his eyes open to make sure no one tailed him into or out of the consulate.

In the intelligence world, spies like Jim worked foreign assets by befriending them, gaining their complete confidence, and learning their vulnerabilities. Then came the pitch—*Will you help me?*—and promises of a better life. Jim had worked many assets this way during foreign postings with the CIA, using these agents to help him collect all manner of intelligence on the Soviet Union and other nations.

Nathan came easy. Jim set a virtual banquet in front of his son's eyes, telling him of the financial relief he could potentially bring to his family. Nathan would do nearly anything to help. Jim told him that this was their secret to keep, and that he chose Nathan for the assignment over his sister and brother. Star was strung too tightly for such work, and Jeremi—now stationed in Florida with the Air Force—was far too practical to even consider such a plan. Jim explained to Nathan it was his choice whether to eventually loop in his brother and sister. For now, they would operate as a two-man team.

Jim spent a few minutes during each visit teaching Nathan basic surveillance detection, a spy skill that would help him see if he was being tailed. Jim coached him on how to assess potential threats to his security—taking mental notes of the people and autos he saw during his travels, focusing vigilantly on those he saw with any frequency. He cautioned Nathan to be wary if his computer suddenly slowed—a sign it might be under surveillance—and warned him to pay cash rather than using his credit card to sidestep paper trails. He also provided Nathan with a cover story for his visit to the Russian Consulate: He'd pose as a student studying Russia's architecture.

Words like "cover story" and "tails" should have scared the bejesus out of Nathan. They didn't. The old man was dangling a new life in front of him, one full of daring, intrigue, and money. Nathan was certain his dad would never put him in any real danger, and it never occurred to him to ask impertinent questions about the potential consequences of his contact with the Russians. Whatever the risks, he was willing to shoulder them. He had pushed all in. And so it was that in the middle of October 2006, a dozen years after Jim began spying for the Russians, he sent them his youngest son.

11

The Russian Consulate, San Francisco

"My father was pleased I actually had the guts to do it."
—Michael Walker, recruited by his dad,
John A. Walker Jr., to spy for the Soviet Union

Northern California, Fall 2006

The Russian Consulate in San Francisco rises in the middle of one of the city's thigh-burning hillsides, a monolith of multicolored bricks in desert shades from cream to adobe, a blend that renders the building tabby-cat orange. The diplomatic establishment rises between the Presidio and Pacific Heights in a neighborhood covered by multimillion-dollar swankiendas, with their postcard views of the great dome of the Palace of Fine Arts and the rust-colored arch of the Golden Gate Bridge.

Nathan parked his little blue Cavalier several blocks downhill of the consulate on a weekday morning in early October 2006. He climbed out looking road-weary but businesslike, having stopped at a rest area just before sunup to shave, slap some cold water on his face, and climb into his black suit. He hiked along Green Street, his back a little stiff from the eight-hour drive. Affixed to the front of the building was a brass plate emblazoned with Russia's ubiquitous double-headed eagle. It read:

CONSULATE GENERAL
OF THE RUSSIAN FEDERATION

A tricolor Russian flag rustled from a pole atop the building. Nathan walked through a wrought-iron gate and made his way down a sidewalk to the public entry, which looked more like a servants' entrance. His dress shoes treaded over steps covered with slip-proof sandpaper strips, and he found himself standing on a landing that overlooked the rooftops of mansions and a little patch of San Francisco Bay. Nathan pushed through a heavy wooden door into a room that looked like a marble tomb. It was appointed with the kind of institutional furniture you find in doctors' offices.

Nathan hooked to his right toward a pair of windows, where he heard a woman's voice behind thick glass asking if she could be of any assistance.

"I'm here to see the chief of security," he said.

As he spoke, he slid a folded note under the glass. The receptionist picked it up and read it. This one, signed by his father, greeted his Russian friends and introduced Nathan as his son. She asked Nathan to take a seat and quickly disappeared.

Nathan crossed the marble floor and sagged into one of the cushioned chairs that made up an L-shaped couch. On the wall was a generic black-and-white clock. He waited for what seemed like a very long time, perhaps forty-five minutes or an hour, before a middle-aged man with a dark mustache and flecks of gray in his short-cropped hair opened a door.

"I'm to understand that you want to speak with me," he said.

The Russian led Nathan down a hallway. They walked up a set of stairs to an office, then into an adjoining room with thick, padded walls—clearly soundproof—and took seats. The older man seemed to be sizing up this twenty-something visitor who had popped into the consulate in a discount suit and hair shaved to the quick.

Nathan reached into his jacket, producing his dad's taped note, along with the envelope Jim had mailed to him. It held the old man's letter and their father-son photo, which had been snapped by an inmate photographer in the prison visiting room. In the image, Jim and Nathan are standing together in front of a rendering of Oregon's iconic Mount Hood, the conical glacier that rises taller than any other peak in the state. Jim is wearing prison khakis, his arm around Nathan, who is dressed in the same suit he now wore in the consulate.

The Russian looked it over closely and rattled off questions.

"Where were you born?"

"Makati," he said. "The Philippines."

"Tell me about your brothers."

A trick question. Nathan explained he had one brother, and a sister. He gave their names.

The Russian wanted to know how he could trust he wasn't an FBI agent wearing a wire.

"Look," Nathan said, "you can search me right now."

The Russian asked him to hand over his watch, phone, and wallet, and Nathan obliged. His middle-aged interrogator slipped out of the office for a moment. When he returned a moment later without his belongings, it was clear to Nathan that he had handed them off to someone else to copy his information and probably search for bugs.

Jim had saved $300 from his UNICOR earnings and released the funds from his prison trust account to pay for the suit. Nathan had needed business attire after accepting a part-time job that August as an insurance salesman for Bankers Life and Casualty Company in Eugene. Jim knew his boy needed to dress up to look the part of an insurance man. But Nathan had proved himself comically inept as a salesman. In the space of two months, he had managed to earn about $500 in commissions, after having paid $300 for his license. Nathan had no stomach for the insurance business, and he felt sorry for the senior citizens he pitched to buy policies. In fact, he spent less time closing sales than he did sympathizing with his aging customers and talking them out of buying policies they didn't need. Within a few months, he would abandon the job.

The Russian glared skeptically at the photo, then at Nathan, and launched into an interrogation. He wanted details of his dad's 1996 arrest for espionage, and Nathan gave him the basic story as he knew it. The Russian seemed unimpressed with his answers. He handed Nathan a set of papers that appeared to be a Russian visa application, and walked him back to the public waiting room to fill it out.

Nathan jotted answers with a ballpoint pen, giving up his Social Security number, date of birth, his mother's maiden name, and the schools he attended. When he finished, he sat and waited. With each click of the plain-Jane wall clock, it seemed ever more obvious that he had entered the consulate under the misapprehension that the Russians were his dad's friends. The meeting was clearly a bust, and he was ready to drive home to Springfield. But somewhere in the guts of the building, the Russian still had his phone, wallet, and watch.

After about an hour, the Russian fetched him from the waiting room and they returned to the padded office.

"I want you to know," the Russian said, "we don't trust you. We have no idea who you are."

Nathan stared back, insulted.

"We want you to come back in two weeks," the Russian said. He handed paper and pen to Nathan and asked him to draw a diagram of Sheridan's visiting room. As Nathan sketched the room he knew by heart, the Russian asked what his plans were if someone caught him visiting the Russian Consulate.

Nathan said his cover story was that he was an architectural student who had come to the consulate to fill out a visa form so that one day he could visit Russia to study its architecture.

In an uncharacteristic burst of salesmanship, Nathan pitched the Russian.

"Look," he said. "I don't have much money for gas. Is there anything you can help me out with?"

The Russian shot Nathan a sympathetic look.

"I have nothing," he said bluntly. "I'm going to give you nothing."

The Russian hadn't shared his name. Only much later would Na-than learn he was Mikhail I. Gorbunov, who was nearing the end of a two-year hitch in San Francisco. It may never be known officially whether Gorbunov was an SVR officer serving under diplomatic cover. But whatever his position, the Russian was smart to be skeptical. U.S. and Russian intelligence agencies had a long history of posing undercover as voluntary spies for each other's services. Gorbunov was smart to be on guard for a false-flag provocation, responding carefully in a way that wouldn't embarrass the federation or get him sent home.

Nathan walked out of the consulate into a gusty afternoon. He climbed into his car and pushed north over the Golden Gate Bridge. He pulled over that evening into a roadside rest stop just south of the Oregon border. He turned off the engine, settled back in his bucket seat, and slept like a stone. When Nathan woke, he still felt like a failure. He dreaded the idea of telling his dad that he came up empty-handed, and on the long slog northward, he tried to figure out what he did wrong. Second-guessing himself was his custom; nobody could pummel Nathan harder than himself. He replayed his conversation with the Russian over and over in his head. He had walked in hat in hand, carrying proof of identity, photographic evidence that he really did know Jim Nicholson; he had even gone so far as to diagram the visiting room. But the Russian had turned him away as if he were a fraud.

He felt as if he had presented a tapped-out credit card to a depart-ment store only to watch a counter clerk cut it in half. Except this was his father's credit card. Nathan was embarrassed for his dad, and thought perhaps they were grasping at straws. He was certain that telling him about his shabby treatment by the Russian would only make his dad feel worse.

Eight days later, he drove up to Sheridan to break the news. Jim was clearly disappointed, but he took it better than Nathan expected. He said Nathan should probably accept the Russian's invitation to return to San Francisco the following Friday, October 27. But he told his son there was no shame in bagging the whole plan. This served only to push Nathan, ever the pleaser, back to the City by the Bay.

Jim phoned Nathan the following day, a Sunday, reaching him at home.

"You have a prepaid call," said the recorded message. It was the voice of a woman without an ounce of personality. "You will not be charged for this call. This call is from"—now came Jim's recorded voice, "*This is Dad, Pa, Daddy*"—"an inmate at a federal prison."

Nathan knew to push 5 to accept the call, which would cut off automatically after fifteen minutes.

"Hey, Pa."

"Hey, Nate, how you doin' today?"

Jim sounded like a Montana rancher, his diction crisp and country. He and Nathan spoke alike, sharing the habit of repeating phrases— "Doin' good, doin' good"—and they even laughed alike. But Jim sounded older, with a little rasp in his voice.

"Hey, I got a verse for you," he said. "God's kind of opened it to me a couple of times in the last couple of days, and so I claimed it for you and me. It's Isaiah 45:3."

"Isaiah 45:3?"

"Yep."

Nathan scrambled for his Bible and leafed to the 45th chapter of Isaiah, verse 3.

"I think you'll see the relevance there," Jim said. "It's really gonna be a good one."

Nathan found the verse and began to read aloud.

"And I will give you treasures hidden in the darkness—secret riches," Nathan read. "I will do this so that ye may know that I am the Lord, the God of Israel, the one who calls you by name."

These were the words of God to Cyrus the Great, as recalled by the Prophet Isaiah. They were words of hope to the oppressed, part of a prophecy that Cyrus, the pagan ruler of Persia, would one day free the Jews from their bondage and return them to Israel.

The verse served as Nathan's code from the prophet Jim that they would succeed with the Russians. They were wary of the CIA's eavesdropping. Agency analysts pored over every call to make sure, among other things, that Jim wasn't giving up classified information.

"Wow," Nathan said. "I like that."

"Yeah?" Jim said. "I claimed it for you and me."

They laughed.

"That's good news," Nathan said. "That's good news."

Four days later, Jim phoned again to ask how Nathan was doing.

"Could be better," he said dejectedly.

Nathan had traded in his Cavalier a few weeks back. The Chevy had a broken window and a big dent in the driver's-side door, and its brakes and tires were tuckered out. He offered the Cavalier in trade, plus $1,000 payable in monthly installments, and drove out of the dealership behind the wheel of a white 2005 Pontiac Grand Am with just 28,000 miles on the odometer. Now, Nathan told his dad, the dealership said they screwed up the paperwork and that he had to pay $1,000 immediately or return the Pontiac.

"Oh, man," Jim said. "Are you kiddin' me?"

"No."

"What?! How could they screw up like that?"

Nathan said he complained to the dealership, telling them they had signed a binding contract. But the dealership was adamant that he pay the thousand or return the Pontiac.

"So what, what's going on now?" Jim asked.

"Well, I got my old car back."

"You got your old car back?"

"Yeah."

"Oh no. With the bad tires?"

"Yeah," Nathan said. "The Lord gives, the Lord takes away, you know? But I'm sure it will work out for the better."

"Yeah?"

Nathan told Jim he hoped there would be a windfall in his future to take away the sting.

"Yeah," Jim said. "I understand exactly what you're saying. I'm just concerned about you. Are you gonna be able to get around in this car OK?"

"Oh yeah. It'll be fine. It'll last for what I need it for."

"Well, you just be careful in it anyway," Jim said. "OK, hon?"

"OK."

"We're praying for big things for you, OK?"

The following morning, Nathan steered the Cavalier onto I-5 and pointed it south. He had invited his cousin, Danielle Rogers, and her boyfriend, Jesse Mickelson, so they could have some fun and take turns at the wheel on the long drive. Nathan told them he was meeting an Army buddy in San Francisco, and he promised to spring for a hotel room.

They crossed the Golden Gate Bridge early on the last Friday in October, a clear, calm morning. They ate breakfast and climbed back into the Chevy. Nathan stopped the car a few blocks from the Russian Consulate and hopped out. He had lied to them, saying he needed to catch his Army friend before his flight back to duty. Jesse climbed behind the wheel, and Nathan told Danielle he would phone when he was ready to be picked up.

"I'll be just a few hours," he said.

A few moments later, Nathan pushed through the big wooden door of the consulate and told the receptionist he needed to speak with the chief of security. The Russian with the mustache appeared in a flash. Now he was a changed man, smiling and guiding his young charge into the bowels of the building. Back in the padded office, he bear-hugged Nathan and apologized for his previous skepticism. It was clear to Nathan that the Russians had vetted his story and now realized they had Jim Nicholson's flesh and blood in their midst. The Russian asked Nathan how his family was doing.

"Doing just fine," he said.

Nathan explained that he was in college, Jeremi had joined the Air Force, and Star was looking to put her degree in zoology to use. As for his dad, he said, he was still in prison and anxious to get out.

"Call me Mike," the Russian said.

Gorbunov was careful not to give himself away completely. In fact, he took active measures to avoid identification. He slid a photograph under Nathan's nose, the face of a man he'd never seen before. Gorbunov told Nathan that if the FBI should ever question him about their conversations, he should describe *this* man, not him. He gave Nathan a moment to memorize the face.

Gorbunov handed Nathan a small paper bag.

"This is five thousand dollars," he said, apologizing that it wasn't more. He asked his visitor to count it.

Nathan said he didn't need to count it. But the Russian was adamant.

"Please, please count."

Nathan counted fifty bills, each imprinted with the face of Benjamin Franklin. He had never held $5,000 in cash. The heft of so many Benjamins felt like a fortune.

Gorbunov told Nathan it was no longer safe to meet in the United States. He asked the young American to write down an address. Nathan plucked a business card from his wallet that read, "Nathan Nicholson, Insurance Agent," with the Bankers Life and Casualty Company logo and the words, "We specialize in seniors." Nathan flipped it over to the blank side and scribbled as the Russian dictated.

JOSE VASCONCELOS 204
COLONIA HIPODROMO CONDESA
DELEGACION CUAUHTEMOC, 06140
MEXICO, D.F.

Nathan had no clue that this, the address of Russia's embassy in Mexico City, was one of the most famous places in the history of espionage. For at least two decades, the embassy served as a haven for spies, with an estimated 150 of them working undercover as diplomats, journalists, clerks, chauffeurs and other positions at the height of the Cold War. Some of America's most famous spies sold U.S. secrets there,

Harold James "Jim" Nicholson, age twelve.

Laura Sue Cooper married Jim Nicholson in June 1973. They passed beneath an arch of swords held by Jim's ROTC comrades from Oregon State University.

Jim's official CIA photo.

Jim tried on Bedouin attire during a family trip to Egypt a few years before his divorce from Laurie.

Jim gave Nathan trigger time with several firearms in his boyhood, including this AKM assault rifle.

Betty and Nick Nicholson still live in Eugene, Oregon, in a small home filled with their arts and crafts.

Jim in Malaysia, 1992, with his children (*from left*) Jeremi, Nathan, and Star. The kids wore the tie-dyed T-shirts that their mom, separated from their father, bought them in the Pacific Northwest.

Neighbors who live near Jim's former town house in Burke, Virginia, know it as "The Spy's House." In 1996, the FBI took the home apart looking for evidence of Jim's espionage.

Jim sports his infamous "KGB is for me" T-shirt at a CIA function. The U.S. government circulated the image widely after Jim's arrest.

John Maguire (photographed in Iraq in the mid-1990s) is the only CIA officer to have spied on another inside the agency's Langley, Virginia, headquarters to help make a criminal conviction for espionage.

Jim pulled up to this post office in Dunn Loring, Virginia, on the night of October 9, 1996, to mail a note signaling an earlier-than-expected meeting with his SVR handler in Switzerland.

FBI agents Steve Hooper, left, and Dave Raymond arrest Jim on the tarmac at Dulles International Airport on November 16, 1996.

After Jim's conviction, John Maguire's colleagues gave him a cup with a handcuff handle that reads: "From Your Unindicted Colleagues In CTC/MSB 1996–1997. Thanks For Not Arresting Us."

Jim's second round of espionage began in the federal prison complex in Sheridan, Oregon.

Nathan and Jim posed for a photo inside the prison visiting room in 2003.

Nathan used the Bible that Jim bought him for his eighteenth birthday to hide some of the money that the SVR had paid him for Jim's messages.

COURTESY OF NATHAN NICHOLSON

Nathan visited his dad at the prison for this photo in 2005, the year before Jim recruited him to serve as his agent in meetings with the SVR.

On Veterans Day 2005, honorably discharged from the Army, Nathan put on his dress uniform and shot a crisp salute in honor of the soldiers who carried on without him.

COURTESY OF NATHAN NICHOLSON

BRYAN DENSON

The Russian Consulate in San Francisco rises from a hillside east of the Presidio.

Vasiliy V. Fedotov, a former KGB general, came out of retirement to meet with Nathan in Mexico, Peru, and Cyprus.

UNITED STATES
DEPARTMENT OF STATE
Tax Exemption Card

MISSION OF			
USSR			

DATE OF BIRTH	EYE COLOR		
01/12/36	GRAY		

HAIR COLOR	WEIGHT	HEIGHT	SEX
BROWN	145	506	M

NAME	
FEDOTOV, VASILIY VASILYEVICH	

SEE REVERSE FOR EXEMPTION INFORMATION

FEDERAL BUREAU OF INVESTIGATION

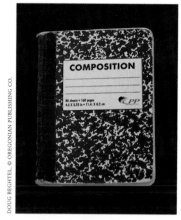

Nathan bought a dime-store composition notebook to take notes during some of his meetings with the spy he knew as "George."

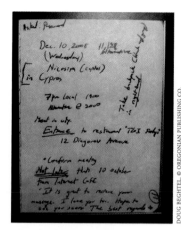

Inside the pages of Nathan's blue notebook, Nathan scribbled the time and address of his 2008 meeting in Nicosia, Cyprus.

The FBI printed copies of Nathan's coded notes to the Russians, which they found in a search of his Yahoo email account.

FBI agents found Nathan's packing list for his trip to Cyprus during a secret search of his apartment in Eugene, Oregon.

Nathan met his Russian handler outside the TGI Fridays in Nicosia, Cyprus, at Christmastime 2008.

Nathan upgraded to a nice third-floor walkup in the Heron Meadows Apartments after the Russians began to pay him tens of thousands of dollars. It was there, for the second time in his life, he would find FBI agents at his door.

Scott Jensen, one of the key FBI agents in the father-son spy investigation, kept eyes on Nathan and attempted to eavesdrop on his prison visits with Jim.

FBI agents played a hole card—this postcard from Cyprus—during a key moment in the FBI's investigation of Jim and Nathan.

Jared Garth, chief division counsel in the FBI's Portland Field Office, served as lead case agent in the bureau's investigation of Jim and Nathan Nicholson.

Assistant U.S. Attorney Ethan D. Knight worked with lead prosecutor Pamala Holsinger to bring the father-son spy team to justice.

Assistant U.S. Attorney Pamala Holsinger, who headed prosecution of the Nicholsons, came to see Jim as ruthless and manipulative.

Nathan's defense team spent untold hours trying to help him understand how destructive his relationship with Jim had become. They were (*standing from left*) investigator Karen Bates, lawyer Thomas E. Price, and investigator Janan Stoll; and (*seated*) investigator Wendy Kunkel and lawyer Jerry Needham.

During hundreds of hours of interviews, Nathan acknowledged his betrayals of his country, and his family. Eventually he came to see that he, too, had been betrayed.

including two men who had served time at Sheridan with Jim. Christopher Boyce, of *Falcon and the Snowman* fame, had passed messages to the KGB through the embassy, sending Andrew Daulton Lee, his boyhood best friend, as his courier. James Harper Jr. sold U.S. missile documents to Polish spies inside the embassy, and in other spots in Mexico, in the early 1980s.

Gorbunov asked Nathan to make sure he reached Mexico City early enough to walk into the embassy on the 13th of December for his next meeting. The Russian told him that before he flew south, his new contact needed answers to some questions. Gorbunov coached Nathan to code all of his questions and answers in a way that only his contact would understand them. His young American friend jotted notes on the blank sides of his business cards as Gorbunov posed questions about Jim's travels for the CIA and the circumstances of his arrest. Nathan's new contact would need answers when they met in Mexico City.

Nathan walked out of the consulate on air, astonished by his good fortune. His dad's plan had actually come together, and he felt ashamed for having doubted him. Nathan celebrated by taking Danielle and Jesse to dinner. They beached up in one of those trendy blond-wood restaurants in Little Italy, where the entrees are "spendy," as they say in Oregon, and the management crams tiny tables so close together that everybody in the joint could practically eat off the same plate. Nathan couldn't tell his cousin or her boyfriend why he was so happy.

On the road home the next day, Nathan's cell rang. It was Jim.

"Hey, Nate, I thought I'd call you and see what kind of hours you're keepin' these days."

Nathan, caught off guard, couldn't tell his dad he had invited Danielle and Jesse to San Francisco on a whim. That was not part of the operational plan.

"I'm on the road headin' back now," Nathan said.

"Oh, are you? Did everything go OK?"

"Yeah, everything went real well."

"Oh, excellent," Jim said. "Excellent."

Nathan chose his next words carefully, making the news of his score sound as if it came from a break in what so far had been a specious run in the insurance game.

"Got a sale," he told Jim. "For about, uh, five, uh, five K."

"OK, uh-huh," Jim said. "Excellent."

The old man's tone was flat. His voice betrayed no excitement.

Nathan said, "Even thinking about making a trip over to Mexico, come December."

"Is that right?"

"Yeah."

"Oh, so business is picking up, huh?"

"Yeah, sure is."

Jim said he was glad to hear that, and deftly switched subjects. He wanted to know how he and the Cavalier were holding up.

"Did you get any sleep at all?"

"Yeah," Nathan said, "I actually just pulled over not too long ago to take a quick half-hour nap."

Nathan neglected to mention that Jesse was now behind the wheel.

Jim asked Nathan if he would buy an MP3 player, load it with some tunes from Enya and other music, and ship it to Kanokwan for Christmas. Nathan said he'd do it, and they talked about eventually moving some money into Jim's prison trust account and perhaps giving some of Nathan's "insurance commission" to Nick and Betty for safekeeping.

"Well, I'm just so, so pleased that everything's going well for you," Jim said.

"Oh yeah," Nathan said, casually slipping in a reference to the source of the money back at the Russian Consulate: "They were just real, real nice."

"Wonderful," Jim said. "Wonderful."

They ended their call, and Nathan continued northward into Oregon.

Jim called back a few hours later, as Nathan's little Cavalier climbed steep, winding passes. He told Nathan he was concerned he might have gotten caught in one of Oregon's infamous inland fogs, which had left the valley socked in. But Nathan told him it was clear sailing. Then Jim got down to the real point of his call.

"How much money were you planning to give to Grandpa?"

Nathan said he expected to drop off $550.

Jim worried that might make his son a little tight, a wink to the cost of airfare and expenses on his forthcoming trip to Mexico City. But Nathan assured him he'd be fine, and told Jim to call after church the following day.

Nathan's trips to Sheridan took on new urgency. With a little more than a month before his rendezvous in Mexico City, he found himself dashing to the prison early on his Saturday morning visits. On one trip, he rolled up his sleeve to reveal questions penned on his left forearm. He read the questions to his dad, who memorized them in his seat.

Jim whispered to his son to go to the bathroom and scrub the notes off his arm.

Inside the restroom, washing ink from his arm, Nathan considered the questions the Russians were asking his dad. They looked innocuous to him, a little bit of Monday-morning quarterbacking to learn how his father had screwed up all those years ago. He didn't understand why Russia would be so concerned about the old man's answers. It seemed to him that the answers were available in court records and news articles. But he was wrong.

The Russians were on a mole hunt to determine which of its spies or former spies had helped point the way toward Jim back in the 1990s. During a seven-year stretch, Moscow had lost several of its U.S. assets— including Jim, Ames, Pitts, and the hugely destructive Robert Hanssen, the FBI agent who was rolled up by his colleagues in 2001. This indicated that one or more of Russia's own intelligence officers had betrayed the motherland on behalf of the U.S. intelligence apparatus. Finding the Russian turncoat who triggered Jim's capture might tell them whether they still had a problem.

Jim would have known instinctively what the SVR sought, and why. But he kept Nathan in the dark.

"I think I know what they want," Jim had told him.

Nathan never thought to ask what he meant.

Jim's original plan was to craft his responses to the Russians on notebook paper. He could buy a legal pad for $1.20 or a composition book for $2.10 at the prison commissary. A two-pack of Bic Cristal pens was eighty-five cents. Jim's idea was to fold his notes into crisp squares and hide them in his prison khakis. Then, when it appeared no one was looking, he would once again slip them under the trash that piled up on the snack tray, and his son would quietly palm them into his pocket, hoping the corrections officers wouldn't take notice.

Nathan, getting into the spirit of the father-son spy collaboration, devised a better plan. A thick red line on the floor of the visiting room marked an out-of-bounds zone for prisoners. On the other side of the line sat two rows of vending machines. Nathan's routine was to cross the line with a handful of crisp bills to buy chips, candy, soft drinks, and other food. He nearly always returned with the old man's favorites—a jalapeño cheeseburger, a Coca-Cola, and a package of Twix, Kit Kat, or Snickers—and some snacks for himself. Nathan always carried a stack of tan napkins from a nearby dispenser, setting the food on a tray between them as they visited.

Nathan's new idea was to get Jim to keep a cache of the napkins in his cell. There he would write notes to the Russians on the napkins, then carry them into the visiting room folded in a pocket of his khakis. While they were chatting, Jim would slip a napkin out and drop it on the tray table between them, where it would be camouflaged by other trash. Nathan would pick up the napkin and pretend to blow his nose with it, then pocket the used paper. Or he would carry the wadded napkins to the garbage can and slide his dad's note into his pocket. Then he would retreat to a bathroom stall, pull off a sneaker and sock, and hide the note under his arch. That way, if prison staffers forced him to remove his shoes on the way out, there would be no telltale bulge in his sock.

Jim was impressed with Nathan's smuggling plan, which came with a bonus. If he thought corrections officers were going to flip his cell for contraband, or had somehow figured out that he was communicating with the Russians, he could flush his notes down the toilet. In a pinch, he could even swallow them, literally eating his own words.

He passed Nathan the first round of responses to the Russians on November 4, sliding a folded napkin under the trash. During another visit, December 9, while Jim and Star caught up, Nathan trundled off to the vending machines and brought back sandwiches for himself and his sister, a hot pastrami for Jim wrapped in white paper, and drinks for everyone. After they finished eating, Jim put his arm around Star and quietly palmed a note under the trash.

Nathan began to hide his dad's messages beneath the green felt lining of a wooden box on his nightstand.

Jim phoned Nathan that night and caught his boy heading over to his cousin Dustin's to hang out. Jim made small talk about Nathan's long days without rest. But he'd called with an agenda.

"I just want to let you know," Jim said. "That letter that I sent you? If you want to share that with your friends, that's OK. You know what I'm saying? You know what I mean?"

"Oh yeah," Nathan said. "OK."

"All right, all right. That's great. Well, listen, you just have a great evening tonight, OK?"

"OK, Pa."

The following Monday, Nathan pulled into the parking lot of Springfield's Continental Bank Building, which sat in one of those distinctly American vortexes of concrete, macadam, and glass where you can test the power of the dollar at Target, Sears, Ross Dress for Less, a couple of multiscreen movie houses, banks, insurers, dentists, doctors, and, should you find yourself in need, an STD test. Nathan strode across the institutional carpet of Premier Travel & Cruise, where he plunked down $803.84 in cash for a round-trip ticket to Mexico City. He drove home and packed a PlayStation Portable game console, an iPod, and his Bible into a black-and-gray Alpine backpack.

Before Nathan flew out the next morning, Jim phoned. He was calling to make sure his boy had gotten some sleep before the big trip and that he had wired some money to Kanokwan.

"Hey," Jim said, "did you get that note off to Kanokwan for me?"

"Sure did. And she said that she received it, and that she feels really bad and that you shouldn't send any more."

"Oh really?" Jim laughed.

"Yeah. But she said she appreciates it very much."

Jim wound the conversation down by telling Nathan he loved him.

"Love you, too, Pa, and everything's all set."

"I'm sorry?"

"Everything's all set."

"Good. Did you read that psalm that I mentioned?"

Nathan had read the passage, five lines from the Psalm of David. They offered comfort for the journey in front of him: "Blessed *is* he who considers the poor; The Lord will deliver him in time of trouble. The Lord will preserve him and keep him alive, *And* he will be blessed on earth; You will not deliver him to the will of his enemies."

Jim told his son to have a good week and that he was praying for him every day. He pointed out that his next big adventure at the prison would be performing as a singing elf at a children's Christmas party. He and his boy busted a gut.

"Well," Nathan said, trying to imagine the old man dressed as an elf, "have fun with that."

Sometimes during these conversations, he felt a lot like the old Nathan, the little-boy version nestled in a Virginia bed, his dad seated on his bedroom floor, a Patrick F. McManus book open, fighting through tears of laughter to get out the next line.

12

A Spy Named "George"

"But one thing was for certain: Something would happen next.
Something always did. Especially when you live the life of a spy."
—Maya Bode, *Tess Embers*

Mexico City, December 2006

The Russians picked the perfect time to bring the young man from
Oregon to the city of seventeen million people. Inviting the son of a
notorious American spy to an embassy closely watched by U.S. agents
was risky; bringing him in for the holidays, with the city's hotels packed,
its broad boulevards teeming with taxis, was genius.

Millions of people were pouring into Mexico City from around the
world on December 12 for the feast of Our Lady of Guadalupe and the
four-week run of festivities to follow: the Posadas, Christmas, the Day of
the Innocents (Mexico's version of April Fools'), and Three Kings Day.
Roman Catholic priests would gather at the Basilica de Guadalupe, on
a hillside in the northern end of the city, to bless children in honor of
the Virgin Mary. The city was alive with tourists.

Catholics had made the pilgrimage there since 1531, when according to legend an apparition of Mary appeared before an Aztec peasant
named Juan Diego. The blessed virgin told him to build a church in her
honor. Diego carried news of his encounter to the local bishop, who

sent him back to the hill for proof. There Diego found Mary, who told him to pick roses from a frigid hillside normally covered in cacti. Diego found a pristine bloom of roses and bundled them into his cloak. When he opened it to show the bishop the flowers, they had vanished. All that was left was the image of Mary pressed into its cactus fibers. The bishop had seen his miracle, and he ordered the basilica built at the site of Juan Diego's encounter.

Nathan's flight touched down at Benito Juárez International Airport on the evening of the Guadalupe feast. He climbed into a taxi and asked the driver to take him to an inexpensive hotel near the Russian Embassy. The ride was an adrenaline-packed excursion as cabs and cars honked and careened within inches of one another, brave pedestrians—even little old ladies—willing themselves unhurried through the blur of traffic. They motored along the Circuito, the wide freeway that circles the city's inner neighborhoods, and pulled up to a small hotel on a busy street near the Bosque de Chapultepec, an urban park twice the size of New York's Central Park. Nathan's room was shabby, with a tiny box of a TV and a big latch on the door. It was the best he could do. He had given much of the $5,000 from Gorbunov to Star and Jeremi, telling them that it came from their grandparents' suddenly-booming craft sales, a ruse devised by his dad.

He woke on the morning of December 13, scarfed down the free breakfast buffet, and caught a taxi to the gates of the Russian Embassy compound. Nathan paid his fare near the corner of Maestro José Vasconcelos and Chicontepec and stepped out in tourist attire: jeans, sneakers, and a blue skull cap and dark blue nylon jacket, both reversible. He stood for a moment peering at the massive white embassy that rose from behind a tall wrought-iron fence. The building had once been a rancho out in the boonies. But Mexico City grew up around the property, now flanked by one of the many freeways that helped turn it into one of the smoggiest cities on Earth.

Nathan felt a nagging sense of foreboding. He knew the Russians were his friends, as Jim kept telling him. But the embassy grounds on the other side of the fence were Russian soil, his new contact inside a mystery. Jim had not mentioned to his son that the FBI and CIA kept eyes on the embassy, which had served as a diplomatic Dodge City for generations of walk-in American spies. Nathan found uniformed guards standing near a brass plaque at the main gate. They held a practiced gaze of nonchalance.

"I'm here to see the chief of security," he said.

The guards pointed him down a side street to a rear entrance of the embassy compound. Nathan thought perhaps they'd been advised to keep an eye out for him. He hiked through a gate and up to an entrance that reminded him of the consulate in San Francisco. At the receptionist's desk, he explained that he was looking for the security chief.

A short Russian man with gray hair popped out from behind her and opened a door to invite him inside.

"Follow me," he said in a hushed voice. "Don't say a word."

Nathan followed the old man through the guts of the building. The Russian led him into a room that he could see by the thickness of the door now closing behind him was a private vault. Nathan introduced himself and shook the Russian's hand.

"You can call me George," the old man said.

The Russian would never betray his true name to Nathan. But he was a master spy, a former KGB general who would turn seventy-one the following month. The Russian had once headed KR Line—*kontrazvietka*—during a Cold War posting in the Soviet Embassy's *rezidentura* in Washington, D.C. There he ran counterintelligence operations and kept tight reins on the comings and goings of his own people to ensure that the FBI didn't recruit them from under his nose. The SVR had called on the old spymaster to handle Jim Nicholson's son.

The old man walked directly to a desk and flipped a switch, leaving Nathan to assume he had tripped a recording system. The room's walls were appointed with paintings, and through a window he observed an eye-popping view, a grassy courtyard flanked by lush palm trees. If the Russian was trying to impress Nathan, it was working.

He motioned for the young American to take a seat on a couch, returning directly with a cup of coffee for himself.

"Can I get you some coffee?"

Nathan had seen enough spy movies to be leery of open beverages. He didn't think the Russian would drug him, but he wasn't betting his life on it. On his way in, he had spied bottles of Coca-Cola chilling on ice.

"Coke, if you have it," he said.

The Russian's bushy white eyebrows knit together in what appeared to be a wince.

"You're just like your father," he said with a smile.

The Russian retrieved a bottle of Coca-Cola and handed it to Nathan, who inspected the plastic cap as he unscrewed it. The older man took a seat on the opposite side of the table and sipped his coffee as he posed a series of questions. He wanted to know the name of the hotel where Nathan was staying, the room number, the length of his stay, the cost of his trip, the name of his airline, his flight numbers, and how much money he thought he could legally carry back into the U.S. He also asked Nathan whether he thought he had been tailed.

Nathan said he didn't think so.

"How is your family?" the Russian asked, his voice calm and reassuring.

Nathan told him they were all doing fine, and the Russian smiled. His friendly demeanor put Nathan at ease, but he kept things business-like as he recounted the debts and financial troubles confronting Star, Jeremi, and himself. He explained that his mom was remarried, but living on a tight budget, and he said his dad appreciated Russia's help and was happy to return the favor any way he could.

This was precisely why the old KGB man was there. Spies of his stature would never be called in to service a low-level agent such as Nathan. It was Jim Nicholson's answers he needed, and, for now, Nathan served as little more than Jim's courier and asset. The Russian handed Nathan a piece of blank paper and asked him to diagram the interior of the prison visiting room. Nathan took the paper and sketched a slightly more detailed diagram than the one he had prepared for Gorbunov in San Francisco. He handed it across the coffee table to the Russian.

The old man looked it over and posed questions about the prison's security. He was concerned that Nathan or Jim would be caught smuggling notes. Then, out of the blue, the Russian said something that made no sense to Nathan.

"Let your father know his letters were received," the Russian said.

Nathan reached into his backpack and retrieved a pocket-size composition notebook with a blue marbled cover. He jotted down George's message.

"Do you have anything for me?" the Russian asked.

Nathan handed the Russian a pair of tan napkins. The old man unfolded them carefully and studied Jim's words. One of Jim's pleas was for the Russians to escort Nathan back to his hotel after their meeting. Jim clearly was concerned with Nathan's safety, and he knew the Russians could easily sneak him out of the embassy so that he wasn't spotted by the U.S. government snoops who watched the place.

When George finished reading, he began to pose questions to Nathan, all of which were intended for his dad. He wanted to know Jim's thoughts on how he'd fallen under suspicion in Malaysia in the 1990s. He also wanted to know if Jim believed someone in that region had provided details that put him under investigation by the FBI.

Nathan scribbled furiously.

The Russian wanted to know if Jim thought anything suspicious had happened between the day he applied for the CIA station chief job in Addis Ababa to the time the agency canceled that assignment. Had Jim felt he was under investigation? And how could U.S. investigators have known about his relationship with his Russian friends at that time?

George also posed questions about Jim's debriefing by U.S. investigators: Who debriefed him, and what did they ask him about his relationship with the SVR? Who polygraphed him? The Russian wanted names of the FBI and CIA officials involved, if Jim remembered them.

To Nathan, the tenor of the questions suggested that the Russians were trying to reconstruct how his dad screwed up. But the Russians were trying to figure out how they had failed Jim. They were looking for their own Judas.

As their meeting drew to a close, Nathan's new friend opened an envelope and pulled out a brown grocer's sack folded into a rectangle. The old man unwrapped the package and shook out $10,000 in U.S. hundred-dollar bills. He didn't touch a single one of them.

"Please count the money," he said.

Before cutting Nathan loose, the Russian pulled out a calendar book to set up another meeting. He wanted Nathan to appear at the embassy between 10 a.m. and 1 p.m. on July 10. If that wasn't possible, he was to appear on one of the two following days. The Russian told Nathan that if he needed to make emergency contact sooner, he was to appear at the embassy gate, ask for the chief of security, and return in four days for a meeting.

Nathan reversed his jacket and skull cap so that they were now gray. The Russian walked Nathan to the back entrance and they parted with a firm handshake. There would be no accompanied ride to his hotel. He sent his young asset away on foot.

"Until next time," he said.

Nathan caught a cab to his hotel, keeping an eye out. He was less concerned about the FBI than about being mugged for the ten grand.

That very day, Jim wrote Nathan a Christmas card, telling him to enjoy the blessings rolling in. He also phoned Star, who was down in the mouth because her little hatchback wouldn't start. Laurie was fronting her money for the repairs, which would total nearly $600, and Star worried she wouldn't be able to pay her mom back. Jim told her not to fret; he was working on some things and would send Laurie the money on Sunday. Jeremi, meanwhile, had sent $500 to his mother to cover Star's auto repairs. When Jim found out, he phoned his oldest to say that his generosity was unnecessary, and that he had personally made arrangements with Nick and Betty to pay Star's debt.

Nathan was suddenly confronted with a fat stack of cash and three days in Mexico City. But if Russian intelligence officers were following him—and to be certain of his loyalties, they should have been—young Mr. Nicholson would have bored them silly. He rarely left his fleabag hotel, and never thought about upgrading to a better accommodation. He went nowhere near the all-night mariachis in Plaza Garibaldi, never got stumbling drunk or prowled for prostitutes. Ignacio Garibay, the up-and-coming matador, was fighting that Sunday at Plaza Mexico, the biggest bullring in the world, and there were posters all over town. A lesser man would have paid to change his airline ticket so he could attend the bullfights. But Nathan dodged any such extravagance. In his mind, this was a business trip, and his bankroll belonged to Batman.

He woke the next morning with a backache and hailed a cab to see if he could find a professional masseuse. The driver, laughing, mashed the accelerator. They soon pulled up to a brothel. *"Masaje!"* the driver exclaimed. Nathan, laughing at the miscommunication, lacked the Spanish skills to say he wasn't looking for *un final feliz*. But refusing to climb out of the cab spoke volumes.

Nathan thought he might look suspicious returning from Mexico at Christmastime with no presents, so he took a minor detour from his self-imposed austerity. He conscripted his driver for a day of souvenir shopping. Nathan picked up a ceramic dolphin for Star, perfume for his cousin Danielle, and an enormous black sombrero with gleaming gold *conchos* to plunk on the head of his scrawny cousin Dustin. The cabbie helped Nathan find a good bottle of tequila for his landlord, and Nathan bought his driver an identical bottle for his troubles. He paid twenty bucks to buy himself a Liekens & Braun DVD player, along with a few movies. They swung by a Pizza Hut, where Nathan picked up dinner and took it to his hotel. He paid his driver a hundred bucks, plus a handsome tip, and holed up for the night in his room. America's greenest spy spent the evening watching a Disney movie, *The Incredibles*.

That Sunday, Nathan paid his hotel bill and stuffed stacks of hundreds into his jacket pockets, his backpack, and under the insoles of his sneakers. He was under the $10,000 threshold that would have forced him to sign a U.S. Customs declaration. But he didn't want to lose all his money if he was robbed. Now literally walking on money, he was flush enough to push funds to Star, Jeremi, and Kanokwan, with thousands left over. All in time for Christmas. He felt like an undercover Santa Claus.

Sheridan, Oregon, December 2006

Nathan sat in the prison visiting room trying to contain his excitement. Jim had not called him since he'd returned from Mexico City—he often ran low on phone minutes at the end of the month. Now Nathan spotted his dad cutting across the linoleum floor beaming that thousand-watt smile of his. He climbed to his feet, greeted his dad, and trooped off to the vending machines as Jim waited in the din of the visiting room. The place sounded a little like a high school cafeteria, with peals of laughter and the hum of microwave ovens. Nathan sat down next to him with Cokes and snacks. Jim was dying to know about the trip.

"It went great," Nathan said.

"You're OK? You're not hurt in any way."

Not in the least, Nathan whispered. "We got ten thousand dollars."

Jim smothered his boy in praise, telling him he had handled himself better than many of the CTs he'd taught at The Farm.

Nathan radiated in the accolades. After years of depression and ruined dreams, he was making his dad proud, bringing money home to the family, and succeeding in a new clandestine career that made him feel a bit like Robin to Jim's Batman.

Jim asked his boy to describe the Russian he knew as George. But Nathan's description rang no bells with him.

"Did they have any questions for me?"

Nathan casually unbuttoned a sleeve and rolled up his cuff. He leaned into the old man and began to whisper George's queries right off his arm. Nathan had penned them on his skin with a ballpoint that morning. As he recited the Russian's questions, and listened to his dad's reactions, he could tell the old man and his friends had much unfinished business. Nathan let Jim know he was happy to keep the conversation flowing wherever it took him.

Jim told his son how to safely store the money he brought home, cautioning him not to deposit more than $500 at a time in his bank account. Plunking down large deposits on top of the paltry ones from his earnings at Pizza Hut and Bankers Life and Casualty might raise suspicions, he said. So over the next several months, Nathan stashed money in his Washington Mutual Bank account, twenty-nine deposits of $100 each. Nathan kept most of the cash at his home, but delivered a grand each to Star and Jeremi on Christmas, telling them it was from their grandparents at Jim's behest. It lit him up to see his brother and sister so happy.

To cover all the angles on the home front, Jim masterminded a mosaic of lies to explain the sudden influx of family money. He told his parents that Nathan had finally broken through as an insurance sales-man, a whopper if there ever was one, and he told his oldest children that Nick and Betty's craft sales had gone through the roof.

From their tidy manufactured home in suburban Eugene, Nick and Betty were legitimate dealers of arts and crafts, selling their wares at flea markets and other bazaars. Nick was an expert woodworker who built cuckoo clocks that resembled cathedrals. Betty was skilled at crochet and seldom took a seat without a pile of yarn in her lap. She also had mastered Bunka, a Japanese punch-style embroidery, to create tapestries of old barns, mountains, and other landscapes. But these crafts weren't exactly flying off their tables at local shows.

Jim was nearing the halfway mark of his prison term, a milestone in any prisoner's sentence, and was optimistic about a pair of bills in Congress he hoped would put him on the fast track to get out early. In a letter to Kanokwan, he wrote, "I just know this is going to be a great year for us—not only for what I hope them to do [in Congress], but for other reasons dealing with our future." In another letter to his fiancée,

Jim wrote that Nathan had become his "right hand man," and that Nick had described him as a chip off the old block: "Nathan is exactly as I am—enjoys the same things, enjoys adventure with a little bit of danger like me (maybe too much danger sometimes), loves travel, is disciplined, neat, and full of life."

In the early months of 2007, Jim used the mail to embolden his boy, quoting the Old Testament prophet Jeremiah: "[B]efore you were born, I set you apart and anointed you as my spokesman to the world." And on the first Friday in April, Jim wrote Nathan again: "I can't tell you how much joy it brings me to be in your presence. Not to get maudlin but when I begin my nightly prayers with thanks for all God has done for me, I often can't help crying with gratitude for you kids. I think of how God honored my prayers for you—how you have responded to His call—and I just burst with pride in you, Son!"

Jim's letter noted that he had just watched an inspiring movie about the biblical Abraham in the prison chapel.

"I know we've got missions to accomplish for God," he wrote. "It's been prophesied over us. We've got God's work to do. No man or power can come against us with success when we are on God's business."

13

Faith, Prosperity, and The Door

"Delight thyself in the Lord; and He shall give thee thine desires
of the heart."

—Psalms 37:4

Eugene, Oregon, Spring 2007

Nathan had joined The Door, a nondenominational Christian fellowship
in Eugene that offered contemporary lessons in faith through the filter
of fundamentalism. Congregants spoke in tongues, fasted, and held their
palms to the rafters to welcome God. Pastors pushed tithing—giving 10
percent of one's income to the church—as a way of life. Nathan brought
his cousins to the chapel, but they declared it a cult and didn't return.
The sermons left him so renewed that he shared these messages with
Jim during their Sunday night phone calls.

Christianity had always been part of Nathan's life. But he got serious about his faith early in his Army training, where he felt the whisper
of mortality every time he pulled a trigger, grenade pin, or parachute
riser. During basic training at Bragg, a pastor dipped him in a baptismal
pool in the base chapel. Nathan came up from that immersion with a
deeper commitment to God and manhood.

Nathan was now in his third year at Lane Community College,
where he had met a spirited blonde named Camilla Beavers in speech

class. She was an earthy woman with that trifecta personality men adore: She was sporty, wickedly funny, and effortlessly sexy. Beavers was a jeans-and-T-shirt girl who rarely woke early enough to put on makeup. She adored Nathan, but she didn't see him as boyfriend material. Nathan was the nice guy who listened and laughed as she ranted about the dolts she actually dated.

That spring she and Nathan took in a movie at the cinema complex where she worked in the Gateway Mall. Beavers introduced him to a coworker, Molly Harden, who later asked about him. When Beavers mentioned to Nathan he had an admirer, he remembered Molly as shy and a little plump; he hadn't really been attracted to her. But Molly had seemed nice. Nathan had gone on a total of one date since breaking up with his previous girlfriend, and a part of him—perhaps the spiteful side—thought it might be telling to see how Beavers reacted to his sudden interest in her friend. Nathan called Molly to ask her out.

On the first Sunday in May 2007, he left a meeting at The Door and drove straight to Springfield to meet Molly at the mall. They had talked on the phone about seeing a movie, but nothing on the marquee interested them. So Nathan sprung for a game of miniature golf. They laughed their way through the course, missing one spectacularly errant shot after another. Nathan miraculously ended the round with a hole in one, earning a ticket for a free game. He used the blank side of the ticket to secretly take notes about Molly—what she was wearing, things she liked—so he could impress her later with all he remembered about their first date.

Nathan asked Molly if she would join him at The Door. It was a test to see whether she had the kind of character he was looking for in a mate. She joined him enthusiastically, anxious to get back to church, and Nathan was so impressed he began to fall for her on the spot. Soon they were praying together, professing their love for God, and for each other.

One Saturday that spring, Star was sitting between Jim and Nathan at Sheridan. She was blathering on about something neither father nor son understood when suddenly they began to pick up key words—a veiled mention of secrets, and money. They had been careful to keep their exchanges with the Russians just between them. For an instant, it sounded as if Star had figured them out.

Jim tilted his head forward to face Nathan, eyes wide and imploring, as if to say, *What gives?*

Nathan could tell that the old man thought he had blabbed.

As Star kept talking, Nathan pulled his face completely out of her periphery and locked eyes with Jim. He mouthed three words.

She . . . doesn't . . . know.

With Nathan's next trip to meet the Russian set for that July, the last thing he or Jim needed were complications. Nathan began to drive to Sheridan especially early for their customary Saturday visits. They would talk business in whispers before Star arrived. Jim was still working on answers to the Russian's questions, and he was pondering ways to put clandestinely obtained cash into the hands of Star and Jeremi without exposing its source.

During a visit with Star and Nathan that spring, Jim covertly slipped one of his napkin notes under the trash piling up on the table between them. Nathan was waiting for the right moment to palm the message. Suddenly, Star was standing and gathering their trash to carry it to the garbage can. Jim blurted out that it wasn't befitting for a lady to carry off their mess. Nathan shot to his feet, practically ripping the trash out of her hand.

"This is men's work," he said.

Nathan hustled to the garbage bin, pocketing his dad's note and dumping the trash.

On June 23, 2007, a couple of weeks before his next trip, Nathan told his dad in a phone call that he was running desperately low on money and might not be able to buy him snacks during his next prison visit. Jim told him to drop by his grandparents' place and pick up a hundred bucks.

Here Nathan made a sloppy mistake.

"Hey, Pa, how many more times am I gonna be able to, uh . . . visit before that thing?"

Jim must have winced at the words "that thing." It was just the kind of phrase that might grab a CIA analyst's attention. Jim chose his words carefully, saying they were set to visit only once between now and then. He heard Nathan saying he was thinking about working in a Friday visit. It was clear from his boy's tone that there were things on his mind.

"Anytime you come up is fine," Jim told him. "You know that. . . . You know, things are just on the verge of picking up really good for us."

"Oh yeah."

"Things are really gonna, gonna break loose here. So it's gonna be great."

"Oh yeah, I'm really excited for it."

"Me too," Jim said. "Me too."

Nathan drove up to Sheridan three days before his flight to Mexico City. There they settled on a plan to distribute the next batch of money to Star and Jeremi. They walked methodically through each step of Nathan's next operation, from his flights, to the room he booked near the Russian Embassy, to his cover story if he was stopped by the FBI.

Nathan touched down in Mexico City on July 9, 2007, and checked into a Holiday Inn Express. The next morning, a Tuesday, he presented himself again at the Russian Embassy. This time he carried two notes from his father. Jim wanted their friend George to know that Nathan was trustworthy and Russia's money wouldn't be wasted. Once again, he outlined the dire financial straits faced by his two oldest children, and asked for continued assistance.

Nathan had done his best not to look at the notes. But for the first time, he couldn't resist the impulse to give them the once-over before passing them to George. His dad's carefully penned messages shared details of the FBI and CIA personnel involved in his case. He gave the Russian the first name of a polygraph examiner who put him on the box, and a physical description of an FBI agent who interrogated him. He also sketched out a scheme for the SVR to move him to Russia after he got out of prison.

Nathan handed George some brochures from Monaco RV, the recreational vehicle manufacturer in Coburg, Oregon, where his uncle Rob built cabinets for the interiors of the traveling homes. Some of the RVs fetched a half-million dollars or more. Nathan told George that his dad hoped to one day sell the high-end vehicles to Russia's nouveau riche, set up RV campgrounds, and cash in. Jim hoped to rent or sell RVs as transportation for Russian intelligence officers.

George burst out laughing at the notion of Jim running a spy shuttle for the SVR. Then he drew serious. He told Nathan that when his dad got out of prison, he should reapply for a passport and make his way to a nation near the Russian Federation. Jim had told Nathan that he didn't think he'd ever get a passport after his release from prison. But Nathan had done some Internet research anyway, deciding the most logical choices for his dad's passage to Russia were Finland, Ukraine, Georgia, or Turkey.

As for Jim's future in Russia?

"There will be no problem for him," George said.

Nathan shared with the Russian his dad's plans to bust out of prison. Life inside was wearing the old man down, and he wanted out.

George listened intently as Nathan explained that his dad wanted the Russians to pluck him off one of the prison's outdoor recreation yards by helicopter. Jim's plan was for the extraction team to carry him to a submarine parked in the Pacific Ocean off the Oregon coast so he could escape to the motherland. The Sheridan complex didn't have traditional guard towers, and corrections officers didn't carry firearms inside the institution. But there were guns on the complex, and Jim clearly had prepared himself for the possibility of a shoot-out. His newest tattoo, the work of a prison ink artist, provided his blood type: "O POS."

As comical as Jim's plan sounded, it wouldn't have been the first air escape attempted at Sheridan. About the time he arrived at the prison, officers broke up an elaborate plot in which inmates had built a large hang glider with plans to fly it over the fences. They had gone so far as to build leather britches to protect the pilot in case he landed in coils of razor wire. But they clearly hadn't thought things through. There was no building high enough to launch such a craft.

Dozens of prisoners across the globe—typically assisted by hijackers on the outside—had escaped their confines by helicopter, including a few from federal prisons in the U.S. But the escapes often ended poorly. Jim might have been inspired by something he saw on the news. Just that April, two men posing as tourists hijacked a chopper to evacuate a thief named Eric Ferdinand from a prison in Belgium. It's also possible that Jim concocted his chopper escape plans after watching *Spy Game*, a 2001 film he saw at Sheridan. The movie features a CIA operative played by Brad Pitt who is extracted by helicopter from a Chinese prison minutes before he is to be executed.

George smiled at Nathan. He told him to let his dad know that the Russian Federation wasn't risking an international incident to pluck him off a prison yard.

Jim's latest notes for the Russians answered questions about his travels in southeastern Asia. He wrote that someone seemed to be tailing him in Malaysia in the early 1990s. Also, a contact he made in Singapore—someone "off the grid"—appeared to be tainted, possibly connected to the FBI. Jim wrote that he suspected his computer at The Farm had been tapped, because it had slowed to a crawl.

George poured $10,000 on the table for Nathan. He told his young charge that he was trying to find a secure way to signal their next meeting over the Internet. He gave Nathan an e-mail address—Jopemurr2@ yahoo.com.mx—but he fretted aloud about trading electronic mail, even in code, that might connect them. He asked Nathan if he knew how to communicate without passing standard e-mail.

Nathan couldn't believe his ears. Every teenager in America knew how to hide e-mail from his parents. He stifled a laugh. Was this really the best that Russian intelligence could do?

As politely as he knew how, Nathan explained how to communicate electronically without ever hitting a send button. All they needed was a shared e-mail address and password. They could use the Russian's Mexican Yahoo account, writing messages and leaving them in the draft queue. Instead of sending messages, they would just read each other's drafts.

The Russian perked up, seemingly pleased with Nathan's craftiness, and asked him to jot down the password to the Yahoo account: Florida12.

Nathan scribbled it in his notebook as the Russian pulled out his calendar and said they would meet again on December 11, 2007, at the Russian Consulate in Lima, Peru. He gave Nathan some code names: The Russians would be "Nancy," and Nathan would be "Dick." George told him that if for some reason he could not meet on the appointed date, he was to leave a draft e-mail in their Yahoo account saying, "My brother Eugene is ill. . . ." They would also code the day of their rescheduled meeting. For example, the Russian said, if Nathan wanted to meet on December 16, he would put down a date two days later—December 18.

Nathan could not imagine a scenario that would prevent him from accepting another stack of cash. He wrote the date and locale in his notebook.

Dec. 11-13
10am by local time to 1pm by self
Peru (Lima) Consular Section
Avenida Salaverry 3424

On July 12, Nathan flew home, declaring $9,080 in cash at U.S. Customs. He carried a pearl necklace for Molly, which he valued at $100 but cost twice that much. Nathan presented his sweetheart with the pearls and, in a moment of weakness, showed off the wad of money. Nathan explained that the source of this largesse was a family secret, and that he wasn't doing anything illegal like selling drugs. She would just have to trust him on this one.

*   *   *

At the end of the month, Nathan rented a third-floor walk-up less than a mile from his grandparents' home in Eugene, a major upgrade in his living standards. His carpeted bedroom in the Heron Meadows Apartments overlooked a clubhouse with a spa, an Internet café, and a twenty-four-hour fitness room.

Molly began spending her nights in Nathan's bed, and it was clear she was angling for permanent residency.

"It started with a toothbrush," he said. "Within a month, she was moved in."

He soon discovered his girlfriend had a hedonistic streak. She stayed up late, left dirty dishes in the sink, and rose from his bed when the sun was nice and warm. She quit her job, running up her credit card with a thirty-two-inch television and a state-of-the-art laptop computer that Nathan ultimately paid for. He had made the mistake of introducing her to *World of Warcraft,* a highly addictive Internet role-play game. While Nathan was sitting through drafting classes, he imagined her on the front lines as a Blood Elf, battling the Burning Legion to regain the ravaged territory of Outland.

Nathan found himself mentally tallying Molly's flaws. Her addiction to *World of Warcraft* would have been a deal breaker for most ambitious young guys. Yes, Molly was smart, but it seemed to Nathan that she lacked get-up-and-go. She had a cute face and hair that shimmered like fire when the sun hit it just right. But she often wore her locks in an unfortunate bun. She was sexy, but overweight; Nathan couldn't for the life of him understand why she wouldn't hit a treadmill that sat a hundred yards from their bedroom. "She was," as he explained years later, "a depressed bear." Molly seemed to adore him and always tried to make him happy. But they fought over insane things. Once she criticized the way he prepared Top Ramen noodles, saying he failed to measure the water.

They were at loggerheads. Both were night owls, but Nathan was an early riser. Molly was a homebody; he suffered cabin fever very quickly. Nathan liked to stay fit; she liked cookies. She was unemployed; he was trying to earn a college degree. Nathan knew that opposites often attract, and he decided to give their live-in arrangement some more time to take. But her shortcomings were wearing him down.

Nathan took some of these laments to his dad, who counseled him not to stay with a woman he didn't love.

14

CIA Detects Codes, Espionage, Again

"The concept of surveillance is ingrained in our beings. God was the original surveillance camera."

—Hasan M. Elahi

Portland, Oregon, summer 2007

One day that August, a CIA case officer and another government official presented their credentials at the reception desk of the FBI's Portland Field Office. The receptionist buzzed them into the bureau's fourth-floor reception area in the downtown Crown Plaza building, where they were directed into the office of Dan Nielsen, the acting special agent in charge. The three men exchanged pleasantries next to a picture window overlooking a broad bend of the Willamette River.

The men caught an elevator to one of the upper floors of the field office, where they took seats in a SCIF, an acronym for a bugproof room formally known as a Sensitive Compartmented Information Facility. The room, designed to allow agents to review classified files, was decorated in standard FBI Spartan, with a few chairs and computer workstations. The CIA officer had scarcely sat down before launching into the reason for his visit. The agency's analysts had uncovered apparent evidence of the further adventures of Harold James Nicholson.

The FBI hadn't abandoned the investigation it opened against Jim five years earlier. But the trail ran cold when agents couldn't prove the package Jim smuggled out of prison in the capable hands of former cellmate Phil Quackenbush ever found its way to the SVR. The feds believed Quackenbush mailed the envelope to Nick and Betty Nicholson. If that was really the case, it was anyone's guess where it might have turned up—or even whether it ever reached Jim's parents.

What the CIA man said next breathed new life into the moribund case: Langley's analysts had detected peculiarities in Jim's phone calls and correspondence with Nathan. Father and son appeared to be talking in code, with suspicious discussions of money. The CIA was especially piqued by an August 2, 2007, letter Jim mailed to Nathan. "Anyway," he wrote, "if you get the chance I'd recommend hopping down to S. America to check it out. Brazil, Argentina, Chile or Peru could be great places to visit. Peru would be the cheapest although Brazil might not be too bad either. I'd steer clear of Colombia and those countries along the top." Jim's letter appeared to encourage Nathan to fly to one of four cities in South America where Russia held strong diplomatic ties: Brasilia, Buenos Aires, Santiago, and Lima.

Nielsen walked out of the SCIF on two wheels. He knew he'd need to quickly assign a team of investigators to the top-secret case. The Portland office had its own counterintelligence squad, but Nielsen and top counterintelligence officials at headquarters lacked confidence in its supervisor. Nielsen couldn't recall a single espionage case ever worked by the unit. He ran through a mental index of the sharpest minds in the building, knowing he would need his best people to reignite the Nicholson case.

Within twenty-four hours, Nielsen picked four middle-aged white men—three agents and an intelligence analyst—and brought them into his office. He asked the men if they wanted a piece of a closely guarded national security investigation, a priority case guaranteed to disrupt their lives. When each man said yes, he briefed them on the allegations and got them to sign papers promising not to divulge the nature of the investigation to anyone else, a process known as being "read in." Nielsen explained they needed to move quickly and carefully to learn where Nathan was going, and who he was meeting. Job one was to put a stop to whatever Jim was doing.

The FBI's assistant director for counterintelligence had ruffled feathers at the Washington Field Office by assigning the case to Portland's agents instead of their own highly regarded CI group, which handles many of the nation's counterspy operations.

The case was so closely guarded that Nielsen considered moving the Nicholson investigation out of the FBI's downtown headquarters into a rental space. He was concerned that other staffers, a curious bunch by nature, might pick up on the probe by office osmosis. Squads of FBI agents, analysts, and support staff occupied several floors in the Crown Plaza building, their workspaces set up in bullpens where they shared snippets and snatches of their cases with colleagues. That kind of collegiality was verboten in an espionage case. But Nielsen knew the men he chose could keep their mouths shut.

Nielsen's easiest pick was Jared Garth, a supervisory special agent with a background in counterintelligence. He had worked Chinese counterintelligence cases out of the busy New York Field Office before being assigned to headquarters, where he continued his CI investigations. Garth now served as the chief division counsel in the Portland Field Office, making him the FBI's top lawyer in Oregon. Garth and two other investigators would be named co–case agents. But the Nicholson case would be Garth's to run.

He was deeply familiar with national security law, including FISA, which would allow agents to secretly tail Nathan and tap his phone without a standard wiretap order. He was smart, but down-to-earth, the kind of agent you could take for a beer without fear he was sizing you up. Most days, he comported himself like a wisecracking frat boy. But he could turn surly in a hurry when things weren't going his way.

John Cooney was another easy choice. He was a native Oregonian who spoke Russian. He had spent five years in the Los Angeles Field

Office, where he worked on the Russian foreign counterintelligence squad. He came to Portland shortly before the 9/11 attacks, where he investigated domestic terrorism. Cooney helped take down The Family, a multistate ring of eco-arsonists that hit such targets as logging company offices and a ski resort under construction in Vail, Colorado, causing $40 million in damage. Cooney was a clever street agent who could pull your life story out of you, warts and all, between train stops.

Scott Jensen was the oldest of the bunch, the son of a Ford mechanic with the looks of an aging Marlboro Man. When he was a schoolboy, his grandmother gave him a book about the FBI; from then on, all he wanted was to be an agent. Jensen worked his way up from the bottom rungs of the bureau, first sorting fingerprint cards in the Hoover Building. His big break came when Ronald Reagan declared his War on Drugs. Jensen made his bones as an agent in the Chicago Field Office, where he investigated Colombian cocaine dealers, before taking over a one-man office out in the scrublands of eastern Oregon. There he hunted down fugitives, fraudsters, kidnappers, pedophiles, bank robbers, and extortionists.

Jensen, whose wit was drier than desert cheat grass, referred to himself as the "Special Agent in Charge of Pendleton," a small town in Oregon best known for its annual rodeo. He earned a reputation as relentless, coolheaded, and one of the very last men on earth you'd want cold-trailing you. The FBI assigned him to Portland in 2002, where he jumped feetfirst into the investigation of Ward Weaver III, who murdered two of his daughter's middle-school classmates before raping his son's girlfriend. Weaver, whose old man sat on California's death row for a similar run of rape and murder, cut a deal for life in prison.

The Nicholson investigation team set up shop in a small room with a keypad lock on the fifth floor of the Crown Plaza building. The secure workspace comfortably fit four people, although it could hold five or more in a pinch. The space quickly filled with computer gear to run wiretaps and a GPS tracking system so investigators could keep tabs on the doings of young Nathaniel James Nicholson.

Jensen drove out to Sheridan with Nielsen and Garth to meet the warden and Lieutenant Debra Payne, who worked in the prison's Special Investigative Services. The FBI men shared only that Jim was under investigation, a strictly need-to-know case in which they required help running operations inside the prison. Jensen soon began a weekly fifty-mile drive to prison to secretly collect Jim's outgoing mail. Jensen carried Jim's letters to his office, photocopied them, and sent them off to the CIA. Langley's analysts then copied Jim's letters and mailed off his originals to their intended recipients.

The fourth man assigned to the team was Bob Feldman, an FBI intelligence analyst. Feldman was ideally suited for the case. He was already embedded as an analyst in the Portland FBI's counterintelligence squad, so he understood the spy world. As Feldman read through Jim's correspondence and pored over his history, he discovered their lives were uncannily similar. Both were dependents of Air Force personnel, spent portions of their childhoods on Okinawa and other air bases, earned officer's commissions through ROTC, and entered military service just after the draft ended in the 1970s. About the time Jim joined the CIA, Feldman went to work as an electronics warfare officer aboard Boeing B-52D Stratofortress bombers. While Jim climbed through the ranks of the CIA, Feldman ascended to lieutenant colonel in the Air Force. In a way, Feldman felt an affinity to Jim. But he shared the bureau's revulsion for his betrayals.

Jensen reached out to the CIA to obtain all of Jim's letters and phone recordings dating back to 1997 so that he and Feldman could pick through this mountain of potential evidence. Feldman spent countless hours, earphones clamped on his head, listening to hundreds of Jim's phone calls. He and Jensen hoped some word or phrase might jump out at them—any little clue that might tell them what Jim and Nathan were plotting.

Investigators were intrigued to learn Jeremi held a secret security clearance in the Air Force, where he labored as an electronics warfare maintenance technician, a job that potentially gave him access to classified files. They were positively flabbergasted to learn Jeremi's girl-friend was Russian. Jeremi had met Anastassia "Nastia" Suvbotina on Elena's Models, a matchmaking website that featured no shortage of former Soviet-bloc women ready to uproot and pledge troth to Western men. Jeremi had flown to Nastia's home near the Volga River earlier that year, and brought her back to the U.S. Eventually they would marry.

Jensen and Feldman listened to recorded phone calls between Jeremi and his dad, trying to pick up code or some hint they might be co-conspirators. In time, they concluded Jim had kept Jeremi in the dark, and that it was just a jaw-dropping coincidence that Jeremi, who had an entire planet to comb for a wife, found his bride in the same country to which Jim literally sold The Farm.

Investigators determined that the frequency of Jim's contact with Nathan—in prison visits, and by phone and letter—had ramped up markedly in the last year. The FBI's investigators hoped to spy on Jim and Nathan—physically and electronically—to find out what they were up to. Government lawyers in Washington moved swiftly to get the Foreign Intelligence Surveillance Court's approval to eavesdrop on the Nicholsons. Eventually agents would tap Nathan's cell phone and computer, plant a GPS tracker on his Chevy, obtain his bank records, search his apartment, and put surveillance teams on him—some of them from as far away as Phoenix.

Lieutenant Payne quickly got into the spirit of the FBI's work, offering advice to Jensen and running interference for him at Sheridan. Agents briefed only one other person at the prison complex about their investigation: Warden Charles Daniels. Payne couldn't even tell her colleagues in the prison's Office of the Special Investigative Supervisor that she was helping in the FBI's probe of Jim. Instead she gave a cover story that they were involved in a "contraband" investigation. This was a timely lie. Earlier that year, the FBI had arrested thirteen people, including three prison workers and Cold War spy James Harper, for their roles in an elaborate tobacco smuggling ring in the newly "smokeless" facility. Single cans of Bugler had fetched $600 on the prison compound.

Keeping an eye on Jim, a professional spy housed in a highly secure facility, posed enormous obstacles. Jensen and his colleagues came up with several plans to run surveillance operations on him. They considered sending in an undercover team of technical agents, posing as maintenance workers, to bug Jim's cell and the visiting room. They soon realized that bugging the visiting room was the most viable plan, and they thought about planting bugs under every chair. But the space was an echo chamber of human voices laid over buzzing microwave ovens, coins jangling out of a change machine, and the hum of refrigeration units, major impediments for hidden microphones. The place was noisier than a bag of marbles in a garbage disposal. The agents thought about sending in an undercover crew to install carpet in the room to absorb the noise.

Jensen ran these operational plans past Payne, and recalled her pouring cold water on every one of them. Prisoners are creatures of habit, she explained, and they'd be extremely suspicious of new faces popping in to make repairs in the confines of a cell or laying carpet in the visiting room. Besides, Payne told Jensen, someone was bound to blab to the prison's powerful employees union about the sudden appearance of a nonunion crew, which would cause an incendiary response. The chair-bugging idea was hit or miss at best, because seating in the visiting room was first come, first served. If they bugged a few of the roughly seventy chairs in the room, there were no guarantees Jim and Nathan would sit near enough to the hidden microphones to pick up their voices. Bugging all the chairs was expensive and required tech agents to isolate only the Nicholsons' chats; the FBI had no legal authority to eavesdrop on others.

Investigators took notice of a letter Jim wrote to Nathan on the first day of autumn. They found it odd that his missive included not only Kanokwan's address, but her banking information. The idea of Nathan's sending money to a Thai national, his father's supposed fiancée, left the FBI to wonder just how far past the fences the Nicholsons might be swinging.

On October 11, a Thursday, Nathan drove to Premier Travel & Cruise in Springfield, a few miles from his apartment, and paid $1,160.70

in cash for round-trip airfare to Lima, Peru. His departure was set for December 10, with a return flight three days later.

It's not clear whether the FBI had legal authority at that point to tail Nathan. But one thing is certain: Agents had no clue their young suspect had a ticket to leave the country.

On the 13th of October, a hazy Saturday, a team of FBI agents secretly entered apartment 388 in the Heron Meadows complex. A judge on the Foreign Intelligence Surveillance Court had granted the FBI permission for a limited search of Nathan's residence, and agents now performed a swift sneak and peek. They copied hard drives of computers and took photographs of Nathan's photos, papers, letters, notes, and other documents. Agents uncovered an IRS W-2 form that showed Nathan had earned $9,756.66 in wages as a part-time Pizza Hut driver.

The FBI had taken special precautions to make sure that neither Nathan nor his neighbors caught them in the act. Garth and another agent stood on the roof of a nearby store to make sure no one observed the entry or departure of the search team. The FBI had also mounted a video camera on a utility pole on the perimeter of Heron Meadows, which gave investigators in Portland a live feed of traffic in and out of the apartments.

Nathan and Molly drove up to Beaverton that day to fetch Star and take her out for dinner to celebrate her twenty-sixth birthday. They headed eastward over the Cascades, past stands of ponderosa pines and rim-rock canyons toward a high-desert rail stop just north of Redmond, Oregon. Nathan parked his Chevy on a red lava-gravel lot, and they climbed aboard the Crooked River Dinner Train for its Saturday night murder mystery ride. They planted themselves at a table in an orange railroad car for the three-and-a-half-hour dinner excursion out to Prineville and back. A couple of dozen actors dressed in Wild West costumes—including saloon floozies and six-gun-packing cowboys—would serve dinner.

More than one hundred passengers delighted in the interactive show, a whodunit murder mystery that played out piece by piece in the 1954 diesel locomotive that hauled them eastward at thirteen miles per hour as the sun set over the rocky shoulders of Mount Washington. The unhappiest passenger on the train had to be Scott Jensen. He had boarded the train posing as a tourist, his wife in tow for a bit of cover. His job was to serve as the eyeballs on Nathan during the thirty-eight-mile trip, making sure Nathan didn't slip the bureau's cover, jump off the train, and hightail it for his car. Jensen's seating assignment was a nightmare. His ticket had put him on the wrong railcar, his seat facing away from Nathan. This forced him to abandon his wife for much of the journey to stretch his legs, hit the bar, or drop into the men's room just to catch a short glimpse of his target.

Behind them, on the remote train station's parking lot, FBI tech agents slipped into Nathan's Chevy for a search.

Late that evening, when Nathan and his companions reached the lot, he keyed the remote to unlock the Cavalier. The alarm beeped twice, an indication someone had either entered the car or bumped into it while he was on the train. Nathan didn't give it a lot of thought, figuring it was probably a malfunction rather than something more threatening. Either way, he said nothing to Star or Molly. But over the next few months, the remote would hiccup again and again.

The FBI investigation was in full swing by late fall, when agents began to keep closer tabs on Nathan's travels. By the end of the year, a team of agents would sneak into his apartment and plant a bug in his living room.

In the early hours of December 5, 2007, Jensen and another agent assigned to the team, Kirk Danielsen, crept up to Nathan's Chevy to abscond with his little auto and to plant a GPS tracking device inside. They had secretly created a spare key to enter the car, but they found it so close to the curb that they couldn't disarm the alarm system. When they slipped the key into the lock, the Chevy's alarm went off, which they remedied by starting the car. Jensen pulled a dummy car—an almost identical Chevy Cavalier—into Nathan's parking spot in case he happened to look outside. He and Danielsen then eased out of the Heron Meadows complex and drove to a fellow agent's garage nearby, where they installed the GPS inside the engine compartment. Later they returned the Cavalier to its space at the curb.

Nathan called Star a few days later to say he and Molly were heading to the Oregon coast on the 10th of December. He told his sister they wouldn't be back for three days. It was a bald-faced lie concocted by Jim to give Nathan cover for his trip to Peru. Nathan knew that if Star called him while he was away and failed to connect, she'd probably freak out and summon the family posse for a drive down to Eugene. Star would probably understand if she couldn't catch him at the coast. Cell coverage was hit or miss in some of Oregon's beach towns, and there were so many dead zones over the coastal mountains that phones were about as valuable to telecommunication as paperweights.

The FBI had wiretapped the call, but investigators weren't covering the wire around the clock. And they missed it.

Nathan found his gate at Portland International Airport at about 4 a.m. on Monday, December 10, 2007. Outside, a light rain fell on the dark tarmac as he rang Molly to let her know he'd reached PDX safely. He said he'd miss her while he was away. They sounded like clingy teens as they exchanged a multitude of sleepy I love yous. Nathan had told her before he left that he was flying to Peru to collect more money, another dangerous trip but nothing illegal. Just family business.

At a little after 8 a.m., the Nicholson investigation team began trickling into its office cubbyhole. When Danielsen turned on the Global Positioning System map on a computer screen, Garth looked down at the dot representing Nathan's Chevy, which blinked back at them. As he peered at the screen, Garth could see that the car was nowhere near Nathan's apartment in Eugene. It was parked on the north end of Portland, next to the Columbia River, at Portland International Airport.

"Holy shit!" he shouted.

Garth was still losing it when Jensen and another agent who covered the airport grabbed their jackets and bolted. Jensen's SUV made the twelve-mile drive to the airport as if it were burning rocket fuel. He stalked onto the garish green carpet of the main terminal and walked down the row of airline counters, flashing his creds and asking clerk after clerk whether their manifests showed a twenty-three-year-old traveler named Nathaniel James Nicholson.

A counter agent at Continental Airlines punched keys and nodded. She said Nathan had caught a 6 a.m. flight to George Bush Intercontinental Airport, in Houston, with a connecting flight to Lima, Peru, that afternoon. He was returning in three days, she said, with a layover in Houston, where he would clear Customs. Jensen phoned his office with the news. He then hooked up with TSA officials to review surveillance video of Nathan moving through the PDX screening area.

Back in the Crown Plaza building, Garth sheepishly walked into the office of his boss, David Ian Miller, the special agent in charge. He broke the news that their boy had bolted. Miller took it in stride, looking past the lapse. Like any good field supervisor, Miller was less interested in problems than solutions.

Garth said he planned to phone the Houston Field Office and get it to put an agent on Nathan's flight to Peru; the agent could tail Nathan from the airport. First they had to run the plan through FBI headquarters. But Daniel Lee "Dan" Cloyd, the bureau's assistant director for counterintelligence, vetoed the plan. Any attempt to follow Nathan's ride from the airport—likely by taxi—was fraught with complications. It wasn't like you see in the movies, where a detective jumps into a cab and says, "Follow that car!" This was an espionage investigation with big implications; one poorly executed tail might expose the FBI and blow up the case.

With Nathan out of town, investigators wanted to look inside his apartment for clues about whom he might be meeting. First they had to find out if Molly was at home without letting her know who they were.

A female FBI agent knocked on the metal door that day with a flyer in her hand. It was one of the oldest moves in the FBI playbook. Agents would find flyers for a new pizza joint or Chinese restaurant lunch special and then knock on a suspect's door pretending to be handing them out in the neighborhood. The idea was to see whether anyone was in the dwelling before they slipped inside to search the place.

When Molly opened the door to accept the flyer, agents knew they'd have to circle back another time.

Nathan checked into the Melia Lima Hotel that night. His room, walking distance from several embassies and the United Nations complex, was by far the nicest of his travels. He woke early the next morning, hit the breakfast buffet, and caught a taxi down Avenida Salaverry toward the Pacific. When the car passed Avenida Juan Pezet, Nathan saw the Russian flag rising from the embassy compound, its pole-mounted security cameras peering from atop cream-colored walls.

The cab stopped and Nathan paid his fare, overtipping as usual. As he stepped out to look for an entrance, the polite driver pulled behind him to make sure he got in OK. Nathan was trying to find his way into the consulate, one of the buildings behind the wall. He strode along a sidewalk, backpack on his shoulder, to a wooden door. But he discovered the consulate hadn't opened yet. At the suggestion of the taxi driver, he tried the intercom to reach someone inside. But he got no response. Now the driver was pressing the intercom and talking in Spanish. Tinny voices came from the speaker, and they sounded Russian.

It was like a brick hitting a beehive. The consulate came awake all of a sudden, a uniformed guard bursting into view pointing a military rifle at Nathan and shouting words so fast he didn't know what language he was speaking. The guard now jerked the business end of the barrel toward the street, his intent unmistakable as he continued shouting. Nathan slowly moved backward, shaking his right hand as if to say there'd been a mistake.

*   *   *

"These Russians are gonna *shoot* me," Nathan told the driver, chuckling nervously.

Another guard appeared and pointed him toward the gate, where Nathan found his way into the consular office. There, the Russian he knew as George stepped from behind a curtain to welcome him to Lima. The old man led him down a hallway, reminding him not to speak, and they took seats in another soundproof room. There, George upbraided him. First, he told Nathan, he had failed to signal his intention to meet by dropping an e-mail in the draft file of their shared Yahoo account. Second, he'd showed up so early that he spooked the security team.

Nathan apologized profusely for his failure to signal the meet. He had completely misunderstood George's instructions, thinking they weren't supposed to use the Yahoo address unless he couldn't make the Lima appointment. In fact, he didn't think they were going to execute the shared account until after the meeting in Lima. He promised George that he would follow through the next time. Nathan figured he'd screwed up so badly there might not be a next time.

He passed the Russian his dad's latest note, along with the letter Jim had mailed him about visiting South America. Nathan sipped a Coke as the old spy read through everything. When George appeared to be finished, Nathan relayed a few of his dad's verbal messages. Jim wanted him to know that he was a Christian and doing well, and that he was hoping to be freed sooner than expected. He also wanted Nathan's handler to know how grateful he was for Russia's help and to let him know that Jim's family still needed the money, and that its funds were being put to good use.

George had no questions for Nathan, who was beginning to think he held no value to the Russians. Then George spilled a sack of hundred-dollar bills on the table.

"Please count."

Nathan thumbed through the money and found that the Russian had given him $12,000, part of which was for his travel expenses. He explained that he couldn't accept that much cash. Taking more than $10,000 back into the U.S. without declaring it at Customs was illegal, Nathan said. He watched the Russian's expression soften. The old man raked back two grand.

The Russian pulled out his calendar to arrange their next meeting, and Nathan reached for his notebook. The Russian had always told him to write his notes in code, so that only he could understand them. But Nathan felt he couldn't afford to screw up again. He scribbled the notes exactly as George dictated them so that he knew precisely where to go. He misspelled "Nicosia," and "Cyprus," but he got the address right.

Meet in City.
Entrance to restaurant "TGI Friday"
12 Diagorou Avenue

The Russian handed Nathan a camel-colored baseball cap to wear to their next meeting, telling him that he should carry his backpack in one hand. He gave him a *parol* to remember. The Russian would approach and ask, "Can you show me the way to the general post office?" To which Nathan would reply, "It should be somewhere here. Let me show it for you."

Nathan took careful notes of the confirmation message the Russian wanted him to leave in their Yahoo account no later than October 10, 2008, preferably from an Internet café. The note was to begin, "Hola Nancy . . ."

When their meeting came to a close, George's driver took Nathan to a shopping mall, where he caught a taxi to his hotel. The driver who had helped him get into the Russian Embassy without bloodshed later phoned Nathan, wondering what had become of him. Nathan felt like a jerk. He had put the cabbie's business card in his wallet with the promise that he'd call for a ride back to the hotel. For all he knew, the guy had been sitting in his taxi the whole time. Nathan told the driver to please drive over to the Melia Lima Hotel. When he pulled up, Nathan trotted out to apologize in person and pressed a $20 bill in his hand.

A light rain fell across the tarmac at Houston's Intercontinental Airport on the morning of December 13. Continental Flight 591 banked over the six-hundred-square-mile city as daylight crept over the oil refineries east of town. Traffic was already crowding Interstate 45, ten lanes of commuter hell that bottlenecked weekdays from The Woodlands, a suburban township twenty-five miles north, all the way into town. Nathan's flight was late reaching Houston. But he would have ample time, if there were no delays, to clear Customs and catch his flight to Portland.

Jared Garth and John Cooney had spent the previous night in the Best Western Plus Intercontinental Airport Inn, one of those soulless lodgings a few minutes from the airport. Cooney had flown in from Philly to meet Garth, and the two ate dinner at a nearby Hooters. The two agents woke well before dawn and were waiting at the airport hours before Nathan's plane landed. A Houston FBI agent showed them to an office near U.S. Customs, which looked into the international terminal and its secondary screening area. She gave Garth a blue blazer and a U.S. Customs and Border Protection badge to wear around his neck.

The Portland agents had arranged with their new Customs contacts to put Nathan through a secondary search to see what he brought home from Peru. An FBI technical agent would join Cooney in the back office so that when Customs officials pawed through Nathan's belongings, they could pluck out his laptop and secretly deliver it to them to mirror the hard drive.

As Flight 591 debarked, Garth took his place outside, posing as a Customs supervisor. Nathan popped into a restroom to recheck his money, making sure it was divided into multiple hiding places. Soon Garth saw Nathan's head bobbing through the crowd. He watched, trying not to make eye contact, as a Customs officer pointed Nathan and a few other passengers to a row of tables for secondary screening. Nathan carried only his backpack.

A dark-haired officer about Nathan's height handed him a Customs declaration form to fill out. Nathan lied on the paper, saying he had carried $6,000 in cash into the country. When Nathan finished with the form, the officer looked it over and asked why he was carrying so much money.

"I maxed out my credit cards," he said.

Nathan lied again, saying he left the U.S. with $6,500, and volunteered that he had been saving his Veterans Affairs checks since May to afford his trip. The officer dug through Nathan's wallet and backpack, pulling out items he thought the FBI agents hiding behind the one-way mirror might like to see. He set aside a digital camera, a PSP video-game case choked with $4,000 in cash, more clumps of cash from his pack, and his blue pocket notebook.

Nathan silently freaked out as he watched the notebook disappear into an office behind a one-way mirror. The book held 160 pages, many full of notes about his family, the address of the Russian Embassy in Peru, his secret Yahoo account with George, their code names, and questions posed by the Russian about his dad's espionage. Nathan began to calculate how much money he'd really brought back with him, certain he was over the $10,000 limit, meaning Customs could seize all of it. But a portion of the cash remained hidden in tiny zippered pouches on the straps of his backpack, and no one had looked there yet. The Customs man returned without his wallet, PSP, camera, and notebook.

Nathan felt his heart racing.

Garth and Cooney, now working together behind the one-way glass, were disappointed to see that the Customs man hadn't brought them a laptop. Nathan had left it at home. But their eyes lit up when they opened Nathan's little blue notebook. Its pages held the mother lode of his adventures over the last year or so: cryptic notes, dates of meetings in foreign countries, and a Yahoo address with a Mexican suffix.

The two agents had failed to bring a camera with them. Garth fired up the photocopy machine, printing pages of Nathan's notebook. But some of the pages had been written in pen, others with pencil. The photocopier, even on the darkest setting, wasn't picking up the lighter lines. So Garth grabbed the oldest tool in the book, his notepad. He scribbled Nathan's notes line by line, working feverishly so as not to spook his target. Meanwhile, Cooney pulled out papers from Nathan's wallet to take notes, including the name and phone number of his taxi driver in Lima: Eduardo Tapia.

Nathan stood by the Customs table trying to look serene as the officer fired questions. He wanted to know why Nathan wrote $6,000 on his Customs declaration form, yet the search had turned up $7,013 in cash inside Nathan's belongings. Nathan said it now occurred to him that he'd carried $9,000 to South America, not $6,000, and had spent a few grand in Peru. The Customs officer now asked what he'd been doing in Peru. Nathan regaled him with a dazzling pack of lies. He said he had flown to Lima on the spur of the moment to find a romantic place to propose marriage to his girlfriend. He had hoped to meet with an Army buddy in the coastal town, but that hadn't panned out. As he rattled off lie after lie, he felt way over his skis, the consequences of the last couple of years now undeniable.

Fifteen minutes passed. Thirty. How long was he going to be questioned? How long could he keep from melting down? Somehow he found a way to make friendly conversation with the Customs man. Then, suddenly, the officer stepped away.

Nathan tried to imagine the next scene. Federal agents flashing badges, their words echoing through the airport: *Is your name Nathaniel James Nicholson?* His father had given him subtle warnings. So had the Russians. They had used words like "cover story" and "surveillance" and "FBI" and "paper trails" and "computer slow-downs," words that now blazed in big capital letters in the temporal lobe of Nathan's brain, reminding him that he had avoided looking at any clue that might have helped him understand the gravity of what he was doing—that might have helped him avert the mess he now found himself in. He had put his safety in the hands of his father and his Russian friends, with confidence none of them would put him in real danger.

And here it came, the Customs man striding purposefully toward him, carrying his PSP and his camera and the notebook.

"Everything is good to go," he said.

And suddenly, throwing the backpack over his shoulder, Nathan was thanking him and sprinting for his gate like a kid racing into summer with a stolen Popsicle.

15

Keep Looking Through Your New Eyes

"A man that flies from his fear may find that he has only taken a short cut to meet it."

—J.R.R. Tolkien, *The Children of Húrin*

Sheridan, Oregon, Christmastime 2007

Nathan drove to the prison on December 15, still freaked out by the Customs stop in Houston. He feared he'd blown everything. In the visiting room, he struggled to keep his voice low as he recounted to Jim the searing questions about his travels and the money, and the horror of watching his notebook vanish behind one-way glass. He could only hope that whoever thumbed through those pages figured his coded scribbles were the work of someone playing childish games. He told Jim he had kept his breathing even, talking jovially, making himself believe his lies.

"Sometimes in the CIA," Jim told him, "we did simulations like that." He had trained CTs back at The Farm to stay cool when unexpectedly stopped for a hostile run of questioning; during these exercises, they learned to keep their covers at all costs, even under prosecutorial and sometimes brutal interrogations. "I think you actually did very well. You performed better than some of the people I trained."

Nathan appreciated his dad's reassurances, but it was clear to him that he had slipped up somehow and possibly compromised them. He pointed out that on his pass through PDX, his Chevy hiccuped again when he keyed the remote, another sign things weren't what they seemed. On the upside, Nathan noted, the Russian had paid them another ten grand and wanted to meet again next year, in Cyprus. He asked his dad whether, after everything that had happened, it was wise to make that meet. It seemed awfully risky. There was panic in Nathan's voice.

Jim pondered this and said that if they thought it wise they could abandon plans to meet the Russian in Cyprus. But it was a year off, giving them plenty of time to think it through.

Nathan knew his covert meetings with the Russians—not to mention the sacks of money they paid—had rejuvenated his dad. Their venture made the old man's life behind bars more bearable. Nathan sensed that he was desperate for their arrangement to continue, and that his dropping out might scotch his father's plans to move to Russia after prison. He didn't want to hurt his dad, but his anxieties were torturing his ulcerous gut. He sometimes caught himself feeling suspicious of strangers, wondering whether they might be federal agents. Only later would it dawn on him how deeply he'd been drawn into the spy world.

"I was like a lobster in a pot," Nathan would reflect years later, "heated slowly until it was too late."

As Nathan talked to Jim that day in the visiting room, a team of FBI agents crept into his apartment. In his bedroom, they found $3,500 in hundred-dollar bills tucked inside a leather-bound study Bible. They located Nathan's blue notebook—the one Garth had pored through in the Houston airport—and discovered that several pages had been torn out. Agents captured digital images of the money and a trove of Nathan's personal effects, including letters and handwritten notes. They slipped out quietly, leaving the apartment precisely as they found it.

As Nathan hugged his dad goodbye at Sheridan, Jim reminded him to give a portion of the cash to his grandparents, who lived just a mile from his apartment. They would disburse the money to Star and Jeremi so that neither of his siblings knew its true origin. Nathan wasn't clear what kind of story Jim told Nick and Betty about the cash.

Moscow's money carried less allure to Nathan now. He didn't really need it. Uncle Sam was providing him more financial support than the Russians. The GI Bill's vocational rehabilitation fund was paying for his books and tuition at Lane Community College. Veterans Affairs sent him another $541 a month in disability pay. In early 2008, he would begin a paid internship at Burton Saw & Supply, which sold and repaired machinery used by wood-products companies.

Nathan remained grateful to the Russians, burning through their money while supporting perpetually unemployed Molly. He took her out to dinner and chick flicks, bought her *Guitar Hero* for the Wii, and paid her phone and credit card bills. Much as Nathan tried to buoy her spirits, she stayed indoors playing *World of Warcraft,* her moods dodging into dark corners.

Molly had previously made a halfhearted attempt to break free of Nathan, telling him their life together wasn't exciting enough for her. Nathan viewed her unhappiness as flagging self-esteem and, with spring approaching, began plotting an escape of his own. Her preemptive breakup had shattered any faith he held in their relationship, and no one in Nathan's circle understood why he tried to make things work with Molly. Even Camilla Beavers, who had introduced them, thought Molly was a train wreck. Dustin eventually sucked up his guts and drew his cousin aside.

"I gotta be honest with you," he said. "None of us like Molly."

Dustin's candor left Nathan dumbstruck, but he told his cousin that he appreciated hearing the truth about how everyone felt. Of course, Dustin hadn't been completely candid. He didn't tell Nathan that he thought Molly was lazy, overly emotional, incapable of admitting when she was wrong, a sore loser at board games, and a leech sucking the life out of him. Dustin also didn't tell his cousin he took active measures to provoke Molly. Whenever they were all looking for something to do, he would suggest something requiring physical exertion. Dustin knew this would drive Molly crazy.

He recalled one such excursion not long after Nathan and Molly began to date, when they all drove out to Mount Pisgah, about eight miles southeast of Eugene. They parked at the foot of the mountain and started hiking uphill. "We can still *see the car*," Dustin said, "and she's complaining about her feet hurting." This left Molly with two options. She could trudge up the mountain, or she could sit in the car and wait for them to get back. "Those were the options as *most guys* would see it," Dustin recalled. "But Nathan discovered a third option."

Dustin watched his cousin put his unhappy girlfriend on his bad back. He piggybacked her halfway up the two-and-a-half-mile climb before she declared herself too tired to continue. Nathan let her take a seat and pushed for the summit with the others.

One Saturday in March 2008, Nathan met Star at the Malay Satay Hut, a Malaysian restaurant in a shopping center on the southeast end of Portland. Nathan ordered an avocado milk shake and unburdened himself about the state of his relationship. Molly had finally gotten a job—she was cashiering at Target—but getting out of the house during daylight hours hadn't improved her moods. Meanwhile, he was thriving at Burton Saw, where his bosses would soon award him with a dollar-an-hour raise. He was reverse-engineering machinery that broke in the normal course of work in lumber mills, drawing designs for replacements on a computer.

Nathan told Star he didn't know how much more he could take on the Molly front. He was planning to take her off the full scholar-ship under his roof, although in truth it had turned into more of an athletic scholarship than an academic one. He agonized aloud about the impending breakup before asking Star if she thought he was doing the right thing.

"It's the right thing," she told him. "You're both *miserable*."

Nathan drove home to Eugene, reaching Heron Meadows sometime before midnight. Molly could see he had something on his mind. They took seats on the living room carpet, where Nathan began the windup. They had had done their best, he said, yet they remained unhappy. Now it was time to part ways. Molly protested, saying she *was* happy. But Nathan said it was clear they weren't, and it was over. He was awful at this breakup business, unable to comprehend why he suddenly felt sweaty and cold at the same time, unable to get a good read on Molly's emotions. But he was about to get an object lesson in breakup histrionics. Molly went white. Her palms shot to either side like that dying soldier in *Platoon*. She looked at the heavens and shouted, "*Why*, God?!"

She began phoning people—her dad, her grandmother, her uncle. Soon people poured into the apartment to question Nathan and console Molly. It was hours before Nathan helped them haul the last of her stuff out of his place. She refused to assist in the move, and Nathan could hear her on the parking lot three floors below, shrieking hysterically: "Don't leave me!"

Neighbors glared at Nathan for days after that.

An FBI agent was forced to listen to the entire excruciating conversation, which was captured by the bug planted in Nathan's living room.

At the end of March, Jim mailed Nathan an article from a travel magazine about the architecture of museums around the world. One of the museums pictured was in Beirut, which Jim described in his note as "audaciously risky. . . . But if that city could ever be peaceful, it would be a good place. The weather there (Mediterranean) is very pleasant. Cyprus would perhaps be a safer place to build such." The letter and magazine piece were intended to help Nathan solidify his cover as a young architecture student touring Cyprus for research.

On May 21, 2008, Nathan walked out of his apartment and crossed the driveway to the Heron Meadows clubhouse, where he parked himself in the Internet café. He sat back in one of three high-backed chairs and logged into the Mexican Yahoo account, just as the Russian had instructed, and tapped two words into the subject line: "Hola Nancy!"

"Hello sweetie," he wrote. "How are you? I'm good. Sorry for taking so long to write to you. . . . You know how work is and all. Anyways, things are good. It looks like I will still be able to go on that vacation! I will keep you updated on that though. I am very much looking forward to it, and to seeing you again! Well, hon, I thought I'd just say 'hi' since I had the time!"

The Russian had told him to check the draft folder of the Yahoo account from time to time after writing the note. One day several weeks later, Nathan logged in to find that the e-mail had been deleted, a clear signal his message had been received.

Nathan used one of Heron Meadows' PCs rather than his Fujitsu laptop to avoid leaving a trail that could connect him to the Russian. But the FBI, electronically monitoring every keystroke Nathan made on the Jopemurr2 account, covertly obtained records from Qwest Communications Corp., which showed he'd logged on to a desktop computer literally a stone's throw from his apartment.

On July 28, 2008, Nathan punched up Orbitz on his laptop to research flights to Ercan International Airport on the Turkish side of Cyprus. He discovered that the cheapest way to fly onto the island was through Istanbul, and that he'd have to catch a taxi across the Green Line—the United Nations Buffer Zone—onto the Greek side of the world's last divided city. The Turks held the northern end of the island since a coup d'état and war in the mid-1970s. Greek Cypriots had their own capital on the south side of Nicosia.

Three days later, Nathan turned twenty-four. His dad had mailed him a card a few weeks early to make sure it cleared the CIA's censors in time to reach him on his birthday. Jim's note read, "You have been brave enough to step into this new unseen world that is sometimes dangerous but always fascinating. God leads us on our greatest adventures. Keep looking through your new eyes. I understand you—and me."

Nathan ate it up, the old man reaffirmed how much they were alike. Jim made him feel that he was destined for great things, based in large part on his performance with the Russians. And God himself had blessed their pursuits.

Star called him one day, inquiring about his future. She wondered if it was true that he was considering a degree in architecture. Nathan offered a cryptic response.

"I'm just sort of waiting for more excitement to happen," he told her, "waiting for more big changes in our lives."

Star replied that she hated big changes, and Nathan certainly understood. They had shared the cataclysms of their childhood—the marital breakup that left them all shattered, and the arrest of their father, which left them broke. Nathan explained that he liked changes when they were for the better.

"Like winning the lottery or something."

A month would pass before Nathan sat down at a computer in the Lane Community College library to drop the final "Hola Nancy" note. He left it in the draft box of the Yahoo account, confirming he would indeed make it to Nicosia for the December meet.

The FBI had him covered the whole time.

A team of FBI agents watched Nathan on the morning of November 17, 2008, when he walked into a shabby cinder-block office on the west end of downtown Eugene, about four miles from his apartment. A sign hanging from a pole outside read "Bonaventure Travel." Nathan walked out about an hour later with papers in his hand. The FBI learned from Airlines Reporting Corporation, an outfit that keeps records of billions of dollars in annual airline-ticket sales, that someone had paid $1,584.41 in cash that day for round-trip tickets from Portland to Cyprus, with layovers in New York and Istanbul.

Nineteen days later, Nathan finished his internship at Burton Saw and packed his bags for Cyprus. He was scheduled to land on the isle in the early morning of December 10. The FBI had to be certain that Nathan wasn't onto them. Government lawyers fretted over his upcoming flight much the way they did in 1996, when Jim was readying for his fateful trip to Singapore. If Nathan had detected he was under surveillance, he could exploit his trip in Nicosia by popping into the Russian Embassy. There he could seek asylum. Prosecutors at the U.S. Attorney's Office in Portland knew they needed more evidence to prove Nathan was involved in an espionage-related offense. They needed the money shot: Nathan meeting a Russian spy.

The FBI's formal position is that its agents never ran surveillance operations on Nathan in Cyprus, and that the host country was unaware of its presence. While there's nothing illegal or immoral about keeping an espionage investigation under close wraps, not giving the local spy service a heads-up can cause political troubles if things go south.

This much is known: One FBI agent from the Portland Field Office and a surveillance team from Washington, D.C., flew to Nicosia to confirm that Nathan was serving as his dad's agent. The bureau knew from their young subject's handwritten notes that he planned to meet his Russian handler outside the T.G.I. Friday's at 12 Diagorou Street for their 7 p.m. appointment on December 10. What they didn't know was whom he planned to meet.

It's not clear what role the CIA played in tailing Nathan in Nicosia, if any. What is known is that the FBI shot video of Nathan, wearing his camel-colored cap, meeting a short man under streetlamps in front of the red-and-white-striped awnings of the T.G.I. Friday's. The meeting was captured by at least two runs of video, one taken from across Diagorou Street near a sports-apparel shop, the other from inside a window of the T.G.I. Friday's.

The surveillance team lost Nathan after he ran his recognition dialogue with the Russian and they hiked down the sidewalk to a palm-flecked side street. They climbed into a waiting sedan, which shuffled into traffic and disappeared. Later that night, Nathan strode into the Hilton Cyprus, a five-star hotel since the day it opened in 1965. He glided past the reception desk, where wall-mounted Rolex clocks told guests the time of day in Sydney, Tokyo, Nicosia, London, and New York. He passed a row of expensive gift shops in a marble hall and caught a glass-fronted elevator. Nathan carried his Alpine backpack to his room, where he would spend much of the next few days guarding $12,000 in U.S. cash.

A professional spy might have let his hair down a little bit. But Nathan stayed keyed up. He recalled the two Russians who stopped him during his surveillance detection route, asking where they might get a bite to eat. Were they part of George's team? Maybe. Probably. But who could be certain? He remembered telling George about the secondary searches he'd endured at the airports in Houston and Portland. The old spy had shrugged it off like it was part of the game. Nathan had grown fond of George, but he never got the impression the Russian gave a damn about him.

"I knew I was a nobody to them," Nathan later told me. "I couldn't shake the feeling that they didn't care if I was caught or not."

This was Jim's field, not his. Nathan was slow to recognize how deeply he had trespassed into this secret world, where truth sheds its skin like a snake and highly trained professionals play for keeps. He often wondered why his dad taught him to lie for a living, sending him into meets with contacts such as George. Nathan would never feel completely at ease in their world, would always feel like an intruder. Why had Jim pulled him into this? Perhaps it was all that remained of his former life that he could impart.

Nathan knew precisely why he put himself in play outside that T.G.I. Friday's. He'd gone because the old man picked him, no one else, to make contact with the Russians. He'd gone because his dad was counting on him, and because of the money. And he'd gone, God help him, for the thrill of meeting a Russian spy in a city built in the Bronze Age, wrung out by jet lag but wide awake and feeling a whole lot like a junior varsity James Bond.

When Nathan's flight touched down at JFK, he noticed a very tall man moving among the herd of travelers into Customs. The man looked familiar, and it occurred to him that he'd seen him once or twice before on this trip. But he couldn't be certain. The specter of someone possibly following him raised the hairs on the back of his neck. And when the man moved through Customs so fast he barely broke stride, Nathan had to wonder if he was a federal agent. When Nathan presented his passport, he found himself yet again pulled aside for a secondary search, questioned about his travels before he was allowed to board. He slept fitfully on the connecting flight to Portland, too keyed up to lose himself in sleep.

He figured there would be plenty of time for rest when he got home.

16

FBI Offers a Mulligan

"The irony of breaking a spy case is simple. Finding a spy is
terrible news. Not finding a spy is worse but not news."
                                    —Louis J. Freeh, former FBI director

Eugene, Oregon, December 15, 2008

Nathan opened his apartment door, woken by the pounding.

He felt a blast of frigid afternoon air, a lull between snowstorms
that would deliver the valley its deepest snow in forty years. The two
men on his stoop wore jeans and dour gazes. Nathan hoped they were
solicitors of some sort, Jehovah's Witnesses maybe, passing out *Watch-
tower* tracts and saving souls. But deep in his heart, he knew they meant
trouble. He had prepared himself for the possibility of this day and
was determined to follow Jim's script, a cover story for every occasion.
But now, wobbly with jet lag, he wondered if he possessed the acting
chops to carry it off.

John Cooney and Jared Garth held out FBI credentials and introduced themselves.

Nathan braced himself as he heard Cooney say they were looking
for help with an investigation. He fought an instant of pure out-of-body
terror. For the second time in his life, the FBI stood on his stoop. This
time, there was no Uncle Rob to soften the blow. He was all alone.

Cooney told Nathan the FBI had arranged with the management at Heron Meadows to use a vacant apartment in the complex to have a conversation. He said they could go there if it made him feel more comfortable. Cooney didn't mention he'd also come armed with a search warrant. He'd break that bit of news when the time was right.

Nathan held the door wide and invited them in out of the cold.

The agents found themselves standing just inside the door. They looked around casually as Nathan rustled a pair of bar stools from the kitchen. The place was done up in twenty-something Spartan, with hanging prints of painted tigers on white walls. The agents had heard his voice on wiretaps, watched him in the Houston airport. But this was the first time they had met their young suspect close enough to smell his breath.

Remembering his manners, Nathan asked the lawmen if they cared for something to drink. When they declined beverages, he took a seat on his beige faux-leather couch. This left him staring upward at the agents perched on his bar stools.

Cooney told his suspect he was under no obligation to speak to them, his participation purely voluntary.

Nathan said he was happy to help.

Cooney possessed a gift for disarming people. He knew plenty about Nathan, certainly enough to get him talking. His best play was to get his subject comfortable, ask a few dunker questions, and just let him talk. Cooney told Nathan he was aware he had served in the Army, attended classes at Lane Community College, and had no criminal record.

Nathan stopped him cold, saying he wanted to correct something. He told them he did have a blemish on his record.

The agents perked up. This was news to them.

Nathan explained that once, while camping out at the Oregon coast, a ranger had cited him for pulling dry bark off a tree to make a campfire. He was fined $500, but a judge had allowed him to pay half. Nathan's guests had to stifle laughter. His "crime" was one of those

only-in-God's-Country infractions that wouldn't exactly give him brag-
ging rights with the Gambino family.

Cooney asked Nathan if he considered himself a person of honor
and integrity, and if he'd be willing to help his country.

"Sure," he said.

For the next hour, Cooney got Nathan to tell his life story, from
his birth in the Philippines to his parents' divorce, his dad's arrest, his
years growing into manhood in the Willamette Valley, his enlistment in
the Army, and his parachuting accident. Cooney chewed gum as Nathan
talked, eyes planted on his subject. Eventually, he asked Nathan about
his foreign travels.

Nathan told the agents he had flown to Mexico a couple of times to
study its architecture, and that he had just gotten back early that morning from Cyprus, where he had hoped to meet some Army buddies but
failed to connect. He told them about his trip to Peru, saying he had
gone to scout a romantic spot to propose marriage to his old girlfriend,
who was no longer in his life.

Cooney explained to his young subject that it was easy to forget
some details of his vacations, but that the FBI needed the complete story
of his travels. He cautioned Nathan that lying to them was a crime.

"Would you do anything for your family?" Cooney asked.

"Yes," Nathan said.

He told the agents his family stood only behind God in importance
to him.

Cooney told Nathan he could see he was jittery and that it was
perfectly natural to be nervous talking to the FBI. But candor, he explained, was in his best interest. He reminded Nathan again that it was
a violation of federal law to mislead federal agents, and he steered his
suspect back to tales of his foreign travels.

Nathan regaled Cooney and Garth with a spectacular mix of truth
and bald-faced lies. At one point, he got up to find a map of Nicosia to
show the agents where he stayed at the Hilton, the castles he toured, and
a restaurant that a woman who worked at his hotel had recommended:

T.G.I. Friday's. Nathan said he hadn't had the chance to eat there. He also said he carried $10,000 to Cyprus, but had spent only about $300, on cab fares and pizza, carrying cash because he didn't trust banks. He told of his U.S. Customs stop on the way home from Peru and how an officer had carried some of his belongings into a back room.

Cooney asked if he had had any contact with foreign officials or people involved with terrorist organizations.

"No," Nathan told him.

Garth took notes and texted on his phone. He was keeping fellow investigators updated on the doings at Heron Meadows. The FBI had set up a command post five miles east, in the bureau's downtown Eugene office, where agents and federal prosecutors were keeping tabs on teams of FBI agents who had fanned out across the country to interview Nathan's entire family, including Jeremi and Nastia in the Florida Panhandle.

At precisely 2:55 p.m., more than ninety minutes after Cooney and Garth first knocked on Nathan's door, their suspect's phone rang in his bedroom. The last thing the agents wanted their young suspect to do was pick up the call, get an earful from some irate family member, and clam up. Cooney said he preferred that Nathan not answer.

Nathan obliged him.

Cooney said he was puzzled by some of his answers about his travels, and he reminded Nathan again that it was a mistake to lie to them.

"Hypothetically speaking," Nathan said, "what would happen if I quit talking?"

Cooney explained that he was free to end their chat at any time, although he hoped he would help them.

Nathan was already fed up with Cooney and Garth; he felt like a captive in his own home.

Perhaps sensing Nathan's growing testiness, Cooney dropped the hammer. He said the FBI knew more about his travels than he was telling them.

"You show us all your cards," he said, "and we'll show you ours."

"I haven't done anything illegal," Nathan said.

Cooney told Nathan that the FBI helps people who help them, and that he was going to give him a onetime chance to tell his story straight. He said to think of the opportunity as a do-over, like when you whiff a golf shot on the first tee.

"A mulligan," Cooney said.

Nathan took a deep breath, mentally tallying all those moments over the last several months when things felt amiss. He knew the FBI agents weren't sitting in his home without evidence. He was tired of dodging their questions, exhausted by the lying. He looked at the agents, and they at him. And then he began.

"It all started about two years ago. . . ."

He talked for hours, a purge of the last couple of years, guided only by gentle prodding by the agents. Nathan told them of his dad's disgruntlement with the government, how Jim felt the CIA had let him down. He spoke of the old man's scheme, back in 2006, to reach out to Russia for help. Nathan said his dad hoped to get out of prison and leave the U.S. And he told them he had smuggled his dad's notes out of Sheridan's visiting room, carrying them to Russian diplomatic stations in San Francisco, Mexico City, Lima, and Nicosia. When Nathan had wrung himself dry, the agents told him they'd appreciate it if he wrote it all down, and they moved him to the empty apartment downstairs.

Nathan spent an hour or two writing a detailed confession as he continued telling his story. When he was through, the agents presented him with a search warrant. Nathan heard one of them reading it, and he posed a question of his own.

"Am I going to be arrested?"

"Not tonight," Garth said.

He frisked his suspect and a team of FBI agents tromped into Nathan's bedroom. The agents asked Nathan to take them to the money and not force them to find it. So he led them to the Bible on his nightstand and handed over ninety-five hundred-dollar bills. He also pulled the blue notebook out of his backpack.

Later, sitting in the living room and more relaxed, Nathan could hear the search team working through his closets and drawers, a reminder of that November day a dozen years back. After a time, he heard a few of the agents cackling in his bedroom. He tried to imagine what they had found, and it occurred to him they had probably stumbled across a bright orange T-shirt that read, "FUGITIVE (YOU NEVER SAW ME)." Nathan remembered the infamous photograph of his dad, distributed by the government after his 1996 arrest. It showed Jim, tanned and bearded and fit, wearing a big grin and a goofy red bandanna. Emblazoned in black on the chest of his dad's white T-shirt were the words "KGB is for me." Nathan knew his dad had picked up the shirt at a CIA function and that the back of it read, "CIA all the way." But his old man would forever be remembered as the Russian mole with the KGB T-shirt. Nathan now wondered if he might be remembered as the spy's son with the "fugitive" shirt.

Garth and Cooney led Nathan downstairs, where he could see an agent poring through his Chevy. Other agents carried out bagfuls of his belongings, including his passport and laptop.

The agents handed Nathan their business cards, thanked him for his help, and headed for their car. It was long after dark, about eight hours after they first banged on his door.

Monty Waldron was having a helluva week. The young FBI agent, just a little more than a year out of Quantico, had spent the last few days knocking on doors with a swarm of more than two hundred pissed-off cops and federal agents. Three days earlier, a pair of antigovernment wing-nuts planted a bomb outside a bank in Woodburn, Oregon. The device blew up when an Oregon State Police explosives expert tried to take it apart, thinking it was a hoax. The explosion killed the state trooper and a police captain, and it maimed the local police chief. Authorities would eventually identify Bruce Turnidge and his son, Joshua, as the culprits, and a jury would send them to death row.

Waldron had been pulled off the case to drive to Sheridan and toss Jim's cell for evidence. Until that day, he'd never heard of Jim Nicholson. He met with Payne and presented her with the warrant to search Jim's belongings, explaining that they needed to do it covertly. Payne arranged to clear every prisoner from Unit 4-B, Jim's cellblock. It was lunchtime when Waldron, accompanied by Payne and an evidence technician, reached cell 205L. Jim shared the space with a younger prisoner, Kyle Minchey, who was serving time for stealing cash, guns, and a car from his father-in-law's home. Waldron began to bag and tag some of Jim's papers, an address book, and a Swintec 7000 typewriter cartridge.

Detectives of yesteryear sometimes got lucky by laying out their suspects' typewriter ribbons and reading the keystrokes backward. Federal agents in Oregon had once used the technique to take down legendary ecoterrorist Rod Coronado, who had eluded authorities while sinking whaling vessels in Iceland and launching a multistate firebombing campaign against the fur industry. The feds found Coronado's typewriter ribbon in a storage locker in the little town of Talent and reconstructed a letter in which he sought funding for his arsons. FBI analysts at Quantico would similarly read Jim's typewriter tape in reverse, sending Jensen a thick paper report on its contents. But it would turn up nothing incriminating.

Jensen drove to the prison that morning with Tony Buckmeier, a counterespionage supervisor from FBI headquarters who had played a material role in Jim's previous espionage case. Buckmeier had spent the last two decades poking into spy cases involving Russians and Cubans, as well as ferreting out media leakers, from an office in the Hoover Building. He flew to Oregon to take part in the bureau's new case against Jim, mostly because of his vast knowledge of the former CIA man and a lot of guys like him. Buckmeier was an excellent choice to put in an interview room with Jim, especially in the off chance he coughed up the oyster about his latest crimes and started naming Russian spies.

Buckmeier and Jensen took seats together at a table in a private room next to the prison visitation center. Corrections officers brought

Jim in, where the agents introduced themselves. Jensen played things folksy. He told Jim that, as he knew, the CIA analyzed all his mail. Well, he said, some of the agency personnel back East had seen some anomalies in his correspondence.

"This stuff flows downhill," Jensen explained, trying to sound like a weary bureaucrat trying to clear up a few things up before heading home to the wife. "I'm here to pester you about it." Jensen told Jim it was the letter he'd written to Nathan that August that had caught the CIA's eyes. He reminded Jim that the letter went six pages, outlining his health and a whole lot of information about his kids' financial troubles. "I gotta tell you," Jensen said, "it would have caught my attention, too."

He handed Jim a photocopy of the curious letter, and Jim put on his reading glasses. The former CIA man told the FBI agents they had it all wrong—this letter was little more than a journal entry intended to document his good health.

Jensen gave him a puzzled look.

"Really?" he said. "That's funny."

Jensen placed a postcard on the table under Jim's nose.

"Greetings from CYPRUS," it read in big yellow letters. "The Island of Aphrodite."

Classic Jensen. It was his hole card. He had carried it in to get a read on Jim's expression the instant he recognized, once again, that the FBI had been through his underwear drawers. Jensen and Buckmeier hoped that literally laying their card on the table might put him on his heels. Jim studied the card for a long moment, looking stricken.

Jensen seized on Jim's discomfort by outlining what they already knew: Nathan had met with a Russian spy on three continents, and it was clear that Jim was pulling the strings. Jensen told him that he and Nathan were suspected of acting as agents of a foreign government and laundering the proceeds. That very day, he said, agents were searching Nathan's home and car, along with Nick and Betty's house, for evidence of their crimes.

Jim interjected, "Are you holding Nathan?"

Jensen told Jim that Nathan wasn't under arrest and neither was he. But he assured Jim the government had enough evidence to file felony charges.

"I don't believe he has committed a crime," Jim said. "Don't you have to have him doing something with a foreign agent?"

Jensen and Buckmeier betrayed nothing. They didn't say a word about the surveillance team in Nicosia. They had all the video they needed of Nathan and his Russian buddy in front of the T.G.I. Friday's, his son ducking into the backseat of a blue sedan.

"We're not getting into a legal debate," Jensen said.

He told Jim he wanted to ask more questions about the letter, but first he had to read him his Miranda rights.

"If you're charging me with a crime," Jim said, "I need to have an attorney."

The agents assured him he wasn't charged with a crime.

Jim explained that Nathan had traveled abroad to meet Army buddies with money he had saved from the military and a couple of recent jobs.

Jensen looked Jim in the eyes and played the shame card, saying he could save his kid from a raft of shit.

"It's time to cowboy up," he said.

Jim's voice box tightened and his eyes glistened.

"I'd do anything for my children," he said.

Yeah, Jensen thought, *like turn your kid into a Russian spy*.

Jensen said they couldn't talk further until they read him his rights.

"You've clearly been watching him very closely," Jim said. He told the agents it was apparent they were trying to implicate him and Nathan in a crime. Jim said he personally had no quarrel answering their questions, but he wanted to look out for his son. He sealed his speech with words he knew would end the conversation.

"I'd like a lawyer."

"Sorry to hear that," Jensen said.

The agents handed Jim over to corrections officers, who took him to the hole. There Jim would spend twenty-three hours a day alone with his thoughts.

Jensen and Buckmeier made their way to Jim's cell, where they joined Waldron in picking through their subject's things. They leafed through several books, including *The Thompson Chain-Reference Study Bible;* the *New Spirit-Filled Life Bible;* and *Discipleship Essentials: A Guide to Building Your Life in Christ.* One of the bibles was dog-eared, underlined, highlighted, and annotated in the margins by Jim's hand in such a way that it appeared to be code. The agents also seized a language book.

Jim was learning Russian.

Nathan waited until the FBI team cleared out of his apartment to check his voice mail. He listened to the first message, the one from Cooney as he stood on the porch. Cooney had pulled one of the oldest ruses in the FBI playbook, pretending to be a tow truck operator about to haul off his Chevy.

Nathan dialed Star first.

"Nathan, are you OK?" she asked in a panic.

"Yeah, I'm OK. Are you OK?"

"I'm good," she said. "What's up with the FBI?"

"Well, it's kind of a long story, to be honest with you."

Star asked if he was in jail.

"No," he said. "I wouldn't be calling from my cell phone if I was in jail."

"Are they gonna put you in jail?"

"No, no, no. I'm not going anywhere."

"You're not?"

"No."

"I've been *very worried*," she said.

"So has everyone else," Nathan said. Laughing nervously, he told Star that their cousins were heading over to his apartment to check on him.

Star was at her place with her new boyfriend, Josh. She told her brother the FBI had taken down Josh's name and Social Security number.

"They what?!"

"Yeah," Star said, "'cause he was here when they came."

"Oh my God. Is he there right now?"

"Yeah," Star said.

"Tell him I'm *so* sorry to have him, um, meet my family in such a manner."

Star handed the phone to Josh, and Nathan apologized for their weird introduction.

"Yeah," said Josh. "Not a problem."

"I bet that's quite the shock there."

Josh said Star had given him the skinny on the Nicholson family history, so the FBI's sudden appearance wasn't entirely out of the blue.

Nathan laughed, playing along: "Oh, you know, just regular business."

"Standard procedure," Josh said, laughing.

"I'm really kind of embarrassed you had to go through that there. I apologize, once again."

"Not a problem, man."

"Nice to meet you anyway," Nathan said.

"Awright," he said. "Here's your sister."

Star then blurted out the question on everyone's mind.

"So what *happened*?!"

"Holy cow," Nathan said. "Well, it's a really long story. I don't know if you want to spend time on the phone right now when your boyfriend's there or not."

"We're watching *Grumpier Old Men*," she said, her tone suggesting the movie could wait.

"OK," Nathan said. "I'll tell you what I can before the cousins head over."

"OK."

He began by explaining he had just been trying to help the family.

"Traveled to several places," he said. "And, uh, I apologize for lying about who I was seeing."

"You lied?!"

Star was hurt. Nathan rarely lied.

"Uhhh," he said with a painful sigh. "I'm sorry. You know, um, it wasn't that I didn't feel I could trust you guys or anything. It was only for the sole purpose to try to protect you guys."

"OK, so the FBI is OK with you?"

"Yeah," he said, "they're OK with me. I'm not going to prison or anything like that. But what was going on is, I was transporting some information . . . and, uh, you know, getting paid for it. . . . And that's what the whole deal was about."

"Are you a snitch?"

"Am I a snitch? No! No, no, no."

"You're not a professional snitch?"

"I don't even know what the information was."

"Whose information was it for?"

"Well," Nathan said. He dreaded this. "It was—it was for the Russians."

"Dude!"

"But um, you know, it was nothing illegal or anything like that."

"'Nothing illegal'?"

"If it was, I'd be in prison."

"OK."

"OK? So there's nothing to worry about as far as that goes."

"OK."

That's all it was, Nathan said, explaining that he went to Mexico twice, and to Peru. Star knew none of this.

"Dude!"

"And to Cyprus. Which was this last time here."

"Dude! Dude!"

"Well, I'm telling you what it is," he intoned, "I'm telling you what it is. I'm sorry you had to find out this way. We were planning on telling you when it was all said and done."

"Uh-huh."

"The time obviously came quite a bit sooner than was anticipated." He explained that the FBI had carted off some of his things, including his computer and passport.

"Dude," Star said, "you're going to crash."

"I know. But they left my TV—and my Wii."

"Well, yeah," she said, "those don't have any information in 'em."

Star asked if the FBI would return his things.

"They should, 'cause there's no information on any of those things."

"Yeah," she said. "But last time something like that happened, we never got anything back."

Nathan explained that on the way home from Cyprus, he'd been stopped at the airport in New York. This was because he was flying home from Turkey, a high-drug-trafficking area.

Star tried to lighten the mood.

"We would prefer you to be a gigolo."

Nathan laughed and reassured Star he wasn't going to jail, and that he still had his car.

"Did they make noises about throwing you in jail?"

"No," he said. "They were all very polite, very well mannered."

Star said the FBI sent two female agents to her place, and they were mean.

"Aw, Sis, I'm sorry."

Star, clearly looking for reassurance, asked again if he was OK.

"I'm doin' all right," he said. "You know, just a little concerned about *Christmas* now because I was planning on using that money for presents."

"They took your Christmas money?"

"Yeah," he said, "because the information I gave the Russians was, um, worth ten thousand dollars."

"Aw, dude!"

"And I was planning on giving you and Jeremi some of that money."

"Aw, dude. No, no, no!"

"Like the past years, and, uh . . ."

Suddenly it was becoming clear to Star. The money that had helped her and Jeremi stay afloat financially during the hard times of the last couple of years had not come from her grandparents—it had come from the Russians, in payments to her baby brother.

"That was you?!"

"Yep."

"Dude! You're not supposed to do that. Thank you. Don't think that I don't appreciate it. But, but, but, you know, *seriously.* It just sounds kind of like what Daddy did."

"Well," he said, "I understand that."

He explained that all he had done was pass information to the Russians on the details leading up to their dad's arrest. Nothing big, he said.

Star sighed deeply.

Nathan said the information was to help the Russians check their own security, to see where they went wrong.

"You're sure it's not illegal?"

"I'm positive," he said. "I'm so sorry for having you worry so much. And once again, I'm sorry for lying."

"That's OK, dude. But shame on you."

They talked about Christmas, which was huge to Nathan and his siblings. When they were little, it meant their dad was home, the tree was buried in presents, and they were safe.

"I love you, dude," Star said.

"Love you, too, Sis. And enjoy your little visit there."

Before they hung up, Nathan tried to lighten the mood with his impression of Josh: "Hey, Star, how's it going? What, the FBI? They want my Social Security number?"

There was a pause as Nathan reflected.

"That poor guy," he said.

"Yeah," Star said, clearly unamused.

Nathan turned morose. "My poor family."

"Be *good*," Star said.

"Well, you know," he said with a laugh, "our family's full of adventures, right?"

Later that night, Nathan learned that Jim had been put in the hole, and he blamed himself for his dad's miseries. He could only imagine the dank confines of Jim's isolation, a small bed in a cold concrete cell, cut off from his family and his close circle of inmate friends. Nathan's own comforts, a warm bed in a house full of food, suddenly seemed too good for him. So he punished himself. He stalked into his bedroom and yanked the comforter and sheets off his bed and carried them to the living room. There he slept on the floor, hating himself.

"I felt equally responsible for what had happened," he told me, "and I didn't feel that it would be fair if I wasn't disciplined."

Discipline was on the way.

For many months, a federal grand jury had convened secretly in Portland to review the FBI's evidence against the Nicholsons. Jurors came to view Jim as a driven spy willing to sacrifice his own son to build himself up. They wondered how a father could rope his flesh and blood into such a mess. Many of them felt sorry for Nathan, and loathed Jim.

"There was zero empathy for that guy in that room," grand juror Dave Clemans recalled. Nathan seemed so naïve and gullible, said Clemans, who worked as a surgical nurse. It was easy to feel bad about what Jim had done to his boy. During his eighteen-month term as a grand juror, Clemans had heard the government's evidence in hundreds of criminal prosecutions. There was never a time that he doubted the FBI's case against Jim. During an interview, Clemans asked if I had ever heard the saying, "You can indict a ham sandwich." *Only about a million times,* I was thinking. "Well," he said, "that ham sandwich is fucking *guilty*."

Jim mailed Nathan a letter from the hole on January 9. "My Dear Son (and treasure of my heart)," it began, "I have been going through near total torment in worry over you these past four weeks." The prison had cut off Jim's phone and visitation privileges, and he had not heard from Nathan. He had learned just the day before from his old attorney Jon Shapiro that Nathan wasn't in custody. But it was killing him to think about what was ahead. "I am a broken man—nothing but shattered shards on the potter's floor," he wrote.

"Son, I know you can't talk about stuff now as everything is probably stirred up, but are you OK? Are you hurt in any way? I know how they are and I'm sure they probably tried to terrify you, bully you and all that. I don't know what's going on but I know *you* and you are selfless, noble, kind and good to the core."

Now Jim offered his son advice, telling him to go to the college's legal aid office to prepare paperwork granting power of attorney to Star, Laurie, or Nick. He told Nathan to think about moving in with his grandparents or one of his cousins until things blew over, and get his finances in order. "We'll get some money on your account if you get stuck in a jail so you can buy shower shoes, etc. (Don't go barefoot into a prison shower if you can help it.) . . . No matter what, this too will pass . . . Remember, God is working here and my love for you is beyond description. I just hope my phone and visiting privileges are restored soon. I need to hold on to you. Love You Son, Pa."

Jim's letter would not reach Nathan for more than five years.

Cut off from his father, stung by the ruinous turn of events, Nathan buried himself in the opening weeks of the winter school term, and he clung to his family and friends.

He shot a text to Camilla Beavers on January 11, 2009, trying to learn when she was heading back to Oregon from her new home in Austin, Texas. Nathan's unrequited crush was turning twenty-two at the end of the month, and he wanted to take her out with friends to celebrate. His text included a cryptic line about hoping he wasn't in jail by then.

His phone rang almost immediately.

"Explain," Beavers began.

"Explain? It's a long story, really."

"Well, I have about fifteen minutes for you to explain it. Now go."

Nathan told her the basics. The Russians. The travel. The money. He said the Russians had been nice to him and asked if he might consider moving to Mexico City, where he could attend school on Moscow's dime. But he'd declined their generosity, saying the VA already paid for his schooling.

"My friend's a spy," Beavers declared. "Not a spy, you're just . . ."

"I'm just the messenger."

Nathan told her about the grand jury that was meeting in Portland. His grandparents were supposed to testify in a couple of days.

"I'm one hundred percent sure that they are going to be able to make a case out of it," he said. "Obviously they're going to find me guilty, because I already said, 'Hey, I did all this.'"

Nathan explained that he didn't know what the government planned for him. At that hour, he didn't know whether he was going to prison or whether the FBI might consider flipping him as a double agent. He thought perhaps the agents might send him to his scheduled meeting with the Russians in Slovakia to help the bureau identify his handler, George.

"You're gonna be a spy's spy?"

"I don't know."

Nathan told Beavers the FBI searched his home and car, and froze his bank account.

"In hindsight," he said, "I didn't really think I was doing anything wrong."

Beavers then asked what Jim had done to land in prison.

"Well, he gave information to the Russians. ..."

"Yeah, but like what type of information?"

"Nothing that jeopardized any lives, or anything like that," he said. "I don't really know one hundred percent what it was."

Nathan honestly didn't know the half of it. He never looked deep into the records of his dad's arrest and conviction. At twelve, when the feds put his father away, Nathan put on blinders rather than shatter his comfortable illusions about his dad. Did he really need to know the intimate details of Jim's betrayals? It would have been searing to learn that during the years he was drawing closest to his father—from ten to twelve—his old man was quietly betraying his nation's secrets to the likes of Sergei Polyakov. It had been bad enough to see a *GQ* magazine headline that dubbed his dad "The Spy Who Sold the Farm." Did he really need to know that Russia's money paid for the family trip to Disneyland?

Beavers couldn't understand why Nathan was in trouble.

"We're not, like, against the Russians, are we?" she asked. "I mean, last time I knew we weren't worried about that at all."

"We really aren't," Nathan said. He explained that Hollywood plays up U.S. government paranoia about Russia.

"I've never been paranoid against Russia," she said.

"Yeah, yeah," Nathan said. "And they're cool people, they're *really* cool people."

"Yeah," Beavers said, "and they have cool accents."

"*Yeah*, they do."

Nathan blurted out that the Russians' cash payments were gifts, and there was a remote chance the FBI would give him the money back.

"Which," he said, "would be freakin' sweet."

Beavers laughed. She was curious about the messages Nathan couriered between his dad and the Russians. She wondered if Jim might have passed the notes—through him—in code.

Nathan said he doubted it.

"Unless you're just not aware of it," she said.

"Yeah," he said. "Unless I'm just so naïve and oblivious to everything."

Beavers told him she had to get back to work. She was on break at LensCrafters.

"Keep me updated," she said, "on the whole you-might-be-going-to-federal-prison thing."

Nathan laughed. "Hopefully not," he said.

Not long after that conversation, a man popped into LensCrafters wearing jeans and carrying a file folder. *Great,* Beavers thought, *another customer who thinks his prescription is the Holy Grail.* The man introduced himself as an FBI agent and asked if they might talk. They took seats in a back office, and he asked her about a bracelet Nathan had given her. He seemed surprised she was wearing it.

The agent asked Beavers about Nathan's mentioning something in their recent phone call about the FBI's seizure of his computer. Beavers had made a joke about all the porn Nathan downloaded. Now the agent, scribbling notes, was asking about Nathan's religious faith, and it occurred to Beavers that he was trying to get her to say something bad about Nathan. She was furious. Nathan was one of her best friends, a sweet-natured guy without an ounce of guile. It was a short interview. On his way out, the FBI man handed her a card in case she remembered anything.

Nathan learned from his grandparents that his dad was worried sick about him. He felt certain that any letter he mailed to Jim would be returned. But on January 18, 2009, he wrote his father anyway.

"Dear Pa, I'm sorry. I'm sorry for all of the trouble I've caused you and our family. I don't know what is going to happen to me—No one seems to have any answers for me." He let his dad know that he was still in school, and living cheaply. "I see this time period as 'pruning from God.' It hurts, and our lives go into a bit of shock—but as a result we will bear more fruit than before! . . . Try to keep your spirits up—God has not forsaken us. I love you, Pa, and I am proud to be your son! . . . Surely God is watching over us to give us what we need to carry on! *Hold Fast!* Your loving son, Nathan."

It's unclear whether Jim ever received the letter.

On the afternoon of January 28, 2009, a gray and gusty Wednesday, Jared Garth rapped on Nathan's apartment door. He stood for a moment before knocking again. Nathan roused himself from a catnap on the living room floor to answer the door. He instantly recognized Garth as one of the FBI agents who had interviewed him there. He didn't know the other agent, Kirk Danielsen.

"Do you know why we're here?" Garth asked.

"Yeah," Nathan said.

Garth delivered the bad news. One day earlier, the grand jury in Portland had handed up an indictment against Nathan and his dad for laundering money, acting as agents of the Russian Federation, and conspiring with each other to commit those crimes. Nathan faced six felony charges, which carried the possibility of decades behind bars.

The agents let Nathan brush his teeth and pull on a pair of jeans. He wore a black T-shirt with a soccer player performing a bicycle kick at the moon. It read, "DARE TO DREAM." Garth allowed Nathan to text Beavers and explain that he couldn't take her to dinner for her birthday, and that it would be a while before he saw her again. "Sorry," he wrote. The agents took Nathan's phone, keys, and wallet, which held three dollars. Garth pulled out the FBI's standard Miranda form, an FD-395, and read him his rights. He asked Nathan if he understood them.

"Yes," he said. "I'd like to speak with a lawyer."

Garth handed him the form to sign. Nathan was so nervous he accidentally scrawled his name on the line waiving his rights to speak with a lawyer. Garth caught the error and let Nathan scratch out his name. When he signed the correct line, Garth cuffed Nathan's wrists behind him. The agents locked his apartment door and walked him downstairs to a dark blue Ford Crown Victoria, the classic cop car. Danielsen crawled in next to Nathan in the backseat.

They were just under way on the 115-mile drive to Portland when Nathan asked what would happen to him. Garth said he was taking him to the Justice Center Jail, and that he would be appointed a lawyer from the Federal Public Defender's Office. Nathan would appear before a U.S. magistrate judge the next day.

Heading north on I-5, Garth couldn't resist asking Nathan if he remembered his face from the Houston airport. He explained that he'd

been standing a few feet away when Customs officers searched Nathan's
bags on his way home from Peru. Nathan didn't remember seeing him.

"How long were you guys investigating me?"

"For a while," Garth said.

He asked Nathan whether he'd ever read up on his father's arrest in
1996. Nathan said he'd done enough reading online to find conflicting
accounts of how much money the Russians paid his father. Nathan's
take on the conversation was that the agents thought he was just like
Jim, and that they meant to put him in prison. He remembered that
after his dad's arrest, Jeremi had given his dad a lecture on his betrayal.
Nathan could only imagine how Jeremi would treat him now.

"I met your friend Jesse," Garth said. "He's got selective memory."

Nathan knew the FBI had interviewed Jesse, who had joined him
on the second trip to San Francisco with his cousin Danielle. He told
the agents neither of them was involved in any way with the Russians.

"I want you to know that I had them drop me off a couple of blocks
from the consulate in San Francisco," Nathan said. "I didn't want it to
be obvious. I think they stayed in the car a few blocks away."

Farther up the interstate, Danielsen asked Nathan why he had
been sleeping on the floor of his apartment. Nathan started to explain
that it felt wrong to sleep in comfort with his dad laying his head in
an isolation cell. But his throat tightened as he talked, and he felt tears
burning down his face. The agents changed the subject.

Garth steered the Crown Vic into downtown Portland shortly
before 3 p.m., and eased down Second Avenue, a couple of blocks from
the Willamette River. He turned into the opening of an underground
parking area, wending into the bowels of the Justice Center, stopping
at a pair of tall, yellow folding gates. The agents plucked Nathan out of
the backseat and Garth walked his suspect toward the olive-green door
of the booking room, where he spied another agent turning in a collar
from out on the Umatilla Indian Reservation.

Forced to wait, Garth brought Nathan close for a chat. Garth was
forty-five years old, with kids of his own, old enough to be Nathan's dad.

The veteran agent locked eyes on his suspect and, surprising himself, burst into a lecture.

Garth pointed out that Nathan had slept on the floor in solidarity with his old man. Now here he was, going to jail, for a plot concocted by Jim.

"You might blame your mother for the divorce," Garth said. "But it was your father who sold out his country."

Garth told him his dad got a fair deal twelve years back, a chance to serve his time in Oregon and see his kids on weekends. Instead, he used the training he got in the CIA to manipulate his own son.

Nathan wept.

"It's time," Garth said, "for you to be your own man."

At 2:56 p.m., Nathan stood at a gray desk, where booking staffers wearing latex gloves patted him down for weapons, took a "slap print" of four fingers, and began a battery of questions that included, "Are you feeling suicidal?" The next few minutes were a blur of shame. They moved Nathan to a brightly lit photo station with sea-foam green walls. A police ID tech stood him in front of a gray background and told him to look up. Nathan stared at the camera, a pair of comic goggle eyeballs taped above its lens. The camera often captured perps with expressions of bewilderment, anger, or mirth. Nathan's mug shot—with his pursed lips, razor-cut hair, and red-eyed anguish—came out another way.

He looked as if he had just walked off a battlefield.

17

Inmate 734520

"When it comes to espionage, we'll never forgive, we'll never forget."
—Daniel Lee Cloyd, U.S. counterintelligence official

Portland, Oregon, early 2009

After spending half his life visiting the old man behind bars, Nathan got his own taste of the caged world in a concrete tower called the Justice Center Jail. His keepers in the downtown lockup dressed him in blue scrubs and heavy rubber slippers made in China. They quartered him in an eighth-floor cell, in a housing area that reeked of disinfectant. Nathan saw from his cell window an eighteen-story federal building partly named after a former member of Congress, Wendell Wyatt, who died that very day at age ninety-one. The voices of men caromed off the jail's sand brown walls, but Nathan had never felt so alone.

Blue pay phones on a nearby wall read "Charge-a-Call." Nathan wanted to phone home—to Laurie, Star, Jeremi, anyone—just to let them know what had become of him. But he had no number to call. Like many Generation Xers, Nathan dialed names out of the address book on his cellular phone. Without his cell, he was completely cut off. He placed a call to the one number he'd been given, the Oregon Federal Public Defender's Office, which occupied a high-rise a few hundred yards away. But an after-hours recording said the office was closed. Nathan put his head down that night on a mattress so thin it felt harder than the carpeted floor he'd slept on in his apartment. He wore a white jail-issue wristband with his inmate ID: 734520.

The following morning, jailers herded Nathan and other inmates into the bowels of the jail and handed them sack lunches to eat before their court appearances. Deputy U.S. marshals put Nathan in what they call a "three-piece suit"—handcuffs, leg irons, and belly chain—and loaded him into a fourteen-passenger van. The trip that followed was unique to inmates appearing in federal court. The van pulled out of the underground garage, turned left, and traveled a shade over a hundred yards to a sally port, where buzzers sounded and the van descended into the bowels of the Mark O. Hatfield U.S. Courthouse.

Fifty miles away, deputy U.S. marshals prepared to bring Jim to court under full motorcade. They cuffed and shackled him, seating him in the back of an unmarked car they call a "slick top." Jim's transport headed east toward Portland, trailed by a Chevy Suburban loaded with five heavily armed deputy marshals. Scott Jensen, the FBI agent who had slipped the "Greetings from CYPRUS" card under Jim's nose, sat in the front seat of the lead car. Jensen hoped his suspect might volunteer a few thoughts on the ride. But Jim ignored Jensen, clearly annoyed by his presence.

It had been a hectic few hours at the office of the Federal Public Defender, which sat in a high-rise across the street from the federal courthouse. A panicked e-mail that morning alerted staffers that they would handle the defense of a father-son duo in a spy case bound for the nightly news. Investigators spent the early part of the day boning up on Jim's previous espionage to prepare for the arraignment.

Deputy marshals locked Nathan in an interview room to meet his lawyer, Thomas E. Price. The two found themselves on opposite sides of a heavy screen. Price was a slender man with wavy salt-and-pepper hair. The fifty-year-old lawyer had spent half his life as a mental health counselor and private criminal defense lawyer. Now he was working his first "duty call," representing a group of criminals, one by one, as they prepared for appearances in Mag Court. Picking up the Nicholson assignment was luck-of-the-draw for Price, putting him squarely in the middle of a huge case on his first week as a lawyer in the Federal Public Defender's Office.

Price explained to Nathan that at 1:30 p.m. they would appear together with Judge Janice M. Stewart, a federal magistrate, and he would enter a plea to the criminal charges. The answer, Price hastened to add, was "Not guilty." He told Nathan not to utter a word during the Mag Court proceeding; he would do the talking for both of them. Price would ask for a jury trial. Nathan would not see his father, who would be arraigned separately. It would be a swift proceeding, Price explained. Later they would meet to plan his defense.

Nathan thanked him profusely.

Price's first-blush impression, based on the government indictment and the FBI's forty-eight-page criminal complaint affidavit, was that Nathan was in a world of hurt. Nathan's confession to the FBI put the defense in a deep hole right from the drop. That afternoon he watched his young client shuffle into Stewart's eleventh-floor courtroom in ankle chains. Nathan stole a look into the gallery for a friendly face, spotting Jared Garth in the back of the courtroom with other FBI agents. "Eyes front," a deputy marshal warned him. The arraignment was over in minutes. Nathan reached the jail before dinner.

Supervisors in the Public Defender's Office designated Price as Nathan's primary counsel. This meant the office would have to farm out Jim's defense to a lawyer in private practice, because it is a conflict of interest for one law office to represent multiple defendants in the same case. Codefendants often turned on each other—even fathers and sons.

Steven T. Wax supervised a staff of two dozen lawyers in Oregon's Federal Public Defender's Office, which he opened in 1983. He phoned Sam Kauffman, who worked at the Portland law firm of Garvey Schubert Barer, and asked if he would represent Jim. Kauffman, who was on a panel of lawyers appointed to serve as court-appointed counsel for indigent defendants, already held a security clearance. Taking on a high-profile client such as Jim didn't hurt his public profile, but the downside was the lousy remuneration. The U.S. Judiciary paid its contract lawyers about $100 an hour, compared with the $320-an-hour rate Sam charged his regular GSB clientele. For the second time in Jim's criminal career, he got top-flight legal defense paid for by the country he betrayed.

Kauffman was a chiseled ultra-distance runner who liked the in-tellectual stimulation of complicated national security cases. He had a big, boyish smile, but you rarely saw it in court. He had spent the last several years defending Guantánamo detainees, cops accused of criminal misconduct, and corporate officers suspected of antitrust violations. He had a reputation as a tough litigator in corporate cases, the guy who could negotiate behind the scenes to keep his clients out of jail and their names out of the news.

Jim's 1997 conviction for conspiracy to commit espionage ensured that he would serve prison time into his sixties. It would be up to Kauff-man to defend Jim against the new charges, which carried the very real chance that his client would never take another breath in the free world.

Nathan faced the possibility that he would give his youth to the U.S. Bureau of Prisons. The money-laundering charges alone carried up to twenty years in prison, and a furious judge, under the right condi-tions, could potentially stack them in a way that would put him away for decades.

Wax picked a seasoned hand as Price's co-counsel in Nathan's defense. Gerald "Jerry" Needham had served as a defense lawyer for twenty-six years, more than half of that time on Wax's watch. Needham, a native New Yorker with an accent straight out of Queens, had been known during his formative years with the Legal Aid Society in Man-hattan for his cutthroat cross-examinations. He didn't have an ounce of bullshit in him.

Neither Price nor Needham had ever tried a national security case. But their office held a natural skepticism for FBI operations, a trickle-down of distrust from the top. Wax's award-winning 2008 book *Kafka Comes to America: Fighting for Justice in the War on Terror* chronicled stories of two clients whose lives were derailed in the name of national security. One was Brandon Mayfield, an Oregon lawyer and Sunni Muslim wrongly jailed as a suspect in the 2004 Madrid commuter train bombings. The FBI mistakenly matched Mayfield's fingerprints to those lifted from a bag of bomb detonators in Madrid. They bugged his bedroom, tapped his phones, and accused Mayfield of mass murder. The government later acknowledged its error, freed Mayfield, apologized, and paid him and his family $2 million to settle a lawsuit.

Nathan had spent so much time visiting his dad behind bars, the penned-in world seemed almost natural. But being locked in a jail was jarring. He felt cut off from everything and everyone he knew. He still hadn't heard from his family. His mother had chewed him out on the phone after the FBI came to visit, as had Jeremi. Nathan was ashamed of himself and began to think jail was precisely where he belonged.

Fifteen minutes in the Justice Center Jail is all it takes to catch up on the state of American corrections, a business based on minimalism and risk management. Inmates sleep on thin mattresses laid over concrete platforms, eliminating the need for box springs. They brush their teeth and move their bowels on a sink-and-toilet combination that looks like an abstract sculpture in stainless steel. Seats in common areas are attached to tabletops with built-in chessboards so that no one gets beaten to death with a stool. Even the undergarments—pink and unadorned—serve as minimalistic cost savers. Previous runs of T-shirts—white with the words "Multnomah County JAIL" stenciled on them—walked off on the backs of local thugs who wore them for street cred.

Nathan fell into the familiar rhythms of confinement, his hours metered by the movement of food carts, the brightening and dimming of fluorescent lights, and the ceaseless murmur of men's voices. Now he appreciated the terrible loneliness his dad had lived under all these years. Like Jim, Nathan prayed for a miracle and killed time. He read, played chess, and shot hoops in an open-air gym. He prayed most evenings with other Christians. The meals were a dark comedy. Nathan would recall the stinging taste of noodles kept so long in containers they had fermented.

The day after Nathan's arraignment, Tom Price and defense investigator Wendy Kunkel paid him a visit to talk about his case. Nathan was completely freaked out. "He was sobbing," Kunkel recalled, and was astounded to be facing prison time. Nathan told Price and Kunkel that his father promised him their scheme with the Russians wasn't illegal. "What have I done?" he asked her. "I love this country!" It was clear to Kunkel that Nathan was in deep denial, having failed to grasp that his principle betrayer was his own dad.

The following day, January 31, 2009, Nathan was summoned to the visiting room, where he found Star, Laurie, and her husband, Bill. They all had a good cry. Nathan could see that his family was worried sick about him, and he tried to cheer them up. He told them he was going to be fine and not to worry. But it broke Star's heart to see her brother wearing jail scrubs. Bill and Laurie were going through a rough patch financially, and Bill had to sell blood to put a little money on Nathan's jail commissary account.

On the ninth day of February, sheriff's deputies mustered Nathan and other inmates at 5 a.m. They shackled their prisoners and herded them into a green Freightliner truck for the drive to Multnomah County's Inverness Jail, which is designed for long-term inmates. Deputies put Nathan in a dormitory that held fifty-nine prisoners. The jail opened in 1988, a dozen miles from downtown near a scenic crook of the Columbia River and the sandy beaches of Government Island. But Nathan's dorm overlooked a walled-off basketball court with a metal grate over the top. He could see daylight from the window, but the days were short and gray.

Nathan's legal team worried he might commit suicide. The group now included three full-time investigators, all of them mothers. The mom squad made Nathan a special project, popping by the jail as often as they could to keep his spirits up. None of the women were going to nominate Jim as father of the year. They were floored by Jim's betrayal of his son, and they weren't certain how to break it to Nathan how badly he'd been used.

"As a mother," Kunkel told me, "I was furious. All three of us were fit to be tied."

They wondered why Nathan failed to comprehend his father's betrayals. Kunkel saw a flicker of recognition in Nathan's eyes during some of their conversations at Inverness, a hint that he was coming to grips with what his dad had done. But she soon came to understand his blind loyalty to Jim. She recalled one particular meeting, sitting in a visiting room as other inmates passed their window. Nathan told her the story of that day at Fort Bragg when he nearly slit his wrists. He told her about the call from Jim that jarred him from his suicidal fugue. Nathan put his head on the table and wept.

"I felt I owed him my life," he said.

Kunkel teared up.

"You think you owed him your life?"

"Yeah."

Members of Nathan's legal team talked about him constantly, wondering if he would ever come to terms with how wickedly his father had worked him over. In their minds, Jim had treated his boy like one of the garden-variety foreign assets he'd handled overseas. He had put his boy in play in a dangerous game. And for what? To pull the wool over the government's eyes? To massage his magnificent ego? The defense team would eventually have to broach these concepts with Nathan to show him that Jim had pulled his strings like a puppet master. They knew that Nathan and Jim—should they go to trial—would probably cross swords.

The defense's immediate strategy was to prove Nathan could be trusted on the other side of the bars. The defense team knew they would get a much-needed boost if they could persuade a judge to cut him loose from jail as he awaited trial. This would give lawyers and investigators twenty-four-hour access to their client. Instead of driving to the jail and navigating a metal detector to ask him questions, they could talk to him face-to-face.

But the key reason to get him out was to rehabilitate his character in court, show he was a good guy. Springing him from the jail would build momentum. If Nathan was released and kept his nose clean, the judge would almost certainly take that into consideration and reward him with a lighter sentence. They also knew that if Nathan fled, he was going to prison for a long time.

Nathan's trial was set to begin on the last day of March, less than two months away. But the date was a placeholder. The pace of national security cases in Oregon's federal courts was nothing like those in the Eastern District of Virginia, where Jim had been convicted nearly a dozen years before. Spies and terrorists were regular features on Virginia's "Rocket Docket." But national security cases were rarer in Oregon, and federal judges there had much less experience dealing with highly classified files.

The Justice Department was preparing to disclose thousands of pages of evidence to the Nicholsons' defense teams, a mountain of discovery that would include the FBI's massive trove of investigative files, wiretaps, and video surveillance recordings, and the CIA's storehouse of Jim's phone calls and correspondence dating back to 1997. Jim's letters, handed over by the CIA, ran more than eleven thousand pages. There was so much work ahead for lawyers and investigators on both sides that the judge eventually reset the Nicholsons' trial for October 27. In the meantime, the judge docketed a hearing to decide whether Nathan belonged in jail until then.

The Honorable Anna J. Brown, a Clinton appointee, had a reputation as a no-nonsense judge with a maternal streak. Brown seemed to take dizzying steps to make sure jurors and defendants fully understood the procedures in her courtroom, the rulings she made, and what they meant. Her deliberate nature was sometimes read as sloth by eye-rolling lawyers who preferred more expeditious proceedings. But rarely, if ever, did her decisions need clarification.

Brown's meticulous nature may have been an inheritance. She grew up in Portland answering her German-speaking parents' questions in English to help them learn the language. She was the first American-born citizen in her family, which fled East Prussia during World War II, dodging the Red Army on its way to Germany. Seven years after the war ended, her family sailed to the United States aboard the *Homeland*, passing through Ellis Island and eventually settling in Portland.

On the morning of March 31, 2009, Brown entered her courtroom in a black judicial robe and took her seat to hear arguments on Nathan's detention. Her hair was short and straight, mostly gray, and her face was broad. She was fifty-six years old, an age where people remind themselves they've accumulated some wisdom, but not all of it. Taped to the penholder on her desk was a slip of white paper from a Chinese fortune cookie. It read, "Keep your feet on the ground even though your friends flatter you."

Brown stared down from her bench at Nathan, sandwiched between his lawyers. Behind him in the gallery sat his mom, Star, Nick and Betty, and more than a dozen other supporters. On the desk in front of Brown was a report recommending that Nathan be released from jail as he awaited trial. The papers had been drafted by a division of the court known as U.S. Probation and Pretrial Services, which had performed a thorough background investigation of Nathan and found he'd pose little or no danger if cut loose. Prosecutors held a different view. They knew a great deal about Nathan's connections, and his tutelage in Jim's school of spycraft, and believed he'd probably flee if the judge set him free. If Nathan bolted for Russia, and was granted asylum, they'd have a tougher time making Jim's charges stick.

The chief prosecutor in the Nicholson case was Assistant U.S. Attorney Pamala Holsinger, an attractive former Marine JAG officer with straight blond hair and a strong jaw. She had blue eyes that she could narrow into an incandescent glare. Holsinger had spent nearly two decades in the Department of Justice prosecuting criminals of every stripe—including terrorists, gangsters, drug traffickers, fraudsters, corrupt public figures, and child-porn collectors. Her opinion of Nathan was that he had performed as his turncoat daddy's little soldier, and she wanted him behind bars.

Holsinger called her first witness, John Cooney, who recounted the FBI's key accusations against Nathan. The veteran agent highlighted the details of Nathan's confession, beginning with the genesis of the father-son plot, the crumpled notes he smuggled out of Sheridan, the cash payments by the friendly Russians, the code names, the Yahoo dead drop, the surveillance detection run in Cyprus, and the coded notes about the meeting in Slovakia that Nathan would never attend.

Prosecutors played much of the wiretapped phone call between Nathan and his sister on the night the FBI searched his apartment. Nathan listened impassively, hearing him tell Star about the messages he passed to the Russians for their father, and Star scolding him: "It just sounds kind of like what Daddy did." His heart dropped, knowing he had publicly humiliated his sister. Prosecutors also played his call with Camilla Beavers. He heard himself describe the Russians as "really cool people" and declare, "Well, obviously they're going to find me guilty."

"Special Agent Cooney," Holsinger said, "through your investigation, was there any indication that any other family members might be involved with the defendant and his father?"

"Yes," Cooney said. He explained that Nathan's impression, based on their interview, was that Jim had discussed their proceeds from the Russians with Nick and Betty. "There's also a notation in the notebook . . . to the effect that the grandparents 'know the situation'; they are trustworthy and will 'help with the cover-up.'"

Nathan's grandparents sat behind him in court. Nick and Betty weren't charged with any crime. But Nathan felt as if he'd thrown them under the bus. He wanted to strangle Cooney.

"In your experience," Holsinger said, "are you aware if there's been situations where the government of Russia has taken in or harbored a fugitive from justice in the United States?"

"Yes," Cooney said. He recounted the case of former CIA officer Edward Lee Howard, who was fired by the agency and fell under investigation by the FBI for suspected espionage on behalf of the Soviet Union. Howard had slipped the FBI's surveillance. "In 1986, he surfaced in Moscow and began to reside in the Soviet Union." (Cooney didn't provide the court with the epilogue to the Howard story: He was reportedly found dead in his dacha in 2002, the victim of a broken neck, having taken a bad fall.)

Holsinger questioned Cooney about foreign diplomatic stations, such as Russian consulates, and the use of passports to leave the United States. Cooney explained that foreign consulates were exempt from the jurisdiction of U.S. laws, and that passports were a convenience for foreign travel, not a necessity. Holsinger was not so subtly telling Judge Brown that if she freed Nathan, he could race over the Canadian or Mexican borders into the arms of his Russian friends.

Jerry Needham began his cross-examination of Cooney by getting the FBI man to acknowledge that Nathan was just twelve years old when his dad was caught spying for Russia and that there was no evidence Nathan took part in those crimes. Needham established that Nathan's travels over the last few years were under his own name, not an alias, and that when the FBI learned Nathan was flying to Cyprus, they let him go.

"You seized his passport in connection with this investigation?"

"That is correct," Cooney said.

"Did the passport stamps or markings on the passport correspond with the information concerning his trips?"

"I did not look at his passport, so I can't answer that question."

"And the passport is in the possession of the FBI?"

"I would assume it's in our evidence, yes."

"OK, and the passport was in his name. Correct?"

"To the best of my knowledge, yes."

"When did you—the FBI—start surveillance of Nathaniel Nicholson?"

Holsinger shot to her feet to object.

The Department of Justice will go to almost any length to hide the genesis of its national security investigations and surveillance operations. Holsinger did not want to compromise the secretive means the FBI had used to identify and snoop on the Nicholsons. She told Judge

Brown it wasn't relevant for the defense to know when the FBI began eavesdropping on Nathan.

The judge asked Needham to explain why it was relevant.

Needham said he wanted to put it on the record that the FBI had been tailing Nathan for many months; if agents thought he was a risk to flee the country, they could have arrested him much sooner.

"Maybe," Needham began, "the agent could just give the court a ballpark area, how long . . ."

Holsinger objected.

"The objection is overruled," Brown said. "Answer the question please."

"By the fall of 2007," Cooney said, "a full investigation into Nathan Nicholson was initiated."

Needham fired away at Cooney, establishing that Nathan had no criminal history, received an honorable discharge from the Army, kept no guns or illegal drugs, attended community college, worked part-time jobs, and was aware several weeks in advance of his arrest that a federal grand jury was deciding whether to charge him. He also established that Nathan had phoned Jared Garth, prior to his arrest, to let him know he was planning on taking a trip to the state of Washington with friends.

"What did Agent Garth tell him?" Needham asked.

"I don't know specifically what he told him," Cooney said, "but he did not tell him *not* to go. I believe he asked him if he planned on leaving the country. And I think apart from that, he just told him to have a good trip."

"And did Mr. Nicholson reply that he had no plans on leaving the country, or words to that effect?"

"I believe he did, yes."

Needham had deftly let Brown know his client made no move toward Canada.

"Isn't it fair to say that from the time period he was interviewed until he was arrested, all of his phone conversations had been monitored?"

"Yes," Cooney said. "I believe that is correct."

Now it was Holsinger's turn. The prosecutor asked Cooney if Jim—in spite of the monitoring of his mails and phone calls—had still found ways to smuggle messages to the Russians.

"That's what our investigation has determined, yes."

"Special Agent Cooney, based on your training and experience, if the Russian government wanted to take care of the family members of one of their most successful and valuable spies, what message would that send to other people they might want to recruit in the future?"

"I believe it would send a message that the Russian government is prepared—and has the capability—to support family members of people who have worked on their behalf."

Needham now questioned Cooney.

"You indicated that the Russian government would somehow want to send a message that they would take care of spies, or something to that effect. Correct?"

"I said that is my belief, yes."

Under questioning, Cooney acknowledged that Moscow had not, as far as he knew, given any money or assistance to the family of former CIA officer Edward Lee Howard.

Tamara Pinkas, one of Nathan's teachers, later took the witness stand as a character witness. She testified that Nathan had been a student of hers for three terms in 2008 at Lane Community College, including six months where he worked as an intern drafter at Burton Saw. He was professional, she said, reliable, responsible, and always made his deadlines.

Assistant U.S. Attorney Ethan D. Knight, Holsinger's co-counsel, cross-examined Pinkas. Knight was a rising star in the U.S. Attorney's office, just thirty-four years old. He had attended Lincoln High School, just up the street, where he was a national schoolboy champion in constitutional law. He was now an adult version of that funny, self-deprecating, mildly nerdy kid in school, the one born with the sardonic string of one-liners.

Knight began by politely questioning Pinkas about Nathan, getting her to acknowledge that she supervised his internship in 2008 but didn't take attendance.

"And during this period," he asked, "you had no knowledge of the fact that he was communicating with agents of the Russian government, did you?"

"Oh, none whatsoever."

"And you had no idea that he actually traveled to Cyprus at the conclusion of his period with Burton Saw?"

"I did not know that."

"Thank you," he said. "No further questions."

It was now Price's turn to flesh out Nathan's good character.

He began by noting that after the FBI questioned Nathan—and continued tapping his phone—his client went nowhere. In fact, he said, the wiretaps proved that Nathan paid his bills, plugged away at school, and tried not to fret about the grand jury.

Knight offered counterpoint.

He said there was no measure that Brown could impose that would prevent Nathan from fleeing. He said Nathan traveled in secret to foreign locales, hid his trips from even those closest to him, and maintained a clandestine relationship with Russians, who even gave him a code name.

"The defendant was effectively, sight unseen, able to walk into a consulate on U.S. soil," Knight said, "identify who he was, and establish a relationship that enabled him on five subsequent occasions to . . . communicate with Russian handlers in four different countries, including the United States, and be protected and . . . receive money and, more importantly, receive instructions for future meetings."

Knight noted that Nathan and his Russian handler had talked about the possibility that Russia would fund his education in Mexico, and that the Russians could provide him safe harbor in any of their diplomatic stations.

"Let me ask you about that, Mr. Knight," Brown said. "The evidence is that the nearest consulate is in San Francisco, and there might be some kind of diplomatic mission, or something to that effect—said Agent Cooney—in Seattle. Yes?"

"Yes."

"So there's not any place of diplomatic refuge in the district of Oregon. Is that fair?"

"Not a location, no."

Brown asked if fitting Nathan with a GPS ankle bracelet, and tracking his movements inside Oregon, would prevent him from heading for a Russian diplomatic establishment in California or Washington, which would take hours by car. If he's in Oregon, she said, the company monitoring his movements—Satellite Tracking of People—would know if he cut the bracelet off or was on the move.

"I'm assuming," Brown said, "that the defendant would have to physically get into the boundaries of the Russian sovereign space— that is, the consulate or some other physical space—in order to be beyond the jurisdiction of the United States government while still on U.S. soil?"

"Yes," Knight said.

"If we can keep him in the District of Oregon, there isn't any way the Russian Federation or some other foreign government can take him from us, can they?"

"Not if he's here they can't."

Knight reiterated his point that by all appearances, Nathan was an upstanding citizen, going to school, keeping in touch with his family, but that in fact, he'd been traveling the world to meet Russian spies.

"The defendant effectively led two different lives," he said, "and is now asking the court to be placed back in the same environment where he was, with essentially the same support network that he lied to repeatedly. . . . This is someone without a criminal history, without contact with the system, who now faces a series of offenses with an aggregate maximum sentence of one hundred years. . . . It's the government's theory—and laid out quite explicitly in the defendant's own statement—that he was receiving money, at the very least, for his father's prior espionage activities, and that the Russian government was now taking care of the family and providing them money."

Price got one last chance to make the case for Nathan's freedom.

He told the court that Nathan didn't flee after learning he might be charged with felony crimes, remained optimistic, assured his family everything would work out, and even considered applying for a VA loan to buy a house in Corvallis so he could transfer from Lane Community College to Oregon State. Price said Nathan was ashamed of himself for putting his family under FBI scrutiny, and that after agents questioned Laurie, she called and chewed him out. What did Nathan do? He wept throughout the call, Price said. Nathan was dejected to learn the FBI had seized Jeremi's bank account and that his actions had cost his brother the chance to become an officer. And, Price added, the very idea that the Russians would plot an escape for Nathan, who knew nothing of any value to them, was beyond speculation.

"It is," he said, "fantasy."

Judge Brown thanked the lawyers for their arguments.

"I want to consider all of the matter you've submitted," she said. "I can't make a decision right now."

Deputy marshals cuffed Nathan and handed him over to jailers. It would take Brown a week to sort through the court papers, listen to the wiretapped calls, and weigh in on whether Nathan was safe to release. Nathan learned his fate in jail, by way of a phone call. His defense team gathered around a speakerphone in their downtown office to tell him the news. Brown was cutting him free to prepare for trial.

On April 10, jailers transferred Nathan downtown, where he processed out, collected his wallet, and walked across the street with a court officer to be fitted with a GPS ankle bracelet. Brown ordered that Nathan spend his days at work or in college classes, or a combination of both. He had to spend his nights at the home of his cousin Destiny Fargher, who lived in the lower Willamette Valley with her husband. Destiny was the daughter of Jim's sister, Tammie. Brown permitted Nathan to meet with his legal team, but he was not to apply for a new passport or contact his dad by any means.

Nathan's defense team mobbed him when he walked into their fifteenth-floor office later that day wearing his ankle monitor. Kunkel asked him what he might like to eat for his first meal outside of jail. Nathan thought about asking for sushi, but he didn't want to put them out. He asked for a Big Mac, French fries and a Coke. Kunkel brought him the meal, supersizing it with a Coke big enough to drown a horse.

A brutal heat wave hit the Willamette Valley that summer as Nathan mulled his options. He could take his case to trial, but that felt dishonest. He knew he was guilty of acting as a foreign agent and laundering the proceeds as part of a conspiracy with his dad. Another option was to authorize his lawyers to cut a plea deal on his behalf, which would save the government the expense of putting on a trial; they'd go easier on him, with a reduced prison term. The money-laundering charges each carried up to twenty years' imprisonment. But federal sentencing guidelines favored Nathan, because he had no criminal record and his take from the Russians—$47,000—scarcely put him in league with the likes of Bernie Madoff, the billionaire king of the Ponzi scheme. Price and Needham calculated that Nathan faced roughly five years in prison. But government prosecutors would surely ask for more.

Nathan agonized over his fate, and his dad's. Jim's lawyer was showing no sign of throwing in the towel. In fact, Kauffman filed motion after motion to get the judge to dismiss evidence gathered by the FBI's surveillance operations and force the government to hand over classified materials. Nathan didn't know what to do, and he was forbidden from getting advice from members of his family, since they were likely to be called as witnesses.

Nathan's legal team privately sized him up. He kept telling them how much he loved his dad, but they saw signs he was beginning to second-guess the old man's motivations. They tried to help Nathan understand the seriousness of the crimes he and Jim had committed. Price and Needham eventually presented Nathan with his best option: If he was willing to cooperate with government prosecutors and the FBI, they told him, he could potentially cut a much better deal for himself. But he would have to help the government build its case against his dad.

Nathan wondered if he was hearing them right. His lawyers wanted him to save himself by betraying his own father to the very government the man accused of ruining his life? Nathan imagined how it might feel to sit in the witness box, day after day, delivering a courtroom crucifixion of his dad.

Facing this dilemma, he often hiked Mount Pisgah, a peak rising more than a thousand feet off the floor of the Willamette Valley. After seventy-two days in cages, he enjoyed the pure movement of trudging up the winding trail to the top, barrel chest heaving, to survey the southern end of the valley. Time after time he hiked the mountain looking for answers. He stood on its crown, named after the summit above Jericho and the Dead Sea, where God showed Moses the Promised Land on which he never set foot. Nathan's Promised Land lay before him. He saw fields, farm country, and freedom. He tried not to think about what it would be like to leave this place for prison.

By midsummer, he had made up his mind.

On August 4, Nathan and his lawyers sat down in a conference room in the U.S. Attorney's Office with the government prosecutors who would try him. They were joined by FBI agents Garth, Cooney, and Jensen. Nathan began by telling the agents he had lied about not reading his father's messages to the Russians. He admitted he had read a couple of them. It had all seemed such a romantic notion, he said. The travels. Russian spies. Money. Now he wanted to make things right.

The government refers to such meetings as proffer sessions. Nathan was proffering the truth to barter for a shot at freedom. His lawyers privately explained to him that the prosecutors were now on his side and that he should think of them as the guns and he as their ammo. Their target was Jim. It was during these proffers that Holsinger and Knight got a better sense of Nathan. All they knew about him before was what they heard on wiretaps or surveillance videos. As they talked to him, he seemed to be a very different animal from his dad's globe-trotting asset. Polite. Helpful. Apologetic. He answered every question they asked.

There was no going back now. The next time Nathan saw his father would be in court. The thought of testifying against his dad made him gut-sick with guilt. All along, he hoped Jim would plead guilty in exchange for a lesser prison sentence. But he knew how his dad felt about the government. The old man had rolled over once, copped the plea; only Jim knew how far he was willing to go this time to fight his criminal charges. Meanwhile, Nathan prayed about his decision nearly every night, asking God for answers.

On August 27, 2009, Nathan took a seat at the defense table in Judge Brown's courtroom. He wore his only suit, the black one from his first meeting with the Russians in San Francisco. Under one of his pant legs, Nathan wore a GPS ankle monitor.

It was a little after 2 p.m. when Nathan stood, raised his right hand, and promised to tell the truth. The law required Brown to make certain he understood every right he was about to give up by pleading guilty to charges that he conspired with his dad to serve as an agent of a foreign government and launder the proceeds. She wanted him to know that if she found him guilty, he couldn't vote, hold public office, or keep a gun. She explained that although he signed a plea agreement with the government a few days back, his sentence would ultimately be up to her.

Nathan nodded.

"Do you understand?" she asked.

"Yes I do, your honor."

She also pointed out that he was forfeiting any claim to the $9,500 the FBI seized from his Bible and wanted to know if he understood.

"Yes, your honor."

"Has anyone put any pressure on you to plead guilty when you do not want to?" Brown asked.

"No, your honor."

"Have you considered what it might mean to you if in fact you are called to testify in open court in a proceeding against your father?"

"Very much so, your honor."

Nathan had spent five months imagining just such a nightmare. The thought of it sometimes left him physically ill. He now understood his dad had put them both at risk, and that they had broken the law together in what Nathan came to regard as a poorly executed plan that brought additional shame to their family. Nathan loved his dad and wished him no malice. He prayed the old man would understand his decision.

Brown then asked Nathan if he understood that his plea agreement obligated him to testify against his dad, should he go to trial, and asked whether he was willing to do that.

"Yes, I am, your honor."

Brown found Nathan guilty. She would sentence him after Jim's trial to make certain he made good on his pledge to cooperate with the government.

Nathan left the courtroom feeling like Judas.

Sheridan, Oregon, early 2010

Jim seethed in solitary confinement. He had given six years to the Army, sixteen to the CIA, and thirteen to the U.S. Bureau of Prisons—more than half his life. He felt the full weight of his government's comeuppance from the bowels of solitary. His keepers held him alone twenty-three hours a day in this concrete bunker. They fed him through a slot in a steel door, dressed him in disciplinary orange, and provided him a stubby toothbrush too short to turn into a shank. On weekdays, they let him out of his cell into an outdoor recreation cage for sixty minutes to catch some rays, lay eyeballs on other humans, and walk laps. The cage, made of Cyclone fence, looked like an outsized dog run.

The first few months of 2010 were sometimes bitterly cold. Jim paced in his cell to stay warm; at night he stuffed his jumpsuit between two cotton blankets, tucking in like a mummy. It was difficult to get up in the mornings, the cold showers brutal. Jim looked hard in those days. He had shaved off his beard and instructed his prison barbers to cut his hair high and tight, Jarhead-style. He took out his frustrations in pull-ups, chin-ups, and push-ups. He heard pops and cracks in his elbows and shoulders. But his spirits were good.

One day after working out in early February 2010, one of Jim's favorite corrections officers, a former Marine, tapped on his steel door to check on him. Jim got up and walked over to the door. There, as he described it in a letter to Nick and Betty, he told the CO all the things he'd planned for that day. He would drive over to the coast for clam chowder, then down to Eugene to see his family, and then up to Corvallis to have coffee with Nathan between classes. Then he'd drive to Star's new apartment in Beaverton for pizza.

"He laughed and moved off," Jim wrote, "before I could ask to borrow his car."

He'd been locked up in one cage or another so long he could only vaguely recall what it felt like to be free.

On March 12, 2010, Sam Kauffman drove out to Sheridan for a legal visit, which got Jim out of his cell long enough to hear the latest developments in his case. Kauffman had filed motions for disclosure of evidence, and government prosecutors had already turned over roughly twelve thousand pages—much of it copies of Jim's own correspondence. The haul included a pair of letters Jim sent to the CIA after 9/11 in which he offered his expertise to combat al-Qaeda. Jim's defense team also got a pile of FBI investigative reports, known as 302s, which summarized interviews with Jim's family and fellow inmates, plus Nathan's associates. Now Kauffman waged war with prosecutors over the release of secrets the U.S. government didn't want to disclose.

National security cases such as Jim's force federal judges into procedural thickets. They must weigh defendants' constitutional rights to properly defend themselves and the government's need to protect its investigative methods and sources. The FBI does not part easily with classified files, and its lawyers zealously guard the identity of assets—including the Russian mole whose betrayals in the 1990s helped put Jim in the FBI's crosshairs.

Kauffman had learned that the FBI shot a video of Nathan talking to his dad before he flew to Cyprus. He wrote in court papers that the Foreign Intelligence Surveillance Court's order that permitted the video-taping violated Jim's Fourth Amendment protections against unlawfully gathered evidence. Kauffman wasn't the first lawyer to challenge the constitutionality of the court's secret surveillance orders. But no lawyer had ever won that battle. And neither would he.

The best footage the FBI gathered in the visiting room wasn't obtained under FISA. It was captured by a wall-mounted surveillance camera operated by the prison. Nathan is sitting next to his dad in a blue shirt, the old man leaning in, conspiratorially, holding his hand in front of his mouth to prevent being overheard. A man with rakish hair streaked with gray sits in a seat directly across from the Nicholsons—the undercover FBI agent who had befriended Nathan on the way through the metal detectors. The agent is sitting with an inmate, who served as a prop as the FBI man tried in vain to overhear the Nicholsons' conversation. A camera mounted on the agent's midsection captured audio and video, but it was of poor quality. The FBI never got close enough to capture Jim or Nathan's voices in the visiting room.

The prosecution's better footage was shot in Nicosia, and included the dramatic scene of Nathan running his recognition dialogue with the Russian he knew as George outside the T.G.I. Friday's. Kauffman sought those tapes, too, along with government reports chronicling surveillance operations in Cyprus.

Holsinger and Knight fought against such disclosure. They filed a response that asked Judge Brown to bar Kauffman from questioning witnesses about the names, job descriptions, or employers of those running the surveillance. They didn't want anyone knowing FBI teams were active on foreign soil, with a little help from their friends in the CIA. The United States and Russian Federation both enjoy cozy relations with Cyprus. Their embassies sit ninety yards apart, an eight-minute drive from T.G.I. Friday's.

Jim didn't attend motion hearings in his case, apparently preferring to stay in the hole rather than be hauled fifty miles into Portland in chains. He had no TV or radio, just magazines, letters, paperback books, and a whole lot of time on his hands. He spent many hours scratching out letters with golf pencils (the only writing implement allowed in the hole). He penciled a note to Star after his visit with Kauffman.

"Sam came to see me today," he wrote. "Gave me the update on how the government keeps dragging their feet and throwing up obstacles to the discovery we've asked for. Typical. Hiding behind veils and smokescreens of that tired excuse of national security. I'm not even charged with any violation of 'national security.' Nevertheless, once it is shown how scandalous the government has been in this case . . . not only will they likely lose their case, they will end up very possibly with an investigation and charges against them as a result. Of course, even if they try to cover up for themselves, the jury and public will see it for what it is and accountability likely will be sought against elements of the government through popular demand.

"Once I was feeling like I was tied to the railroad tracks while the government's locomotive bore down on me. Now it's more like two locomotives coming at each other and I'm no longer tied to the tracks. Plus, I'm not even on one of the locomotives, but I am controlling it by remote means. There is no way the government's locomotive is going to come away undamaged. I don't want to go on and on but I would like you to know that the big bully who always seems to get his way, has some weak spots and I know where a few key ones are. He has no fear of me because I didn't fight back last time. This time he gives me no choice. It could be very embarassing [sic] to the bully to be shown for what he really is in public.

"So, you hang on and stay happy. We'll count on God to give us a hand if we need it, but he's already let me see the bully's medical charts. Lots of problems to keep him flinching and smarting when I hit them."

Government lawyers, FBI agents, and CIA analysts read the letter before it ever reached Star, keenly aware Jim's threats were meant for them.

Jim scribbled sweet, sentimental letters to his family from the hole. He often spoke of dreams and his deepening Christian faith. The previous fall, he wrote of closing his eyes in his bunk and joining God and Jesus for coffee at a beachside café: "I plan to keep this practice of meeting God for coffee even after I leave prison." Sometimes, the dreams Jim described sounded like the musings of a man coming unhinged. He shared a dream in which he sat in the witness box of a federal courtroom as a court officer sloshed kerosene all around him. "As soon as I was sworn in," Jim wrote, "the person doing it struck a match. I warned him not to drop it but he did. At that moment, a protective bubble circled me and kept me from being burned." The courtroom burst into flames as if made of cardboard, and he now saw other buildings—the headquarters of the CIA, FBI, and Department of Justice—all aflame.

"I do have the occasional nightmare in which hit teams from the USG try to kill me," Jim recounted in a March 2010 letter to me. "I am more bothered by nightmares of trying to swim against a riptide to reach my young son stranded on a rock and calling for me. I have awakened after slamming my hand into the cement wall at the head of my metal bunk, trying to reach out to him. Intense." He added, "Although these walls close in on me, I am what they molded me into and my training keeps me relatively sane, I think. Relative, that is, to any held this long in solitary who haven't had my training."

Jim's correspondence mourned the distance that his isolation put between him and his children. Star wrote only occasionally, he complained. She sometimes passed indirect greetings from Jeremi, who never wrote. Jim blamed the government, as an Orwellian "Big Brother," for holding his oldest son under the microscope. To his parents he wrote, "I can't let the government take another one of my kids from me."

*   *   *

Jared Garth had gone back to Washington in February, where he met up with FBI agents he knew from his counterintelligence days. They gathered for drinks at an Asian fusion restaurant called TenPenh, which occupied a building next door to the Hoover headquarters building. Joining them were a few retired agents. One of the tipplers was Mike Rochford, who had served for decades as one of the FBI's most devout spy hunters. Graying and growing corpulent at fifty-five, Rochford had once served as chief of the bureau's Counterespionage Section, and he played key roles in the arrests of Aldrich Ames and Robert Hanssen. He had a great reputation, but he wasn't perfect. He'd been accused by some of tunnel vision in the Hanssen case for imposing two years of surveillance on the wrong man—CIA officer Brian Kelley—before learning the real turncoat was a fellow FBI agent.

Prosecutors in the Nicholson case had been looking for an expert witness to tell jurors why Russia remained faithful to Jim so many years after his arrest, and why Jim contacted the SVR. Garth's chance meeting with Rochford at TenPenh was just what they needed. Rochford had an uncanny knowledge of Russia's spy apparatus, its characters and complexities. His recall of the previous three decades of Washington-Moscow spy wars would be gold on the witness stand. Rochford slipped Garth his business card.

Holsinger and Knight knew that Rochford's universe of knowledge could deliver killer testimony about the SVR's fealty to Jim and the reserve fund they were holding for him in Moscow. They were happy to hear that Rochford, who retired from the bureau in 2004, still held a security clearance. They quickly hired him as their chief expert.

The former FBI man had joined the bureau in 1974 as a lunch-bucket file clerk making $5,200 a year. He studied Russian and became a translator before entering duty as an agent in 1979. He was working as a counterintelligence supervisor in the Washington Field Office in the mid-1990s when the FBI arrested Jim the first time. Now he was retired from the bureau and serving as counterintelligence director at the Oak Ridge National Laboratory, a ten-thousand-acre secret city in the heart of Tennessee. The U.S. Department of Energy operated the facility, which played a key role in the Manhattan Project and held some of the nation's most closely guarded science and technology secrets. Rochford's job, which occasionally brought him to D.C., was to keep Oak Ridge's secrets under wraps. He welcomed the chance to help the government win the second game of its doubleheader against Jim Nicholson.

During his FBI career, Rochford earned a reputation as a pitch specialist, the guy who reached out to Russians in their native tongue to convince them to betray their countries. Rochford told me during one of our interviews that he pitched twenty-eight people to help the FBI uncover moles inside the U.S. intelligence apparatus. Perhaps his biggest entreaty came in the summer of 1999, when he hunted down legendary KGB officer Victor Cherkashin. The dashing spy had served as counterintelligence chief in the KGB's *rezidentura* in Washington, one of Russia's most active spy dens. Rochford tracked down Cherkashin in the beachside town of Larnaca, Cyprus, where he offered him $1 million in exchange for his help plugging intelligence leaks attributed to Robert Hanssen. But Cherkashin—who later admitted in a memoir that he recruited Hanssen and Ames—turned Rochford down cold.

Little did Rochford know that his foray into Oregon's father-son spy drama would send him back in time to Cherkashin, Washington, and the ghosts of Reagan-era espionage. He flew to D.C. that spring to review the FBI's classified case files in a secure room in the Hoover Building. While poring over surveillance images of Nathan's meeting outside the T.G.I. Friday's in Nicosia, Rochford made an eye-popping discovery: He recognized the short Russian who served as Nathan's handler. The gray-headed Russian had replaced Cherkashin as chief of the KR Line (counterintelligence and internal security) in D.C.'s Soviet *rezidentura*. Back in the mid-1980s, he was a KGB colonel, a big hitter who would later become a general in the SVR. His name was Vasiliy Vasilyevich Fedotov.

Nathan knew him as George.

Rochford first heard the name "Fedotov" during the FBI's 1985 debriefings of Soviet defector Vitaly Yurchenko, a KGB colonel. Yurchenko steered U.S. spy catchers to two turncoats in their midst—former CIA man Edward Lee Howard and National Security Agency analyst Ronald Pelton—both of whom sold U.S. secrets to the Soviets. It was Yurchenko who told the FBI that Fedotov, a rising star, would replace Cherkashin as the head of KR Line. Rochford spent much of the sticky summer of 1986 tailing Fedotov. The FBI often followed KGB officers in the D.C. area to prevent them from running spy operations, or to catch them at it. But Rochford's tails of Fedotov were overt and obnoxious. He often locked bumpers with the KGB man when his driver would take him outside the embassy's *rezidentura*.

He kept eyes on Fedotov that summer and into the fall, doing a dozen or more shifts behind the wheel of his bureau car. He needed to make sure that Fedotov, a short, thick-necked man with dark hair and those big Clark Kent glasses popular in the 1980s, couldn't run spy ops on his watch. The two men never formally met. But Rochford was certain Fedotov recognized him: He'd been the guy pulling ten-hour shifts in the Russian's rearview mirror. One day, outside the National Air and Space Museum, the burly six-foot-two FBI man stepped out of his bureau car and planted himself next to the surprised Soviet. Rochford turned to Fedotov and said he was glad the Russian had gotten the chance to see D.C.'s great museums.

"Hope you enjoy them," Rochford said, "because your stay here is obviously short."

The United States sent Fedotov packing a few months later, in autumn 1986, and the D.C. chief of Soviet *kontrazvietka* wasn't alone. Government agents expelled eighty Soviets as part of the FBI's Operation Famish, a counterespionage probe that focused primarily on D.C. and New York. Some of the Soviet spies worked for the KGB under diplomatic cover, others for Soviet military intelligence (the GRU). The White House's National Security Council listed Fedotov persona non grata, which meant he was forbidden from turning up in any of the other fifteen NATO countries of that era. It's unclear where he landed, although some U.S. counterintelligence officials think he worked in India before retiring from the SVR.

As Rochford looked into the new Nicholson case, he learned that the SVR had brought Fedotov out of retirement to handle Nathan. Fedotov had taken the contract job, Rochford knew, to help Moscow Center identify the Russian turncoat who'd betrayed Jim Nicholson.

18

A Spy Swap and Reparations

"You were sent to USA for long-term service trip. Your
education, bank accounts, car, house, etc.—all these serve one
goal: fulfill your main mission, i.e. to search and develop ties
in policymaking circles in US and send intels to C [intelligence
reports to Moscow Center]."
                              —Encrypted SVR message to U.S.-based spies

Vienna, Austria, summer 2010

On the morning of July 9, two airliners pulled side by side on a sunny
tarmac at Vienna International Airport.

Four disgraced Russian spies—all of whom had secretly worked for
Western foreign intelligence services—readied to disembark from a Yak-42
government plane. The Russian Federation had just released the four from
prison. The other airliner, a Vision Airlines Boeing 767-2Q8 chartered by the
U.S. government, carried ten Russian spies who had served under Moscow's
deepest cover on American soil. The Department of Justice had taken less
than two weeks to round them up, charge and convict them of working illegally as unregistered foreign agents, and toss them out of the country. The
Russian spies had spent the last decade assimilating as ordinary Americans,
eight of them under assumed names—"legends," in spy parlance—to lay
the groundwork for SVR operations from Seattle to Washington, D.C.

President Barack Obama, briefed on the roundup sixteen days before the arrests, wanted to keep relations tidy between the U.S. and Russia. The administration backed a spy exchange, rather than imprisoning the Russians, as the best option to avoid unnecessary political drama between the two countries.

The competing spies walked across a gangway to switch planes, players in the biggest spy swap between Moscow and D.C. since the Cold War. The airliners roared off less than two hours later, a highly choreographed transfer approved by Obama and Russian president Dmitri A. Medvedev. The scene looked eerily similar to Cold War swaps on Berlin's Glienicke Bridge, known as the "Bridge of Spies." The ten Russians flew back to Moscow, where Prime Minister Vladimir Putin, a former KGB colonel, later joined them in singing such patriotic songs as "From Where the Motherland Begins." Two of the Western spies stepped off the Vision charter in London, and the others—former KGB officers Gennady Vasilenko and Alexander Zaporozhsky—flew on to Dulles.

Getting Zaporozhsky back to the U.S. was a major victory for the CIA. He began his well-decorated career in the KGB in 1975, rose to the rank of colonel in the Russian foreign intelligence service, served as deputy chief of the American Department, and headed the first department of the SVR's counterintelligence directorate. A Russian security official told a newspaper that in the early 1990s, he double-crossed Moscow to work as a mole for the CIA, earning the code name "Scythian." Zaporozhsky gave up information that helped point U.S. authorities toward Robert Hanssen and other Russian moles inside U.S. intelligence circles, including Aldrich Ames, according to published accounts.

It was Zaporozhsky, counterintelligence experts would later confirm to me, whose assistance to the U.S. government helped put Jim Nicholson behind bars in 1996. Zaporozhsky, three months older than Jim, pointed U.S. spy catchers in Jim's direction. Other sources also helped put a target on Jim's tail, but it was Zaporozhsky's tip that helped them winnow the suspects to the CIA's Batman.

Jim and Zaporozhsky weren't all that different. They climbed to the higher rungs of their nations' respective spy services, and picked their nation's pockets to sell secrets to their competitors. The U.S. government reportedly rewarded Zaporozhsky with $2 million in housing and benefits to live in comfort on American soil. But, like Jim, he would go to prison for his betrayals, undone by hubris.

Zaporozhsky's troubles began in 2001, while living in Maryland under the PL-110 Program (the CIA's relocation program for spies and their families). The gray-headed Russian, who had retired from the SVR, was invited to Moscow for a KGB reunion party with old friends. He talked this over with his CIA handlers and FBI agents, and they begged him not to go. But he disregarded their pleas, apparently believing his comrades back in Russia hadn't fingered him as a mole. When he stepped off a plane in the motherland, he was promptly arrested and put under lock and key at Moscow's notorious Lefortovo prison to await trial. The district's military court later found Zaporozhsky guilty of betraying Hanssen—the greatest mole Moscow ever ran inside the FBI—and sentenced him to eighteen years in prison for high treason. The court stripped Zaporozhsky of his military rank and all his decorations, and put him in a highly secure labor camp. His wife, Galina, living in the suburbs north of Baltimore, died while he was in prison.

When Zaporozhsky returned to the U.S. after the spy swap, he quietly slipped out of sight. I made a couple of trips to Cockeysville, Maryland, in hopes of interviewing him for this book. I knocked on the door of his two-story suburban home, nestled in a quiet cul-de-sac full of hardwoods and flowers and perfectly trimmed lawns. I heard quiet music upstairs, but no one came to the door. I left a letter urging Zaporozhsky to phone me. But it, too, went unanswered. The U.S. government has little to gain by allowing Zaporozhsky to go public with his story; he's one of those spies who knows too much.

News accounts of the spy swap focused primarily on the ten Russian spies the U.S. sent packing for Moscow, not the four the West got in return. Many journalists referred to the Russian secret agents as "sleepers"—spies put in place by their governments for later activation. But that wasn't entirely accurate. The Russians were active "illegals" working under Russia's deepest cover. They reported to SVR headquarters at Moscow Center.

The illegals lived in the U.S. under their legends with a long-term goal to become so Americanized they could gather U.S. secrets and identify targets ripe for recruitment inside U.S. policy-making circles. For ten years, the illegals posed as yuppies as they inveigled their way into U.S. culture. They bought homes, took white-collar jobs. Some of them married and raised children who had no clue their parents were foreign spies. They ate American food, rooted for American sports teams, and befriended Americans in financial, political, and government circles. In time—had they not been betrayed by one of their own—they undoubtedly would have helped Moscow Center penetrate the seats of U.S. power. The illegals were the best of the SVR's best, patiently gathering human intelligence and receiving codes by secure wireless.

News reports that summer suggested the illegals hadn't gotten very far in their decade of spying in the U.S., a fiction promulgated by Vice President Joe Biden in an appearance on *The Tonight Show with Jay Leno.* The famously long-jawed comedian suggested in his talk-show interview with Biden that Russia appeared to have come up the better horse trader in the spy swap.

"We traded ten for four," Leno said, sounding flummoxed. "Now, I know our math skills are not as good as they should be, but that doesn't seem fair. Why did we trade ten for four?"

"Well," Biden said with a toothy smile, "we got back four really *good* ones. And the ten, they'd been here a long time, but they hadn't done much."

A monitor on *The Tonight Show* set flashed a photo of one of the illegals, sultry redhead Anna Chapman. In the photo, Chapman strikes a pouty, bare-shouldered, Bond-girl pose in a blue spaghetti-strap blouse, a setup for Leno's next question: "You would know, Mr. Vice President: Do we have any spies that *hot?*"

"Let me make it clear, it wasn't *my* idea to send her back," Biden said. "I thought maybe they'd take Rush Limbaugh or something. That would have been a good move."

A lawyer for at least one of the accused Russian spies downplayed their espionage, saying they hadn't collected much, if anything, in the way of U.S. intelligence that couldn't be obtained through open-source channels. Not long after the arrests, National Public Radio quoted Andrew Kuchins of Washington's Center for Strategic and International Studies: "The kind of information that these folks are coming up with, you can simply get from reading *The New York Times,* watching TV. You don't need to be investing the tremendous resources to have people undercover for eight, nine, ten years. It really reflects, I think, an anachronistic mind-set." But such comments, in hindsight, underestimated how close the illegals came to doing serious harm to U.S. interests.

On Halloween 2011, the FBI publicly released its criminal complaint against the illegals, the culmination of a highly classified investigation dubbed Operation Ghost Stories. The FBI documents, though heavily redacted, showed just how much communication infrastructure the illegals had established and what they were after: U.S. technology secrets, military and financial data, and inside information on political policy. Government officials later acknowledged the Russians were creeping ever closer to Americans in power.

One of the illegals, posing as Donald Heathfield, graduated from Harvard University in 2000 and attended the university's John F. Kennedy School of Government, which has trained a who's who of U.S. policy makers. Another illegal went to work for a confidant of an Obama administration cabinet member. And another posed as Cynthia Murphy, a Montclair, New Jersey, financial planner who made a client of Alan Patricof, a venture capitalist who served as finance chairman of Hillary Rodham Clinton's 2008 presidential campaign. Several days after the U.S. deported the ten Russians, they also expelled twenty-three-year-old Alexey Karetnikov, who had moved to Redmond,

Washington, headquarters of Microsoft, to take an entry-level job with the software giant. The FBI established a link between the illegals and Karetnikov, described as a sophisticate deeply knowledgeable about the company.

The illegals had been highly trained in the English language, countersurveillance, concealing and destroying spy tools, and maintaining their cover professions. They communicated with their SVR handlers in new and old ways, including invisible writing, shortwave radio signals, codes and ciphers (including encrypted Morse code), and the hiding of secret text in ordinary digital photos (spycraft known as "steganography"). They exchanged money and information in dead drops, brushpasses, and in agent-to-agent meetings.

Putin described the illegals as uncommonly brave. "Just imagine," he told reporters two weeks after the spy swap. "You need to master a language like your mother tongue. You need to think in it, speak in it. You need to fulfill the task set in the interests of your motherland for many, many years not counting on diplomatic cover, expose yourself and your loved ones to danger." It was no wonder then that President Medvedev awarded the illegals—at least some of them—Russia's top government honors. The *Kommersant* newspaper reported in November 2010 that the illegals were betrayed by a Russian intelligence officer, and Putin later acknowledged this in a televised call-in show. He told viewers that—unlike during the Soviet days—those who betray Russia would not be tracked down and killed.

"As for the traitors, they will croak all by themselves," Putin said. "Whatever equivalent of thirty pieces of silver they get, it will get stuck in their throats."

The traitor he spoke of was Alexander Poteyev, a colonel in the SVR who may have commenced his betrayals of Russia during a 1999–2000 tour in the United States. Poteyev served as the SVR's deputy head of Department S, supervising the illegals from Moscow Center. A military court found that Poteyev betrayed his secret agents, their financial information, and their communication methods. He also hindered their operations with poor equipment, requiring them to meet in unsecured spots. This allowed FBI agents to spy on the illegals for years to determine what inroads the SVR sought in the United States. Eventually, the FBI sent in undercover agents, posing as Russian spies, to make contact with them.

Poteyev was in Russia in early summer 2010, when he learned the FBI was about to arrest the illegals he had betrayed. He dropped everything, fleeing through Belarus, Ukraine, and Germany before flying to the U.S. with a passport in another name. His wife got a farewell text the next day: "Mary, try to take this calmly. I'm leaving not for some time, but forever. I didn't want to, but I had to. I will start my life from scratch and will try to help the children."

Anna Chapman later revealed that she feared she'd been betrayed while meeting with a Russian spy (in fact, an undercover FBI agent) who uttered a code that only Poteyev and her personal handler knew. On June 26, 2010, Chapman had phoned her father, a former KGB man now working in Moscow's Ministry of Foreign Affairs, telling him of her fears that she'd been found out. The following day, the FBI rolled up Chapman and nine other illegals. Another suspect, identified as Christopher R. Metsos—who delivered pay and expenses to the illegals—was arrested in Cyprus. Authorities there allowed Metsos to post bail. He vanished like a ghost, presumably fleeing to Russia.

The same month the U.S. sent the Russian illegals packing, the FBI opened an investigation of a Houston export company busily supplying Russia's military and intelligence agencies with shipments of microelectronics and other high-tech gear. The company was the center of a secret and highly illegal procurement network, according to the U.S. government. Arc Electronics Inc. founder Alexander Fishenko, a former Soviet from Kazakhstan, bought parts with an array of military uses—detonation triggers, for instance, and systems for missile guidance, radar, and surveillance. The gear wasn't available in Russia, federal prosecutors reported, and Arc officials lied to U.S. suppliers about its plans for the parts, saying for instance that the company was producing traffic lights. Federal investigators learned that the Texas outfit served only as an exporter, shipping an estimated $50 million worth of microelectronics and other technologies to Russia. Much of this was acquired by a shady Moscow procurement firm, Apex System LLC, for which Fishenko was a controlling principle. In late 2012, government agents eventually indicted Fishenko and ten other people in the U.S. Fishenko was charged as the mastermind of the illegal procurement network.

Americans shouldn't be surprised that Russian spies operate on U.S. soil. They also shouldn't look past the fact that the U.S. has been caught in recent years running its own spies in Russia. As long as the two countries remain competitors, it's in their best interests to learn each other's military, economic, and trade secrets.

Russia's incursions on U.S. soil should have sounded a national warning bell about Moscow's reach and its strategy to reclaim a berth on the global stage, according to Michelle Van Cleave, who served as National Counterintelligence Executive under President George W. Bush. Instead, she told me, pundits and would-be experts took to the airwaves to poke fun at Anna Chapman and the gang, describing them as little more than hapless spies playing Bond. Not only was that characterization erroneous, Van Cleave said, but it exposed a national naïveté about Russia's efforts to undermine the U.S.

"It clearly revealed a tip-of-the-iceberg investment by the Russians into building infrastructures within the United States—outside of traditional embassy platforms—to enable its intelligence operations," she said. Van Cleave believes there are at least as many Russian spies operating on U.S. soil today as during the height of the Cold War. "And there may well be more." If this sounds like a continuation of the Cold War, she points out, welcome to the party.

"I think Putin's been rather forthcoming about his own views and objectives, sort of capsulized by his statement a couple years back that the collapse of the former Soviet Union was the greatest geopolitical tragedy of the twentieth century," Van Cleave said. "When you measure that statement against a couple of world wars during that century, you begin to appreciate the magnitude of what he's saying." Van Cleave believes Putin's objectives are clear: to return Russia to global power by neutralizing former Soviet states, consolidating power, and undermining the West's global influence.

Putin is a true believer in espionage as the front end of that spear, and he's been quoted as saying that one deceptive man can beat armies. On his watch, Russian spies have more freedom to romp against the West than the U.S.S.R. ever allowed. Van Cleave notes that Russia's security and intelligence apparatus, parented by Putin, faces none of the encumbrances once imposed by the Communist Party. As a result, Putin's government has become virtually indistinguishable from its spy services, allowing organized crime to permeate Russia's industries. "So," Van Cleave said, "the the power and autonomy of the new KGB—the security service, the intelligence services—are even broader than [in] days gone by."

What surprised Van Cleave was the haste of the 2010 spy exchange. "Nothing wrong with spy swaps; there's a time-honored tradition," she said. "But we only had them for two weeks. Normally you'd take your time after ten years[of] having these people under surveillance. The bureau was eager to get their hands on them to find out what they could about their operations. And yet, after two weeks, you got almost no time to debrief them or pursue follow-up lines of inquiry."

It may never be clear why the U.S. so hastily expelled the Russian spies. Perhaps they were getting too close. But the FBI's position is that its agents let the illegals run with a lot of line before reeling them in, part of a calculated strategy to get the upper hand on Russia's foreign spy service. Robert Anderson Jr., who served as assistant director of the FBI's Counterintelligence Division at the conclusion of the Ghost Stories investigation, described the case as a big win for the U.S.

"I think we got back much more than they got," he said. "For numerous years, we owned every facet of their lives. From that, we could watch how that service would run them, operate them, pay them, communicate with them." Ghost Stories gave the U.S valuable insights on

Moscow Center's intentions, and how it might run future spy operations against the West. The SVR unwittingly handed over its methods and sources. "And that," Anderson said, "allows us to go out and look for others like this that we may not know are there."

The FBI's Portland-based investigation of Jim and Nathan offered another portal into the SVR's methods and sources. It demonstrated Moscow's ongoing devotion to U.S. spies caught betraying their country for Russia—at least for those, like Jim, who might still be able to help them.

From his office in the Hoover Building, Anderson supervised the espionage investigation of the Nicholsons. Briefed every few days on the case—sometimes by video feeds in highly secure rooms—Anderson came to think of Jim as cunning, self-centered, self-righteous, and evil. He felt sorry for Nathan, who had been worked over by a master manipulator.

"If you can do that to your own family, and your own son," he said, "the sky's the limit for your employer and the United States government."

Sheridan, Oregon, late summer 2010

Jim had spent more than twenty months in the hole, where rain occasionally seeped into the hallways, occasionally leaving the floor of his cell a swampy mess. Those who occupied the solitary unit had taken to stuffing towels under their doors to fight against the seepage. Jim was eventually moved to a dry cell, but he remained bitter about having been left in such cold, damp confinement. It gave him one more reason to despise the U.S. government.

He mailed a letter to Star on September 4.

"I didn't tell you why I've decided to go to trial yet, I don't think," he wrote. "I want you to know. Everything I write is scrutinized by multiple readers looking for just anything to use against me. That's fine. As you know they twist things completely out of context sometimes . . . to support whatever pet theory they want to use against me. So, it really doesn't matter what I say—they'll piece the words together anyway. I said that because I want to state clearly that Nathan is not responsible for any of the mess he and I are suffering through (and indirectly the rest of our family). I am responsible for bringing this unholy wrath upon us and I alone."

Jim let his daughter know that neither he nor Sam Kauffman believed the government's charges would stick against him or Nathan. But he wanted Star to understand that prosecutors had indicted Nathan because of him.

For a moment, it looked as if Jim might be falling on his sword to save his boy. He had made a feint at this once before. About a month after his arrest, he sent word to Scott Jensen that he wanted to talk things over. The FBI man had driven out to the prison, listened to Jim's pitch, and carried it back to prosecutors in Portland. Jim had told Jensen that he hoped to protect his son from criminal charges. But it seemed clear to the veteran FBI man that Jim—still in the dark about just how much investigators knew about their scheme—was more interested in fishing for details than striking a plea bargain that would save Nathan. Jensen offered Jim another chance to cowboy up and spare his kid from culpability for his father's crimes. But Jim didn't bite. Holsinger and Knight, unmoved by Jim's entreaty, indicted him and Nathan a few days later.

"Nathan is going to be used by the prosecution to testify against me," Jim wrote to Star. "He has no choice. Not only is this something he must do, I want him to. If for some reason the jury decides to find me guilty of anything, at least Nathan will not be punished overly severely. . . . The government will only be happy if I have to spend the rest of my life in prison. . . . That part is pure political vengeance on the part of someone in government. That's why I and Sam believe I should go to trial."

If only Nathan felt the same way. He wanted Jim to plead guilty so that he had a fighting chance of getting out of prison alive. Nathan was certain that a jury would convict his dad of multiple felonies, and that he was powerless to stop him from stampeding to trial. He was forbidden from reaching out to the old man—even through lawyers—to persuade Jim to throw in the towel. This was maddening to Nathan. He worried that if his father rolled the dice in front of a jury and lost, he'd probably die behind bars. Nathan knew this would leave them both shattered. He also knew that if Jim went away for life, it might destroy his relationship with Jeremi and Star.

"I doubt there's anyone still in the government who knows some of the explosives they seem to be playing with," Jim wrote in his letter to Star. "One must be careful walking through a minefield. At least I know where the mines are. So, that's all. You know me and you know my heart. If I didn't have you kids I would have given up long ago. You keep me going—give me a reason, as Grandma said of me, to live. Prison is not life. So I fight to live because of you. I love you, honey. I'm not giving up on God. But as usual, he's cutting it close. Love Always, Daddy. P.S. This is my 630th day in solitary confinement."

In the final days of summer, Kauffman dug deeper to defend Jim.

He added heavyweight lawyer Robert C. Weaver Jr., one of GSB's owners, as his co-counsel. Earlier in his career, Weaver served as a federal prosecutor, making his bones as the man who brought down cult leader Bhagwan Shree Rajneesh, whose followers carried out the only mass bioterrorism attack on U.S. soil, slipping salmonella into the salad bars of ten restaurants in Oregon's Wasco County. As a defense lawyer, Weaver represented figure skater Tonya Harding, who played a role in the notorious knee-whacking of skating rival Nancy Kerrigan before the 1994 Winter Olympics. More recently, he represented several NBA players on the Portland Trail Blazers, whose criminal scrapes and hard partying off the basketball court earned them the nickname "Jail Blazers."

Kauffman filed a court notice to let the government know he planned to disclose classified information at trial, including details of Jim's days in the CIA, his interactions with Russian spies, and the circumstances of his 1990s espionage. Kauffman's motion noted that at trial he intended to cross-examine FBI or CIA officials and potentially some of their Russian counterparts. He also gave notice that he planned to ask questions in open court about Nathan's first contact with the Russians, and whether Nathan was under investigation before the FBI tailed him on the night of the murder mystery dinner train. Kauffman's filing came under the Classified Information Procedures Act, a 1980 law known as CIPA. The law was intended to prevent willy-nilly public disclosure of U.S. secrets.

Holsinger and Knight objected immediately to Kauffman's notice, responding in their own filing that Jim apparently wanted to divulge information that would damage national security. Their objection pointed out that CIPA doesn't permit defendants to surprise courts with classified evidence and that Judge Brown shouldn't allow the former CIA man to threaten the court with the legal equivalent of blackmail, known as "graymail."

Prosecutors figured Jim was threatening them as leverage for a generous plea bargain. They knew that the CIA's lawyers and their own legal superiors at Justice Department headquarters had no stomach for a trial that might give Jim a platform to divulge U.S. secrets in open court. But if Jim thought he had the government by the short and curlies, he was mistaken. Holsinger and Knight, doing the heavy legal lifting in Portland's U.S. Attorney's Office, were itching to take Jim to trial. They knew that winning a conviction in Portland, before a jury culled from a region teeming with government skeptics, would mark a career highlight.

Judge Brown set Jim's jury trial for two weeks commencing on November 8, 2010.

On October 1, Kauffman and Weaver filed a trial memo that served as a blueprint for Jim's defense strategy: "The charges in this case stem from an ill-conceived, but ultimately successful, plan by Mr. Nicholson and his son Nathaniel Nicholson (Nathan) to obtain financial assistance for the three Nicholson children." The defense wrote that it would dispute little about the facts of Nathan's travels around the world. "Nevertheless," they wrote, "Mr. Nicholson is not guilty of the charged crimes. Simply put, it is not illegal for someone to ask a foreign government for financial assistance, even if that person has previously been convicted of espionage. Nor is it illegal for someone to bring cash into the United States from a foreign country, even if it is brought in covertly." The government, they wrote, had gone to great lengths and spent untold dollars to investigate and prosecute the Nicholsons—but they'd committed no crime.

So there it was. Jim's lawyers had pinned his hopes on the novel notion that accepting money—even from the Russian spy service that owed Jim for his espionage—was nothing more than a gift of financial assistance for the Nicholson kids. The defense didn't believe it was money laundering. This appeared to be a legal sleight of hand, and was unlikely to pass a jury's sniff test. But there was more: The defense wanted Judge Brown to exclude testimony about Jim's 1997 conviction for espionage and his attempts to sneak documents out of the prison before Nathan came along.

Prosecutors had framed their case around Jim's prior espionage, which they maintained was the foundation for his repeated efforts to smuggle messages to the Russians. They had spent hours prepping former prisoners for trial. Steven Meyers was prepared to testify that Jim used him in an effort to talk his brother Randall and his paralegal friend to sneak messages out of the prison. Phil Quackenbush would tell the court he covertly carried out a thick document for Jim. Nathan would testify that he couriered multiple messages between Fedotov and his dad, and Rochford would explain why a retired spy like Fedotov was called in to handle Jim's boy.

The government planned to introduce a jarring pile of exhibits at trial, including the photo of Jim wearing the "KGB is for me" T-shirt, his arrest photo on the tarmac at Dulles, and the certificates of completion he earned in prison for Beginning Russian and Russian II. They would play for the court dozens of phone calls between Jim and his kids, and they would introduce piles of correspondence, Nathan's travel records, and surveillance videos. As a coup de grâce, they would trot out Rochford, who would paint a portrait of Fedotov—under a backdrop of Cold War spy dramas and political intrigue—as a spymaster still intent on harming U.S. security by learning the identity of the Russian mole who'd helped betray Jim.

Zaporozhsky had been back in U.S. hands only a few months and remained under protection. Rochford would never utter his name in court, or anywhere. Zaporozhsky's role in the Nicholson case would remain classified, a secret that counterintelligence insiders shared with me for this book, under condition of anonymity. It remains unclear why the U.S. continues to keep Zaporozhsky under such tight wraps. Russia's intelligence leaders traded him, fair and square, to secure the freedom of their illegals rolled up in the Ghost Stories probe. Russians will probably always consider Zaporozhsky a villain for his betrayals. But he will go down in American history as a hero for helping to expose Jim and other moles who betrayed U.S. secrets to Russia.

Jim's defense team made a bid to reach into that inner sanctum of national security. His lawyers filed a motion to force the government to review its debriefings of Robert Hanssen, who worked in the FBI's Washington Field Office about the time Jim ramped up his espionage for Russia. Jim's lawyers wanted to know if Hanssen provided the SVR with details of Jim's first espionage investigation, arrest, and debriefings. They pointed out that if Hanssen had passed Jim's debriefs to the SVR, the Russians would have already known how Jim was caught—making Fedotov's inquiries a moot point.

"Clearly," the defense wrote, "if the Russian Federation already knew the details of Mr. Nicholson's arrest, that tends to belie the suggestion from the government that Mr. Nicholson was somehow providing the Russians information that would be useful to them in detecting weaknesses in their intelligence operations." They noted that Rochford participated in thirty-five debriefings of Hanssen, suggesting he would know the answers.

The Hanssen debriefs were so closely guarded by the government that it's unlikely Judge Brown would have ordered their disclosure.

As it happens, the argument would never reach the courtroom.

Prosecutors were preparing FBI agents for their turns in the witness box when Kauffman phoned Knight to say Jim might be willing to make a deal.

What followed, as Knight put it later, was a furtive exercise in shuttle diplomacy that commenced with a few phone calls and a couple of meetings in his office. It was an uncommonly busy time for Knight, who was suddenly up to his armpits in another major national security case: An Oregon State University student had met that summer with two undercover FBI agents posing as al-Qaeda terrorists. Mohamed Osman Mohamud, a nineteen-year-old Somali American from a good family in Beaverton, had taken a turn for radical Islam and now planned to help his friends detonate a massive fertilizer bomb during Portland's annual Christmas tree lighting ceremony in late November.

Knight knew that the Mohamud case, arising from a classic FBI domestic terrorism sting, would consume his waking hours. What he didn't know is that Holsinger would eventually join him as co-counsel in that case. At that hour, one thing was certain: Knight was happy to negotiate with Kauffman to see if perhaps they could make a deal. The Mohamud case was already chewing up his workdays, and preparing for an espionage trial wasn't going to make his life any easier.

Jim shuffled into Judge Brown's court at 8:58 a.m. on the second Thursday in November. He slipped into the seat next to Kauffman in a wood-slat courtroom with high ceilings and thermostat problems. The room burned hotter than teenage love. Jim looked older, grayer, and more haggard. His swagger was gone. On the table in front of him were two documents, a total of fifteen pages that spelled out a binding plea agreement. If Brown approved his plea, Jim would look considerably older by the time he got out of prison.

Judge Brown took her seat a few moments later and spent much of the next forty-three minutes asking Jim questions, the ambient notes of a court reporter's keyboard quietly clacking between them. Toward the end, Jim pleaded guilty to conspiring with Nathan to act as an agent of the Russian Federation and laundering the proceeds. Brown took the plea agreement under advisement. She would have to consider whether the eight additional years of prison agreed upon by prosecutors and Jim's defense team was in the best interests of justice.

As Kauffman later explained, Jim wanted to face the charges head-on at trial. But the specter of his youngest son sitting on the witness stand was too much to bear. "Ultimately," Kauffman said, "he couldn't move forward."

Government officials in Washington responded to news of Jim's guilty plea with sterile quotes about Jim's breaches of trust and violations of the oath he took to protect his nation's secrets. But Oregon's top FBI official, Art Balizan, got to the heart of Jim's betrayals: "During his career with the CIA, this country entrusted [him] with some of its most sensitive secrets. Not once—but twice—he betrayed his oath, our nation, and his family. Unfortunately, this is a legacy he and his children will live with from now on."

The most betrayed person in the whole sordid mess was forbidden from attending Jim's plea hearing. A few days earlier, Nathan's defense team had gathered around a speakerphone to tell their twenty-six-year-old client that his dad planned to plead guilty, sparing him from a wrenching stretch in the witness box. Nathan, who had prayed for just such deliverance, was relieved but hardly euphoric. He couldn't stop calculating the damage. He was now a felon facing prison. He had betrayed the country he loved. His dad was a two-time felon who'd be well into his seventies before he was freed. The Bureau of Prisons would certainly move his dad to another prison out of state.

Nathan felt certain the judge would impose a no-contact order, meaning he'd be well into middle age before he could mend things eye to eye with his dad. As he told a psychologist, "This is like the death of my father. I doubt I will ever have the opportunity to talk to him again."

Now it was Nathan who would face the judge.

The night before his sentencing hearing, now living in a tiny studio apartment in Corvallis, Nathan sat down alone to a plate of curry chicken at an Indian restaurant called Nirvana. He drove back to his place and put his affairs in order. He jotted down his financial information—including bank account numbers and passwords—on a single piece of paper, which he left on the floor the next morning before driving to Portland. On the morning of December 7, 2010, Nathan made his way through the Hatfield courthouse metal detector. He wore his black suit and a crisp blue shirt and tie, his face taut with anxiety. He strode across the lobby, passing a quotation from Alexander Hamilton etched into a massive wall of black marble—"The First Duty of Society Is Justice"—on his way to the elevator doors. Outside Judge Brown's courtroom, he handed his car keys to a friend he'd known since middle school.

Nathan took a seat between Tom Price and Jerry Needham at the defense table, with prosecutors Knight and Holsinger off to his left. A box of tissues sat on the table in front of him. Laurie and Bill sat behind Nathan, as did Nick and Betty, along with a few other friends and relatives. A large group of high school girls from nearby St. Mary's Academy, Judge Brown's alma mater, crowded into the gallery. A gavel brought them to their feet at 9:01 a.m.

"All rise."

Nathan stood as Brown settled into her chair.

"Please be seated."

Nathan's sole chance of freedom lay in the hands of the graying judge now shuffling papers on the bench.

Jerry Needham, the lanky lawyer with the Queens accent, told Brown that it was unfortunate she had not had the same chance to get to know Nathan that the lawyers, FBI agents, and defense investigators had.

"I'm sure that your honor would come away from that experience similar to everyone else," he said. "Mr. Nicholson is a loyal, decent young man who would never set out to engage in this kind of conduct or behavior had it not been for his unusual and destructive relationship with his father. He exhibited, through the course of all of his meetings, a great deal of anguish about this particular crime and his behavior, how it has affected him. He never had an ax to grind against his government. . . .

"He has a conscience, and it has deeply affected him that his behavior has caused this rift in his family—the destruction, for the most part, of his relationship with the father who he loves and admired as a kid. He never truly understood his father, however. He never really understood his father's crime. . . . His father afterwards, while he was in prison at Sheridan, told him and his siblings the story—which was a lie—that he had done it all for his family. In the shadow of that deception, their relationship grew."

Needham explained that Nathan's faith in his father was shattered when the FBI came to his door nearly two years back. It was then that Nathan began to reexamine himself against the young man whose father had led him astray. Needham urged Brown to sentence Nathan not to prison but to probation, with one hundred hours of community service to the Department of Veterans Affairs. Imprisoning him, he told Brown, would only disrupt his chances of rebuilding his life.

Judge Brown looked down and asked if Nathan had anything to say for himself.

He stood at attention, shoulders square.

"Your honor," he began, "I would first like to thank you for the time that was allotted to me to help regain and reestablish what I could in my life. Your honor, I—I—I am deeply sorry that this even happened. I am terribly embarrassed. . . . I've hurt my friends and family . . . and I wish to use any and all energy I can to help restore what was once lost, your honor. Thank you."

"What's your plan?"

Nathan lightened a little. He said he hoped to finish his degree in computer science, specializing in software systems. His goal was to design a system that would make houses or cars more energy-efficient.

"Aside from that," he said, "I also wish to have a family of my own someday, your honor, to settle down and to not live such an adventurous life. . . . I also wish to continue abiding by the laws, your honor, and to . . . basically own up to anything that I need to, punishment or otherwise."

Judge Brown had reviewed mounds of paper that recommended she be lenient with Nathan. His defense lawyers, the court officer who wrote his presentence report, and even the prosecutors had all come to the same conclusion about the earnest, gullible, slightly goofy young man now sitting before her. None of them thought he belonged in prison. But the judge's job, guided by federal sentencing guidelines, was to structure a sentence that promoted respect for the law, protected public safety, and took into account the seriousness of his crimes.

"While the defendant's relative culpability, as compared to his father's conduct, clearly is less, the two of them together engaged in a conspiracy to engage agents of a foreign government, and then to launder money received from agents of a foreign government in a manner intended to deceive and to avoid detection," Brown said. "Where that plot may have gone, had it not been detected early by the government and interrupted after . . . this defendant's personal overseas travels on numerous occasions, is only left to speculation."

Her words hung in the air like the notes of a funeral dirge.

Judge Brown then launched into a monologue, as if deliberating aloud. She noted that Nathan quickly took full responsibility for his role in the father-son plot, and agreed to mend his breach by cooperating with the government. Nathan did so, she said, at no small expense to his relationship with his father, his own psyche, and his unresolved anxiety about the terrible crimes his father committed against his nation.

"When I released you from custody, Mr. Nicholson, there was debate about whether that was a wise decision. The lawyers who are joining in the probationary recommendation today argued that I was taking a risk by letting you out and that there was a chance you would flee to seek refuge from the agents of the foreign government with whom you had been dealing. You committed that you would not. You promised that you would follow every condition of supervision that was placed on you. And with every single report I've received since I authorized your release, it has been confirmed that you met each and every one of those obligations. So I'm relieved. I'm relieved that the promise you made was actually borne out by your conduct.

"I think here, for all the reasons that have been written about," Brown said, "it is fair to conclude that a prison sentence is not necessary. And therefore, I decline to impose a prison sentence, but instead will place the defendant on a five-year period of probation." She also ordered him to serve a hundred hours of community service with the VA.

Nathan was free to go home.

On Tuesday, January 18, 2011, Jim shuffled across a patch of courtroom carpet in leg irons. Betty Nicholson was shocked to see her son so bedraggled. He had always put himself together, even behind bars. Now he wore wrinkled BOP khakis with short sleeves, his Ranger tattoo as faded and worn out as his face. His scalp showed more shine than that day nearly two years before when he'd walked into court looking as if he owned the place. Now he appeared resigned.

Nathan and Star squeezed in together on the front bench directly behind their dad. The only thing separating them from Jim was a wooden rail and armed deputy marshals. Nathan had not seen or heard from his dad in nearly eight hundred days, and his gut was knotted with worry over how the old man would treat him after his sentencing.

At 1:36 p.m., Kauffman and the government's lawyers walked into the courtroom out of a door near Judge Brown's bench. She took her seat moments later and got right to business. She was ready to proceed, having read Jim's presentence report, and would accept his guilty plea. But she noted that under federal sentencing guidelines, she could sentence Jim to an additional twenty-five years in prison.

"So, Mr. Nicholson, first I need to be sure you've seen the presentence report, and reviewed it with your attorney."

"Yes I have, your honor."

"All right. Is there anything you would like to say before I impose sentence?"

"Yes, your honor. I do have a statement to make."

Jim asked Brown to forgive him for what would be a long speech.

"We have all the time you need," she said.

Standing now, Jim began.

"Your honor, in my life I have been through several coups. I have been through a revolution, and I have been through a war. I have been marked for assassination by a foreign terrorist organization. I have been hunted by armed gunman in East Asia, and I have been imprisoned in this country. I have gone through a heart-wrenching divorce and custody battle. But the worst day of my life was the day I learned that my young son had been arrested and charged with acts for which I was responsible.

"Your honor, in 1996, when I was first arrested, it was not just my money, my home, my car, and my possessions that were taken by the United States government. It was my children's home, my children's family car, my children's possessions, and their personal savings accounts that were also seized by the United States government, in an effort to punish me. For at that time, on that day, my children were told to pack one bag each. They were then taken to the airport with their pet cats, placed on an airplane, and flown from their home in Virginia to Oregon—a place where they had only visited their relatives. My oldest son was forced to leave college and to get a job, in an effort to help support his younger brother and sister.

"For over a decade I sat, as if in amber, watching from the federal prison while my children struggled to make ends meet. They did a heroic job. After 9/11 and the terrorist attack in 2001, both of my boys entered the military on their own, but with my blessing. My daughter went to get a college degree and set out to pursue a career on her own.

"For the last 766 days, your honor, I have been in solitary confinement. I have been held in a stark cement cell for twenty-four hours a day. I have been separated from my family. Other than letters, I have had no contact with anyone but my legal team and prison officials. . . . During this time, I have concluded that my children never really needed the extent of help that I thought they needed. My children, each one of them, are wonderful, good, caring, smart, and capable people.

"The truth is, your honor, it was not just their need for assistance that caused me to suggest the course of action that I did. It was my pride. It was also the illusion that I was somehow indispensable to my children's survival. Your honor, in solitude, illusions dissolve. It was in my solitude of solitary confinement that I realized that all my children ever really needed from me was my love."

Jim explained to Judge Brown that he sought help for his kids only when Star and Jeremi were buried under an avalanche of student loan debts and struggling to make the rent.

"And it was in desperation that, after all of my prison savings had been expended, that [I believed] they might be helped by only one source—and the only source I could think of at the time was the Russian Federation. Now, I recognize that it was because of my previous assistance to them that they were willing to help my children in their time of need. However, I would also like to add that the Russians owed me nothing. And insofar as their efforts were truly to help my children, I regret the embarrassment that this has caused them as well."

Jaws dropped among the FBI agents against the back wall. The son-ofabitch had just apologized for embarrassing the Russians. Jim's fealty to Moscow was particularly galling to Jared Garth, the FBI's lead agent in the case. He was flabbergasted that Jim failed to offer a single word of apology to the nation he betrayed. Only later did it dawn on him: "Why would he apologize to the United States? He was loyal to the Russian Federation."

Jim's apologies continued.

"I would like to ask my children to forgive me," Jim said. "When I was initially arrested, I could have never imagined that I would fail them again. And I will endeavor not to do so, once more."

Nathan's eyes brimmed, and Star's shoulders trembled under the weight of her sobs.

"I would like to say, your honor, in regard to my young son, that if he harbors any feeling of failure in this regard to let those feelings go. His efforts in all of this were completely selfless. And they were designed only to help his family in their time of need."

Behind Jim, Nathan's face reddened as he wept.

"I love him dearly," Jim continued. "I could not be more proud of him. He has never let me down, and he has never failed his family. Any failure has been mine alone.

"That's what I would like to say, your honor. Thank you."

Judge Brown glared at Jim.

"He's made an eloquent statement today to his family, to his children," Brown told the courtroom, eyes drawing a bead on Jim. "Notably absent from his remarks, however, was any suggestion of remorse for committing criminal conduct against the United States and its interests. What he calls 'previous assistance' to the Russian Federation was *criminal espionage*, for which he was sentenced. He's been in solitary confinement pending today's proceedings because of repeated criminal activity. His 1996 arrest was for a reason. The United States didn't act against him on an arbitrary whim. He committed conduct which resulted in a conviction for *espionage*."

Brown sentenced Jim to the eight-year prison term the lawyers had agreed upon. But from her expression, it appeared to have left a bad taste in her mouth. She punctuated her decision by subtly warning Jim that he would rue the day he broke another law behind bars. If he ever did, she said, "I don't know how anyone will be able to make an argument, Mr. Nicholson, that you should ever do anything other than spend the rest of your life in prison."

Jim nodded somberly. He had just sealed two more superlatives in the annals of American spying. He was already the highest-ranking CIA officer ever convicted of espionage. Now he was the only U.S. spy caught betraying his country twice, and the only American convicted of spying for a foreign government inside the bars of a federal prison.

Brown pointed out that Jim had deservedly spent the last few years in the hole.

"And so the time itself, going forward," she said, "is not going to be easy time. And it wouldn't surprise me at all if the defendant spends it in solitary confinement, too."

Brown ordered that Jim not reach out in any way to Russia or any foreign government, and that he have no contact with Nathan without advance approval of his probation officer. She reminded Jim he was to give no media interviews without telling the CIA in advance so it could make an officer present.

Jim's legal team had negotiated a few lines in his plea agreement to let him spend a few minutes with his family at the end of his sentencing. Deputy marshals would stand by to make sure Jim had no physical contact with them. FBI agents and CIA officers would listen to the conversation to make sure Jim betrayed no secrets to Nathan or anyone else in the closed-door gathering. Brown told the court she was honoring the agreement, but she wanted the get-together to be brief—about ten minutes.

"Mr. Price," she said to Nathan's primary lawyer. "You and your client are free to stay if you wish. We're in recess on this matter."

The courtroom doors closed at 2:18 p.m. Brown walked back to her chambers as the gallery filed out.

When the courtroom doors closed, Jim swiveled in his high-backed chair as his family pressed closer to the wooden railing separating them. Jim had not laid eyes on his family in more than two years.

"Hi, guys," he began.

Jim told Nathan and Star how much he loved them. Through tears, they told him how much they missed and loved him. His parents, Nick and Betty, and siblings, Rob and Tammie, also pushed a little closer to say hello and let Jim know he still had their unconditional love and support. Conspicuously absent was Jeremi, still furious with his father for reaching back to the Russians. Jeremi also remained troubled by Nathan's willingness to take part in Jim's harebrained scheme, which only brought more shame to the Nicholson family name and put their dad behind bars even longer.

After Jim said his goodbyes, deputy marshals guided him through a door in the paneled wall on his way back to the hole. Nathan left the courtroom looking spent, his eyes red. He could muster only one thought before hiking out of the courthouse into a cold rain.

"It was good to see him again."

This was an echo of the teenage Nathan who had told a TV reporter he liked talking on the phone with his imprisoned dad just to hear his voice. That was half a lifetime ago. That boy was a distant memory now. In his place was a grown man who'd made his own mistakes.

As the months passed, Nathan forged plans. He would try to earn a college degree, find a nice woman, and start a family of his own. In the meantime, he was coming to grips with his dad's betrayals, haunted by the old man's words. He recalled phrases Jim had used to inspire him—some of them Bible verses—and he wasn't ashamed to admit some of them still inspired him.

Before you were born, I set you apart and anointed you as my spokes-man to the world.

You have been brave enough to step into this new unseen world that is sometimes dangerous but always fascinating.

God leads us on our greatest adventures.

I understand you—and me.

Nathan and Jim had grown incredibly close during their years as spy and son, and Nathan sometimes choked up, in our many interviews, as he measured that bond against its outcomes. Some of Jim's words carried special relevance now, revealing, in the objective world, what manipulations they were.

Nathan also suffered from what might be called post-traumatic surveillance disorder. Like a soldier who feared mortar attacks long after coming home from combat, Nathan found himself flashing back to his short life as a spy. Paranoia shadowed him. He still drove the Chevy Cavalier the FBI had repeatedly searched. The government still monitored his computer usage. He still found himself hyperaware of his surroundings, and the number of times certain faces or vehicles came into view. Could he ever be certain someone wasn't watching him?

He had been tailed by professionals from the FBI, the SVR, and God only knows who else. The old man had seduced him with scripture and spy tales, goading him into seeing the world with new eyes. But the world Nathan occupied had eventually looked back in condemnation.

There had been times in the past when Nathan read his dad's letters and could hear Jim's voice as clearly as if he were sitting on the bedroom floor reading them aloud. Jim's words were now filtered by Nathan's human education, bathed in the context of an FBI investigation. Some of the words that had guided him into trouble now had double meanings.

Keep looking through your new eyes, Jim had said.

That part, Nathan knew, would come easy.

Epilogue

The Last Asset

The U.S. Department of Justice threw up every obstacle in its power to prevent Jim from talking to me. I had fooled myself into believing that the Bureau of Prisons, one of its agencies, would allow Jim to make good on his promise to give me an exclusive interview. But a little more than a month after his sentencing, the BOP quietly shuttled him out of Oregon. He moved through prisons in California and Oklahoma before he landed, on April 4, 2011, in the same prison complex where the government had executed Oklahoma City bomber Timothy McVeigh for the 1995 murder of 168 people.

The BOP reconfigured its death row facilities at the Terre Haute Federal Correctional Complex in December 2006 to accommodate an influx of mostly Muslim men rolled up in post-9/11 terrorist plots. There the government created the first of two Communications Management Units, perhaps the most invasive lockups in the modern era of American punishment. The government wired the facilities with video cameras and listening devices so that a team of counterterrorism experts in West Virginia could remotely snoop on inmates around the clock. News media nicknamed the facility Guantánamo North.

The government's intention was to monitor Jim as closely as the law allowed to prevent him from reaching out to the Russians. But the BOP, perhaps humiliated by the ease with which Jim had bypassed Sheridan's security to communicate with Russian spies, also planned to shut him down from telling his story.

In the spring of 2011, I wrote to the warden at the Terre Haute complex for permission to interview Jim, and he responded days later: "After a thorough review of your request and established policy regarding news media contacts, your request to interview inmate Nicholson has been denied. Specifically, it is our opinion the interview could jeopardize security and disturb the orderly running of the institution." I asked the warden to reconsider, offering a compromise in which I'd agree to interview Jim by speakerphone, a CIA officer sitting next to me. I closed my letter by quoting forty-five powerful words penned in 1791 by James Madison. But the warden, clearly unmoved by my recitation of the First Amendment, denied my appeal. He was backed by the U.S. Supreme Court, which had ruled in 1974 (*Pell v. Procunier*) that the need to maintain internal security in prisons thoroughly trumps prisoners' free-speech rights.

Jim's liberties weren't as important to me as those of my readers, who had a constitutional right to hear his story. I had written a few letters to him while he was in Sheridan, but the government seized his replies before they could reach my letterbox. Only after Jim's sentencing did the FBI turn over photocopies of his letters.

"In a way," Jim wrote in the first of them, "I feel I should be writing this from an upper room of a house on the South Devon Coast. It somehow would seem fitting. For now that is not possible. . . . Perhaps you can appreciate that sometimes in life bridges blow up seemingly by themselves. Once we cross them we can't get back. I believe this because I tried and failed. We must then go on from where we find ourselves."

Jim complained of writing from a cold concrete cell, putting pencil to lined notebook paper like a schoolboy. He posed questions to me as if he were interviewing a job candidate. There were no "correct" answers, he wrote. All he wanted was honest responses, not those I thought he might like to hear. He asked if I had children and about my relationship with them. "Do you have faith in anything—God, country, family, job, yourself?" he wrote. "Was there ever a time when you lost your faith in anything or everything?" In a postscript, Jim apologized for sounding overly suspicious and acknowledged that thirteen years in prison had degraded his social skills.

Jim cautioned me not to expect too much, offering a hint that he might not be able to articulate why he twice betrayed his country and risked his own son's future: "I don't have answers to some of the questions you might expect me to know. Some things have been a mystery even to me about me." I responded with a five-page letter, but it's unclear whether Jim received it.

In the summer of 2011, months after I sought permission from the BOP and CIA to interview Jim, Attorney General Eric H. Holder Jr. forced Jim to sign a secret document called a Special Administrative Measure, known as a SAM. The papers were ostensibly intended to prevent him from communicating words—by any means—that could harm the U.S. What the SAM really did was crystallize the government's intention to muzzle Jim, trample the public's First Amendment rights, and punish him for exploiting security weaknesses at Sheridan. Jim's own counsel, Sam Kauffman, was not permitted to speak to his client until he, too, signed the document. Forty-nine U.S. prisoners would be held under SAMs by the end of 2012. None could have any contact with journalists.

I appealed directly to the Justice Department's National Security Division. A contact there told me that Jim's Special Administrative Measure expressly forbade him from contact with any journalist. "Not going to happen," he said. "Sorry."

Shut down by the U.S. government, I reached out to the Russian Federation to learn why Moscow Center remained so loyal to Jim. The SVR would not discuss the personnel who handled Jim and Nathan: Sergei A. Polyakov, Mikhail Gorbunov, and Vasiliy Fedotov. I walked into the Russian Consulate in San Francisco, and its embassy in Nicosia, Cyprus, asking to speak to a representative of its diplomatic corps or security detail to get Russia's version of the story. In San Francisco, a tanned first-name-only official who called himself Sergei met me on the street to say, "I don't like spy stories," and claimed ignorance of the

Nicholsons' crimes. In Nicosia, a consular officer told me to e-mail my questions directly to the SVR at Moscow Center. I sent multiple queries in Russian and English. The SVR never responded.

By then, the BOP had moved Jim to the U.S. Penitentiary Administrative Maximum Facility in Florence, Colorado, better known as the federal Supermax. Jim would serve his time in this Rocky Mountain Alcatraz with fellow spy Robert Hanssen, 1993 World Trade Center bomber Ramzi Yousef, Unabomber Ted Kaczynski, and a rogues' gallery of other notorious prisoners. The Bureau of Prisons kept Jim locked in his private cell twenty-three hours a day, limited his correspondence to short letters to close family, and permitted him just one fifteen-minute phone call per month. He would eventually get a janitorial job that for a time provided some more time out of his cell, and $17 a month, Nick and Betty told me. He has not been allowed to communicate with Nathan.

Jim's earliest release date is June 27, 2024. If he gets out then, he will be seventy-three years old and will find himself at a crossroads. He can stay put in the U.S., where Jeremi and Nastia have borne him a grandson (they named him James) and Star bore him another grandson, or he can bolt for the Russian Federation and the pension that awaits him. His decision will prove to his family where his loyalties live.

One of Jim's letters to me from Sheridan noted there were reasons why a "a former Boy Scout, mom and apple pie-loving, flag-waving, country-first young man ended up as an older man in solitary confinement." He asked if I'd seen *Spy Game*, the movie that stars Brad Pitt as a CIA man mentored by a grizzled case officer played by Robert Redford. "Interestingly," Jim wrote, "Pitt's character had also been a Boy Scout before becoming a special operator in Southeast Asia and then a CIA case officer. He said he learned how to shoot well in the scouts. I learned on my uncle's farm as a boy. It's perhaps not atypical to pick someone like this to mold into what the CIA needs. I guess it works pretty well until they expect you to juggle one too many balls at once."

Jim wasn't forced to juggle more balls than a great many of his brother and sister officers in the CIA. He was hardly the first spy to face the strain of long-term covers, lying on cue, keeping secrets from the spouse, and hearing his kids grow up over long-distance lines. The CIA's Employee Assistance Program and Family Advisory Board were designed to help agency families in crisis. These services were available to Jim. But there's no record that he reached out to them, and there were good reasons why he wouldn't. His revealing his problems—a crumbling marriage, infidelity, financial troubles, emotional wounds, disgruntlement with his employer—might have alerted Langley that Jim was in deep trouble. Agency superiors would have thought twice about sending him back overseas, because those vulnerabilities sometimes pushed intelligence officers into the hands of rival spy agencies.

It may never be clear to me why Jim didn't seek help from friends, family, coworkers, or bank officers for financial assistance. I've pored through court papers and other public documents detailing Jim's financial predicament, and it's clear he could have held things together without moonlighting for the SVR. Jim could have sold his town house and downsized his lust for electronics and other extravagances. Jeremi could have gone without a car at college. Star and Nathan didn't require so much *stuff*; they were happy just to have their father around.

The irony of Jim's latest crime is that by the time he and Nathan got things going with the Russians, his kids really didn't need the money. Jeremi was in the Air Force. Star had a fine job. Uncle Sam was taking good care of Nathan as he worked toward a college diploma.

Because I am a journalist, and perhaps not shot in the ass with compassion, I briefly flirted with the notion that Jim was born a conscienceless psychopath motivated by the thrill of pulling the wool over the CIA's eyes. Successful spies, swaggering risk takers that they are, have a native talent to lie through their teeth during the day and check their covers at the doorstep at night. But it's the extremely rare psychopath, I came to learn, who could get past the agency's rigorous screening.

Two psychiatrists with unique perspectives on CIA officers both told me that Jim's love for Nathan and his family demonstrated the kind of empathy that psychopaths lack. Dr. Marc Sageman, who spent seven years as a CIA case officer, and Dr. David L. Charney, who has seen his share of patients from the agency at his northern Virginia practice, both believe Jim is, rather, an extreme narcissist. But Charney pointed out that the same qualities that made Jim a successful spy—superficial charm, grandiosity, impulsiveness, and the knack for burrowing into others like a parasite when he needed something—were also traits of the psychopath.

Charney, a psychiatric expert on the defense team of Robert Hanssen, said that Jim and the FBI's most damaging spy shared one intriguing parallel: Their country and colleagues spurned them after they were unmasked, yet their children still loved them deeply. In that way, Charney said, the children of Hanssen and Nicholson served as the last lines of protection from a disapproving world. Both traitors clung to their kids after the FBI turned their lives upside down. But the most heartbreaking consequences fell to Nathan. As Charney put it, Jim had turned his youngest son—emotionally and literally—into his last asset.

The sun began to set over the rounded shoulders of Oregon's Coast Range mountains on the early evening of June 15, 2013, the sky a smear of pink and plum. The air smelled of fresh-cut grass. The day foreshowed summer and possibilities. The college town of Corvallis, home of the Oregon State University Beavers, was forty minutes in my rearview mirror. Behind me, a few hundred newly minted graduates of the university's School of Electrical Engineering and Computer Science were gathered for cake and photos, most of them still wearing their graduation robes and mortarboards.

Nathan had vacillated for months over whether to cross the stage and publicly accept his diploma. He decided only in the final days to join his girlfriend, Savannah Lee Van Beek, and their classmates for the ceremony. By then, it was too late to be listed in the printed program. The graduates were about what you'd expect from an auditorium thick with computer geeks on the cutting edges of new technologies. Many wore shorts under their gowns. One festooned his graduation cap with a green circuit board. Another rigged hers with a strand of bright orange lights in a display of school spirit.

Master's and doctoral grads had pursued course work in such areas as "Bayesian Optimization with Empirical Constraints" and "Node-to-Set Node Disjoint Paths Routing in Some Interconnection Networks," techno-gibberish that drew quiet chuckles from parents in the audience.

"Look for ways to make the world a better place," the head of the school told graduates before handing out their diplomas. "And laugh a lot."

When the ceremony ended, the new grads filed out as loudspeakers blared Kool & the Gang's "Celebration." The song had been the nation's number one hit on that day in 1980 when Nathan's dad joined the CIA. I lingered for a few moments as the tide of black gowns pushed past. I kept thinking about how far Nathan had traveled in less than a decade, from doting son to broken soldier, spy to inmate, convicted felon to college graduate. Finally he had matriculated, diploma in hand, to his place in the world of commerce. He had met and fallen deeply in love with Savannah on the very campus where his parents met forty years earlier.

I wondered how Jim would learn of his younger son's achievement. I imagined Star would tell him by phone, or Nick and Betty might share the good news by letter. I thought about all the moments in Nathan's life that Jim missed, the birthdays and graduations and the firsts that fathers and sons are supposed to share, from first car to first legal beer. And I remembered what Nathan told me when I asked him what he would ask his father, were they given the chance to one day talk again: "Was it worth it?" Nathan was determined to rebuild his own life, brick by brick, and restore the Nicholson name.

Four years have passed since Nathan promised to tell me his story exclusively. Since then he has given me roughly two hundred hours of his life in face-to-face interviews, on the phone, by e-mail, and via text message. I asked him painful and impertinent questions, poking under the sore teeth of his psyche, which he handled with grace and good humor. His story never wavered. He sought nothing in return. After I sold the rights to this book to movie producers, they wanted to buy Nathan's life-story rights. His plea agreement forbade him from earning a dime from his personal drama. So he signed his rights away gratis. All he asked in return was that they write a check for $500 payable to the U.S. government. He was making amends.

I remember once telling Nathan that he would be about a month shy of his fortieth birthday before his dad got out of prison. I asked what kind of future he envisioned for himself. He told me he hoped to have a faded diploma, a wife, and three kids of his own. He told me with a chuckle that if things went according to plan, he'd have a helluva lot less adventure in his life.

Nathan knew that if he was to achieve these things, he would do it without Jim's guidance. By court order, he was forbidden from communicating with his dad by any means, even through a third party. But Nathan didn't need a judge to tell him he should put some distance between himself and the naïve young man who'd been so easily seduced into serving as his dad's agent. I asked him once, as he sat in a studio apartment not much bigger than a jail cell, whether he believed he had betrayed his country.

"Absolutely," he said.

Never have I heard so much anguish poured into one word.

I thought about Nathan, and of my own son, Holden. I had shared Nathan's story with my boy when he was just twelve, the same age at which Nathan had learned of his father's arrest for espionage. I asked Holden how he'd feel if it were I who had been imprisoned for betraying our country. *I'd be really mad,* I recall him telling me. *But I would still love you.* He said it would take a long time for me to regain his trust.

There is long-held orthodoxy in American journalism that forbids writers from getting too close to the subjects of their stories. We are counseled to keep barriers, however thin, between us and them. For many years, I adhered to this journalistic canon in service of something

I called objectivity. I rationalized away my detachment by thinking of it as the foundation of fairness. Only late in my career did I cotton to the fact that it was a load of crap. Because, in the end, there's only truth.

As I sat in the college auditorium that afternoon, I thought about the steps I had taken to get into Nathan's head and shake out the truth. I had literally walked in his shoes, donning the heavy orange slippers and jail scrubs and shackles he'd worn in two county jails. I had smelled air full of cleaning solvents inside both of the lockups that kept him, felt the sting of ankle chains when I took steps that exceeded their reach. I had walked the cobblestone streets of Nicosia, the polished floors of the Russian Consulate in San Francisco, the carpeted courtrooms of Portland. I had toured Nathan's boyhood town house in Burke, Virginia, thanks to a good-natured tenant aware she lived in "The Spy's House." I had listened to hours of wiretapped conversations between Nathan and his dad and read a pile of letters they'd exchanged. I had spent countless hours interviewing people who knew Nathan, or who had investigated him.

Nathan and I shared our personal stories, some bawdy tales of youth and hormones, even a few secrets. We drank together several times, and I was always horrified by his cocktail of choice, a high-octane mix of light and dark rum, brandy, triple sec, and orange juice called a Scorpion. It was impossible not to grow fond of Nathan, not to feel a kind of paternal pride, especially on that Saturday in June at Oregon State—the day before Father's Day— in the way he had cleaned his own slate.

I found Nathan at the alumni center surrounded by friends and family. He had that goofy look on his face, eyes sweeping the ceiling with mirth, and I pumped his hand, telling him how proud I was to be there and celebrate his achievement. I shot some photos of Nathan and Star as parents nearby snapped pictures of their graduates. A few moments later, I drew Nathan aside and handed him a small gift bag. In it was a box of two-ounce miniatures of booze—enough for Nathan and Savannah to each mix a monstrous Scorpion cocktail.

"Don't drink and drive, kids," I cautioned. And we laughed.

I was speeding home to spend Father's Day weekend with my boy when I got a text on my iPhone from Nathan. I waited until the car was farther up the interstate to defy the traffic laws of Oregon and read the message. Nathan was thanking me again for being there, and he concluded with a little semicolon wink to say thanks for something else I'd left in the bag.

Inside the sack was a poorly gift-wrapped present, a little notebook with a blue marbled cover. I'd picked it up at a dime store. It was almost identical to the one Nathan had carried into his clandestine meetings with Fedotov. I left a short inscription on the first page.

"A new book," I wrote, "one to begin the rest of your life. . . . Godspeed, Nathan."

Four months later, as I was writing some of the words you've already read here, my cell phone dinged again with a text. It was from Nathan. There was a photograph attached. It showed a woman's hand, Savannah's, a diamond gleaming on her ring finger. Nathan wrote three words.

"She said yes."

And so it began.

Author's Note

This book is a work of journalism based on a five-year investigation. I spent hundreds of hours interviewing participants in this story, as well as other people who provided insights about them. Other sources helped set some of the scenes, including one who offered interpretations of biblical events mentioned in the book. Some offered technical or historical assistance. The spine of the narrative was constructed with many thousands of pages of public records, including FBI reports and federal court files in Virginia, Oregon, and New York; military records; contemporaneous news accounts; correspondence between key participants; government-generated reports on espionage; congressional testimony; and portions of more than fifty books about spy operations, the CIA, FBI, tradecraft, and traitors.

Every person in this book is real, and all but a few endured neurotic rounds of fact-checking. As in all journalistic accounts, there are some people who prefer to avoid participation and others whose privacy must be maintained. I intentionally left out the name of one character because he still works for the CIA, and I changed the name of one minor character because I was unable to interview her and saw no reason to intrude on her privacy. For the sake of clarity and continuity, I have referred to Jim's ex-wife throughout the book as Laurie, although her legal name is now Al'Aura Jusme (and she signs her name in the lower-case fashion "l'aurie").

The great bulk of dialogue in this book resulted from phone recordings provided by the FBI or from interviews with two or more participants in those conversations. In a few brief exchanges, I have included dialogue based on the best recollections of one participant. For example, I relied on Nathan Nicholson's recollections of his conversations with Russian officials (backed by FBI reports in which Nathan provided investigators more timely accounts of those conversations). Some of the dialogue comes from contemporaneous news accounts. For example, conversations between Jim and his SVR contacts, and certain facts in those scenes, came directly from David Wise's excellent March 1998 story in *GQ* magazine: "The Spy Who Sold the Farm."

Some readers may ask why I have revealed the identity of the U.S. intelligence source whose assistance to the CIA and FBI helped lead to Jim's arrest in 1996. I named him because Russia has already released him from prison and because his name is already in the public domain. I believe Americans should know that a few foreign-born men and women have imperiled their lives and abandoned their homelands to serve this country, for good pay, and now move among them in anonymity. The untold story of this Russian, as I understand it, is so extraordinary that I hope he will one day sit down with me for an interview. I recognize that one nation's hero is another's traitor.

Some of the thoughts and words ascribed to Jim in these pages came from letters he penned to Nathan, his parents, and his good friends Glenn and Shadley Wiegman, who shared those missives with me. Additionally, a counterintelligence expert shared excerpts from Jim's diaries. Jim's words to Star, in his letters from prison, were filed in government court papers.

Acknowledgments

This book began with a preternatural run of good luck that began in early 2010. I was recently divorced (again), drowning in my efforts to research the Nicholson espionage cases, when I received a series of life changing gifts.

The first of these gifts was Kristin Quinlan, who entered my life and soon became my soulmate, co-conspirator in adventure, and my rock-solid love. Kristin cheered my labors, cooked and sometimes cleaned for me, and let me read portions of the book aloud to get her reaction and catch clunkers in my prose. She patiently put up with my spy obsession and (almost always) forgave me as my keyboard kept me as its mistress. She did all this while running her own household, sending two kids off to college, and managing a growing business. Kristin, the CEO of Certified Languages International, also provided me free translation services as I scoured the Internet and made entreaties—in Cyrillic—to the SVR. This book simply would not have happened, at all, ever, without Kristin. And I can only hope that one day she will consider making an honest man of me in front of God and everybody.

The next gift came in the form of retired CIA officer Brian Kelley. He contacted me to say he had been using my Nicholson articles in *The Oregonian* as teaching tools for his students. Brian recognized I was green in matters of espionage and graciously offered to guide my research into the lives of spies. Brian mentored me in counterintelligence, tradecraft, and all things CIA. He gave me many hours by phone and e-mail and cheered me on to write this book. Brian's backstory made him the perfect tour guide: He once was the target of a massive FBI counter-spy operation; agents tailed him for two years, turning his family upside down, as agents wrongly accused him of the crimes for which Robert Hanssen eventually was convicted. When Brian was exonerated, he could have sued his government. Instead he returned to the CIA to serve his country. He died of a heart attack on September 19, 2011, a few weeks shy of our first face-to-face meeting, leaving a hole in many hearts, including mine. Some of Brian's many friends in U.S. intelligence circles—perhaps in memory of him—offered their time to help me research this book.

My luck continued by putting me in the hands of two talented women. I am deeply grateful to Tamar Rydzinski, my agent at the Laura Dail Literary Agency, and Corinna Barsan, my editor at Grove Atlantic. Tamar had read "The Spy's Kid" newspaper series and reached out to say the story sounded like the kernel of a great book. I had only hoped she could sell it. But Tamar, tirelessly swinging for the fences, turned up several publishing offers. Grove's publisher, Morgan Entrekin, then gave me a treasure in Corinna, one of his senior editors. I've never worked with a better story editor. She's a young woman with an old-school approach: She worked through my early drafts just as the gods of literature intended—on paper, with sharp pencils—and knew where to wield her machete and when to use a scalpel. Corinna instantly *got* the Nicholsons' father-son dynamic. She worked like a scrivener over every line, pushing me hard to drill down on the key characters so that the sum of their deeds—good and bad—revealed the soul of the story.

Closer to home, I owe a truckload of thanks to Margaret Haberman, one of *The Oregonian*'s many talented editors. Margaret understands the proper care and feeding of journalists, and always seems to know the best door to open for her writers. Margaret edited "The Spy's Kid" and later joined two other great friends—Pulitzer Prize–winning feature writers Jacqui Banaszynski and Tom Hallman Jr.—in reading over a section of the book and offering suggested revisions. I love all three of them. I'm thankful to work at *The Oregonian*, which cherishes long-form journalism and where I was greatly encouraged by editors Peter Bhatia and John Killen, veteran photojournalist Michael Lloyd, and publisher N. Christian Anderson III.

I'm indebted to the many people, named and unnamed, who patiently gave me so many hours of their time so that I could tell this story as accurately as possible. I'm terribly lucky and thankful that author David Wise published his excellent 1998 *GQ* story about Jim, *The Spy Who Sold the Farm,* when he did. Had he not spent many hours interviewing Jim and documenting his recollections before the government stifled this rogue CIA officer, there would be no source for details of Jim's meetings with the SVR.

I also owe a significant debt to America's talented national security writers and foreign correspondents for the news they reported on Jim's first arrest and conviction, and the state of present-day U.S.-Russia affairs. I've singled out several of my favorites: James Risen, David Johnston, Ronald J. Ostrow, Stan Crock, Dan Morain, Charlie Savage, Peter Baker, Benjamin Wiser, Scott Shane, Ellen Barry, Annys Shin, Ken Dilanian, Michael Schwirtz, Vladimir Isachenkov, Elaine Sciolino, Kathy Lally, and Will Englund.

I thank David G. Major, founder and president of the Centre for Counterintelligence and Security Studies, whose "Spypedia" website aggregates and analyzes an astounding volume of data on convicted spies. I'm grateful to the Defense Personnel and Security Research Center, which has published rigorous studies on the motivations that drive Americans to spy against their country. I'd also like to thank Oleg Kalugin, a retired major general in the KGB, whose insights and recollections (along with his excellent books *Spymaster* and *The First Directorate*) were invaluable to my research. And I'm extraordinarily grateful to Norman Polmar and Thomas B. Allen, authors of *Spy Book: The Encyclopedia of Espionage,* which became my bible.

The Spy's Son would not have been possible without the men and women of the FBI and CIA, past and present, whose kindness and help drew me into the world of spies and spy catchers. Many are named in these pages, and some are not for reasons I can't share. I owe special thanks to Angela Bell, in the FBI's public information office in Washington, D.C., and to bureau spokeswoman Elizabeth A. Steele in the Portland Field Office, for their considerable help in setting up interviews with agents and analysts and other officials. I'm grateful for the help of several CIA public information staffers, notably Ned Price (now a spokesman for the National Security Council) and Christopher White for helping me to reach contacts in and out of the agency for interviews. Thanks also to Chris Burke, a spokesman for the U.S. Bureau of Prisons, who helped me track the institutional movements of Jim and other inmates.

The following generous souls provided technical assistance, historical context, and in some cases guided tours of the many places and time periods chronicled in the book. I've listed them alphabetically: Captain Raimond R. Adgers, a jail administrator for the Multnomah County Sheriff's Office; Deputy U.S. Marshal Cory Cunningham, who literally brought Jim Nicholson to the halls of justice; Warden Marion Feather and Executive Assistant Kyle Olsen at FCI Sheridan, who allowed me to tour the prison; Frederick P. Hitz, a former inspector general of the CIA, who helped frame my understanding of the agency and those who betray it; author H. Keith Melton, who has probably forgotten more about spies and their methods than I'll ever learn; the journalist Michael Ottey, who shot photos of a statue in Bratislavia, Slovakia, just so I could describe it accurately; CIA historian David Robarge; John Roth, the chief resource manager at the Oregon Caves National Monument; Chief Deputy Michael Shults, who heads corrections for the Multnomah County Sheriff's Office; Matt Wiederholt with the City of Prineville Railway; and Jake and Whitney Zatzkin (who opened the doors to their home, the former Nicholson town house in Burke, Virginia).

I'm also grateful to the many former prisoners who served time with Jim at Sheridan, including the cellmates, workmates, and prayer meeting friends who alternately depicted him as saint and sinner. Some supplied me with UNICOR work records, commissary lists, chow hall menus, inmate handbooks, and annotated maps of the medium-security lockup. Most notably, I'd like to thank Rob Tillitz and John Will for the time they gave me in interviews and written accounts of life inside the prison.

I owe much to First Amendment lawyer Jeff Kosseff, at Covington & Burling LLP, my attorney and former investigative partner at *The Oregonian*. Jeff, one of the smartest humans I know, worked behind the scenes in an attempt to get the Department of Justice to permit an interview of Jim Nicholson. We also hoped to mount a legal challenge to Attorney General Eric H. Holder Jr.'s Special Administrative Measure that forbade Jim from communicating with me. Neither Jeff nor I have given up hope of challenging the SAM in federal court.

I'm also thankful to my best friend, the author Stephen Kelly, who pushed me to report my way into this story and pulled me out of a few panic attacks as my deadlines approached. I am extremely grateful to my family in Texas—my mom, Patricia Jean Denson, and my brothers J.M. "Dutch" Denson and Cavan P. M. Denson—for encouraging this multiyear project even as it took me in directions away from them.

I'll close by thanking Nathan and his family for choosing me to tell their painful but revealing story. I'm forever indebted.

Notes

Chapter Two

27: **"A death sentence awaits me":** "Undelivered speech of Senator Benigno S. Aquino Jr.: Upon his return from the United States of America on August 21, 1983" (as published by the *Official Gazette* by order of the Office of the President of the Philippines Under Commonwealth Act No. 638)

38: **he would deny ever cheating on her:** "The Spy Who Sold the Farm," *GQ* March 1998, by David Wise

39: **Pol Pot, who had superintended genocide in Cambodia:** "Cambodian Genocide, 1975–1978," a paper by World Without Genocide, at William Mitchell School of Law

Chapter Three

52: **the SVR's top official in Kuala Lumpur, Yuri P. Vlasov:** "The Spy Who Sold the Farm," *GQ* March 1998, by David Wise

52: **throw open the door to dialogue between the two spy agencies:** "The Spy Who Sold the Farm,", *GQ* March 1998, by David Wise

53: **a group of Arab terrorists—some battle-hardened by the Soviet war in Afghanistan:** "Malaysia's forgotten, forgiven 9/11 history," Asia Times Online (Holdings) Ltd., by Derek Henry Flood, September 11, 2010

53: **hanging out the shingle:** "The Spy Who Sold the Farm," *GQ* March 1998, by David Wise

53: **He had broken into houses, planted bugs:** "The Spy Who Sold the Farm," *GQ* March 1998, by David Wise

54: **Jim was tortured by nightmares of going to prison:** "The Spy Who Sold the Farm," *GQ* March 1998, by David Wise

54: **[Ames] accused the CIA's careerist bureaucrats of deceiving generations of Americans:** "Spy Voices Shame and Defiance Before Receiving a Life Sentence," *The New York Times*, by David Johnston, April 29, 1994

54: **Ames would acknowledge in a letter:** Aldrich Ames letter to the author, received January 18, 2011

54: **the SVR might be in the market for another highly paid mole inside the CIA:** "The Spy Who Loved Them: Jim Nicholson Explains Why He Spied for Russia," NBC News, Katie Couric, July 14, 1997

54–55: **Jim told Vlasov he was in trouble:** "The Spy Who Sold the Farm," *GQ* March 1998, by David Wise

55: **"That should not be a problem":** "The Spy Who Sold the Farm," *GQ* March 1998, by David Wise

55: **"What did you do wrong?":** "The Spy Who Sold the Farm," *GQ* March 1998, by David Wise

56: **Vlasov gave Jim a mail-drop address in Harare:** "The Spy Who Sold the Farm," *GQ* March 1998, by David Wise

56: **responding with a pass-phrase:** "The Spy Who Sold the Farm," *GQ* March 1998, by David Wise

56: **He turned over the names of more than a dozen assets:** "The Spy Who Sold the Farm," *GQ* March 1998, by David Wise

Chapter Four

62: ***getting down to the business of catching spies:*** "Clinton signing order on new FBI-CIA relationship," The Associated Press, May 3, 1994

62: **ordered the FBI and CIA to share information:** "Clinton Alters Counterspy Net in Wake of Ames Case," *Los Angeles Times,* by Ronald J. Ostrow, May 4, 1994

64: **"tied up in the security purgatory":** *See No Evil: The True Story of a*

Ground Soldier in the CIA's War on Terrorism, Robert Baer, Crown Publishers, 2002

66: **a hulking fellow with a broad face and dark hair thinning above his temples:** "The Spy Who Sold the Farm," *GQ* March 1998, by David Wise

66: **sack held a batch of CT dossiers:** "The Spy Who Sold the Farm," *GQ* March 1998, by David Wise

66: **Polyakov handed him a brown paper package:** "The Spy Who Sold the Farm," *GQ* March 1998, by David Wise

66: **Polyakov was chief of the SVR's South Asia Division:** "The Spy Who Sold the Farm," *GQ* March 1998, by David Wise

67: **prepared him to defeat the test without drugs:** "The Spy Who Sold the Farm," *GQ* March 1998, by David Wise

67: **threw him a curve by putting him through their own single-issue test:** "The Spy Who Sold the Farm," *GQ* March 1998, by David Wise

68: **In July, he mailed the Russians a postcard:** "The Spy Who Sold the Farm," *GQ* March 1998, by David Wise

69: **The KGB reportedly killed at least ten:** "An Assessment of the Aldrich H. Ames Espionage Case and Its Implications for U.S. Intelligence" (Senate Select Committee on Intelligence), November 1, 1994

69: **One of the Jaguars he drove was valued at $49,000:** "An Assessment of the Aldrich H. Ames Espionage Case and Its Implications for U.S. Intelligence" (Senate Select Committee on Intelligence), November 1, 1994

70: **broke things off with Lily:** "The Spy Who Sold the Farm," *GQ* March 1998, by David Wise

73: **The Russian told him that some of the information about Ames was new:** "The Spy Who Sold the Farm," *GQ* March 1998, by David Wise

74: **"You can be greedy and still feel good about yourself":** "Million Idea: Use Greed for Good," *Chicago Tribune,* by Bob Greene, December 15, 1986

75: **honed in on the phone to help knock off the Chechen leader:** "Did NSA Help Russia Target Dudayev?" *Covert Action Quarterly,* by Wayne Madsen, 1997, No. 61

Chapter Five

100: **took as trophies the uncircumcised penises of more than six thousand enemies:** "Eunuchs in the OT, Part 1, Introduction and Summary," by Bruce L. Gerig, 2008

101: **Ames earned a reputation as a talented, if forgetful, spy:** "An Assessment of the Aldrich H. Ames Espionage Case and Its Implications for U.S. Intelligence" (Senate Select Committee on Intelligence), November 1, 1994

Chapter Six

105: ***"It must be gained from what is learned by men":*** *Sun Tzu: The Art of War, The New Translation,* Research and Reinterpretation by J. H. Huang, Quill/William Morrow and Company Inc., 1993

111: **"bull-in-a-china-shop bureaucrat":** "C.I.A. Chief Charts His Own Course," *The New York Times,* by Elaine Sciolino, September 29, 1996

111: **"Shoot-ready-aim"** . . . **"unguided missile":** "C.I.A. Chief Charts His Own Course," *The New York Times,* by Elaine Sciolino, September 29, 1996

111: **$3 billion, 17,000-employee spy agency** . . . **Diet Coke–guzzling** . . . **"Tora Nora":** "Nora Slatkin's Mission Impossible: The CIA," *Business Week,* by Stan Crock, February 26, 1996

112: **quality of foreign assets over quantity:** *Denial and Deception: An Insider's View of the CIA,* Melissa Boyle Mahle, Nation Books, 2006

122: **CIA also credits OTS scientists with engineering the first ultra-miniature camera:** CIA press release, September 16, 2011

Chapter Eight

135: ***"the Bible begins with a betrayal":*** *Paris Review,* "The Art of Theater No. 2, Part 2," Arthur Miller as interviewed by Christopher Bigby, Fall 1999

139: **his client would vigorously fight the accusations:** "Alleged Mole to Plead Not Guilty," *Los Angeles Times,* by Robert L. Jackson, November 21, 1996

146: **Bloch faced no charges:** *Spy Book: The Encyclopedia of Espionage,* Norman Polmar and Thomas B. Allen, Random House, 1998

Chapter Nine

155: **"*you get the chance to see who really loves you*"**: *Suge Knight: The Rise, Fall, and Rise of Death Row Records: The Story of Marion "Suge" Knight, a Hard-Hitting Study of One Man, One Company That Changed the Course of American Music Forever,* Jake Brown, Amber Books Publishing, 2002

156: **The government spent $52 million to build the prison complex:** "Sheridan becomes a prison town," *The Register-Guard,* by Eric Mortenson, May 21, 1989

157: **carried them to Poland's spy service, the Służba Bezpieczeństwa:** *Spy Book: The Encyclopedia of Espionage,* Norman Polmar and Thomas B. Allen, Random House, 1998

158: **only person that was arrested as a result of my action was me:** "CIA Officer Nicholson Sells Secrets to Russia," *Nightline,* June 26, 1997

158: **"It flew in the face of everything that I believe":** 'The Spy Who Loved Them: Jim Nicholson Explains Why He Spied for Russia," NBC News, Katie Couric, July 14, 1997

159: **"the CIA and FBI are very capable of doing that":** "Parents are still not convinced," *The Oregonian,* by Janet Filips, June 6, 1997

160: **Scott Scurlock, dubbed "The Hollywood Bandit":** *The End of the Dream: The Golden Boy Who Never Grew Up,* Ann Rule, Pocket Books, 1998

161: **Scurlock escaped, then took his own life:** Historylink.org, the Free Online Encyclopedia of Washington State History

Chapter Eleven

184: **"*My father was pleased I actually had the guts to do it*"**: "Walker Son Says He Became Spy 'to Please My Father,'" *Los Angeles Times,* by Dan Morain, May 20, 1986

192: **the embassy served as a haven for spies:** "Mexico City Depicted as a Spies' Haven," *The New York Times,* by Robert Lindsey and Joel Brinkley, June 23, 1985

Chapter Fourteen

218: **"*God was the original surveillance camera*":** "Artist Hasan Elahi meticulously documents life after FBI investigation," *The Baltimore Sun*, by Julie Scharper, January 22, 2013

Chapter Seventeen

292: **turned Rochford down cold:** *Spy Handler: Memoir of a KGB Officer—The True Story of the Man Who Recruited Robert Hanssen and Aldrich Ames*, Victor Cherkashin with Gregory Feifer, Basic Books, 2005

Chapter Eighteen

295: *fulfill your main mission, i.e. to search and develop ties in policymaking circles in US and send intels to C*: Unclassified federal criminal complaint, Southern District of New York, June 25, 2010

296: **The administration backed a spy exchange ... as the best option to avoid unnecessary political drama;** "Swap Idea Emerged Early in Case of Russia Agents," *The New York Times*, by Peter Baker, Charlie Savage, and Benjamin Weiser, July 9, 2010

296: **singing such patriotic songs as "From Where the Motherland Begins":** "Vladimir Putin consoles exposed Russian spies with 'singalong,'" *The Guardian*, by Tom Parfitt, July 25, 2010; and author H. Keith Melton.

296: **double-crossed Moscow to work as a mole for the CIA, earning the code name "Scythian":** "Intrigue and Ambiguity in Cases of 4 Russians Sent to West in Spy Swap," *The New York Times*, by Scott Shane and Ellen Barry, July 9, 2010

296: **Zaporozhsky gave up information that helped point U.S. authorities toward Robert Hanssen:** *The Secrets of the FBI*, Ronald Kessler, Crown Publishing Group, 2011

297: **reportedly rewarded Zaporozhsky with $2 million in housing and benefits:** "Intrigue and Ambiguity in Cases of 4 Russians Sent to West in Spy Swap," *The New York Times*, by Scott Shane and Ellen Barry, July 9, 2010

297: **put under lock and key at Moscow's notorious Lefortovo prison:** "Moscow Court Sentences Former Foreign Intelligence Officer to 18 Years in Prison," RIA Novosti, by Maria Lokotetskaya, November 6, 2003

297: **sentenced him to eighteen years in prison for high treason:** "Intelligence Officer Gets 18 Years for Treason," *Gazeta.ru*, by Vita Lukashina, June 11, 2003

297: **His wife, Galina, living in the suburbs north of Baltimore, died:** "Spy swapped in deal with Russia could return to house in Maryland suburb," *The Washington Post*, by Annys Shin, July 11, 2010

299: **"It really reflects, I think, an anachronistic mind-set":** "Spy vs. Spy: Real Catch Is the One Who Gets Away," *Morning Edition*, National Public Radio, by Rachel Martin, July 5, 2010

299: **made a client of Alan Patricof, a venture capitalist who served as finance chairman of Hillary Rodham Clinton's 2008 presidential campaign:** "Russian spies were succeeding, FBI official says," *Los Angeles Times*, by Ken Dilanian, October 31, 2011

300: **The FBI established a link between the illegals and Karetnikov:** "Russian spy worked for Microsoft," *The Guardian*, by Charles Arthur, July 14, 2010

300: **"You need to fulfill the task set in the interests of your motherland for many, many years":** "Vladimir Putin sang patriotic songs with spies expelled from US," *The Telegraph*, by Andrew Osborn, July 25, 2010

300: **Medvedev awarded the illegals—at least some of them—Russia's top government honors:** "Agents Deported by U.S. Are Honored in Moscow," *The New York Times*, by Michael Schwirtz, October 18, 2010

300: **"Whatever equivalent of thirty pieces of silver they get, it will get stuck in their throats":** "Vladimir Putin: Russian secret services don't kill traitors," *The Telegraph*, December 16, 2010

300–301: **hindered their operations with poor equipment, requiring them to meet in unsecured spots:** "Alexander Poteyev, Russian Intelligence Officer, Convicted of Betraying U.S. Spy Ring Including Anna Chapman," The Associated Press, by Vladimir Isachenkov, June 27, 2011

301: **"Mary, try to take this calmly":** "Alexander Poteyev, Russian Intelligence Officer, Convicted of Betraying U.S. Spy Ring Including Anna Chapman," The Associated Press, by Vladimir Isachenkov, June 27, 2011

301: **Anna Chapman later revealed that she feared she'd been betrayed:** "Alexander Poteyev, Russian Intelligence Officer, Convicted of Betraying U.S.

Spy Ring Including Anna Chapman," The Associated Press, by Vladimir Isa-chenkov, June 27, 2011

302: **Fishenko was charged as the mastermind of the illegal procurement network:** "Russian Agent and 10 Other Members of Procurement Network for Russian Military and Intelligence Operating in the U.S. and Russia Indicted in New York," FBI press release, Eastern District of New York, October 3, 2012

Epilogue

323: **reconfigured its death row facilities at the Terre Haute Federal Correctional:** "'Little Gitmo,'" *New York* magazine, by Christopher S. Stewart, July 10, 2011

323: **a team of counterterrorism experts in West Virginia could remotely snoop:** "'Guantánamo North': Inside Secretive U.S. Prisons," *All Things Considered,* National Public Radio, by Carrie Johnson and Margo Williams, March 3, 2011

325: **Forty-nine U.S. prisoners would be held under SAMs:** "Silencing stories: Special administrative measures handcuff First Amendment," by Rachel Bunn, Reporters Committee for Freedom of the Press, *The News Media and The Law,* Winter 2012

Index